Randa ♡

Rude

DEVELOPMENT ECONOMICS

Richard Grabowski:
To my mother and father, whose work and hope sustained me.

Michael Shields:
To Gail, Mary, and Royal.

DEVELOPMENT ECONOMICS

Richard Grabowski

Southern Illinois University at Carbondale

Michael P. Shields

Central Michigan University

First published 1996

Blackwell Publishers, Inc.
238 Main Street
Cambridge, Massachusetts 02142
USA

Blackwell Publishers, Ltd.
108 Cowley Road
Oxford OX4 1JF
UK

Library of Congress Cataloging–in–Publication Data
    Development economics / Richard Grabowski and Michael P. Shields.
        p.   cm.
    Includes bibliographical references and index.
    ISBN 1-55786-706-2 (hc)
        1. Development economics.   2. Economic development.   I. Shields,
    Michael P., 1945–   II. Title.
    HD75.G7   1995
    338.9--dc20   95-38754
                                                                        CIP

British Library Cataloguing in Publication Data

A CIP catalogue record for this book is available from the British Library.

Composition by Megan H. Zuckerman

Printed in the USA by Book Crafters

This book is printed on acid-free paper

Contents

Preface: Development Theory

The student of development economics is often surprised, sometimes pleasantly surprised, by the differences between development economics and other fields of study within economics. The material is often descriptive but the descriptions are bold and sweeping. Hence, the student seldom has to understand specific institutions. The material is theoretical but seldom formal. Hence, the student seldom has to master formal theoretical models. The material is empirical but seldom econometric. Hence the student does not need to master mathematical statistics. Finally, and most important, the material deals with the reasons for poverty on a scale few of the students have witnessed, much less experienced.

These differences may be, to some extent, both desirable and necessary because of inevitable differences in the subject matter. However, the student cannot help wishing that there was more continuity between the methods of development economics and the methods applied in other fields of economics. A consistent and formal treatment of various topics in development economics would go far in bridging the gap between development economics and economics in general. At a minimum, such a treatment would facilitate learning by employing consistent notation within a unified theoretical structure. Understanding of controversies would also be enhanced by interpreting opposing views within the same theoretical framework. The framework would be the mainstream of economic theory that is learned and applied in other courses. It is, of course, recognized that not all problems in development economics or, for that matter, in other areas of economics fit neatly into this framework. It is our belief, however, that real advances can be made by providing a unified theoretical approach to development economics. Insights from alternative views can then be discussed in terms of how they can be accommodated by the main approach.

Development theory can be organized in three different ways. Theories and theoretical innovations could be treated somewhat chronologically. Each theory could be discussed in terms of when and why it appeared, how it is related to other theories, and how theoretical innovations refined or extended the theory. This organization may tend to stress disagreement and ignore interaction between theories. The second approach would be to organize theoretical discussions according to the applied topic toward which they are being directed. For example, one such topic could be the role of education in furthering economic growth and development. The implications of various theories on the relationship between education and the development process would then be discussed. These first two methods of organization are followed, often with some mixture of the two, in the theoretical discussions of most development textbooks. A third method is to organize development theory in terms of the field into which the theory fits. These fields would include choice theory, international economics, public economics, labor economics, and so forth. This is the approach taken in this book. This last approach is best suited to exploring the relationship between development theory and economic theory in general because it focuses directly on how economic theory can be used to understand economic development.

This book's primary audience includes advanced undergraduate students as well as graduate students. However, professional economists may also find this book worthwhile in terms of its approach and content. Some knowledge of calculus is assumed. However, efforts are made to emphasize the economic meaning of all analyses. The student should also have a good understanding of intermediate microeconomics along with some understanding of intermediate macroeconomics. A junior or senior level course in economic development is not necessary, but some background in development economics or other fields covered in the book could be helpful.

If the book is used as a graduate level course, the entire book can be covered in two semesters along with appropriate supplementary readings. However, it could also be used for a one semester course in development. The core sections on growth and development, a unifying theme, and the traditional sector would be covered first. Then the instructor could choose which of the remaining topics he or she wished to cover.

The book begins with a survey of theories of the process of growth and development in Chapter 1. This chapter introduces many models and concepts that are used in later chapters. Chapter 2 reviews the concept of rational choice, its uses and limitations, and introduces the theme underlying subsequent chapters. Chapters 3 through 7 apply concepts discussed in the first two chapters to fields of study within development economics. The theoretical concepts and models relevant to each of these fields are introduced. These models are modified to reflect the institutions and problems of less developed countries and to help organize the theoretical and empirical literature in the field of study in question. Finally, Chapter 8 considers the role of the state in development.

The book emphasizes theoretical concepts and models in development economics. Reference will be made to historical, institutional, and empirical features of less developed countries and how they have influenced and have been captured in the theory. It should be emphasized, however, that the book is intended to be primarily a book on development theory. Historical, institutional, and empirical material will be introduced to understand the development and the empirical implications of the theoretical models.

Because this will not be a comprehensive book on development, auxiliary readings will be desirable. Case studies, descriptions of various cultural characteristics, empirical investigations, and the history of different regions are best covered elsewhere. The book will provide a theoretical thread for these studies that, although present in the literature, have not been integrated into a unified treatment of development theory. In providing a unified treatment of development theory, we hope to make it easier for the reader to apply theory to development problems.

ACKNOWLEDGMENTS

The writing of this manuscript took place over several years. The authors used parts of it to teach graduate level seminars in economic development. The students in these seminars made numerous useful comments that improved the quality of the work. In addition, we would like to thank Professors Stephen Reynolds, Don Clark, Sajal Lahiri, and Vernon Ruttan for reading the entire manuscript and offering valuable ideas. Also we would both like to thank Nancy Mallet, who carefully and meticulously typed the manuscript and its many revisions. Finally, our wives and children put up with us and humored us throughout the ordeal of writing the manuscript. We thank them and promise not to begin another such project for at least six months.

1

Growth and Development: Some Views

Stagnation, both economic and demographic, seems to have been the condition facing humanity for almost all of its existence. Although population size as well as levels of living fluctuated, fundamental changes came slowly until the beginning of the industrial revolution. Individual nations rose and fell with little impact on the lot of humanity. For reasons that remain controversial, the economies of England and, later, other nations experienced sustained and, by previous historical standards, rapid economic growth. The economies of many countries, however, were left behind in this growth process or may have worsened as a result of growth in the expanding economies of the industrializing nations. Some key questions in development economics regard the nature of this apparent transformation from backward to modern economies. First, did this process involve qualitative, structural changes in the societies involved? If so, what was the nature of the mutual causality between these changes and the growth of the economy? Second, what elements of this growth process are subject to control by poor nations today? Third, can poor nations replicate the example of wealthy nations or has the world been so changed by the transformation of some formerly backward economies that the rest of humankind is doomed to dependence and poverty without major structural changes in the world trading system?

All three questions concerning the development process have in varying degrees motivated growth and development theories. In this chapter these theories will be classified into two categories. First, historical theories of how economic development has occurred and is occurring will be briefly reviewed. Second, formal theories of production and growth will be reviewed, focusing on questions of how countries can facilitate economic growth. There is, of course, some connection between historical and formal theories of growth. Formal theories may be in part representations of historical

1

theories. Historical theories in turn may be strongly influenced by formal theories.[1]

HISTORICAL THEORIES OF DEVELOPMENT

Historical theories are theories that explain current events or conditions in terms of a causal chain of historical events or conditions. The theory explains or predicts how these events or conditions evolve. Many historical theories of economic development simply postulate the existence of different phases or stages of a development process and hypothesize about the forces that cause a change in the phase or stage of development. Clearly delineated stage theories have been proposed by Karl Marx, Friedrich List, Karl Bücher, W. W. Rostow, and some members of the dependency school such as Andre Gunder Frank.[2] There are also elements of a stage theory in the writings of classical economists such as Adam Smith and current economists working within the classical tradition such as W. Arthur Lewis.[3] These historical theories will be considered roughly in the chronological order in which they were proposed. The order is not intended to necessarily represent scientific progress from early primitive theories to later more refined theories.

Historical Views of Classical Economists

The classical economists probably had no historical theory, per se. They were deeply involved in matters of economic policy, and their theorizing tended to be oriented toward the creation of a theory of value. They were, however, concerned with growth and tended to emphasize the extension of markets as a key element in this growth. Adam Smith saw economic prosperity as the result of increased specialization and trade. He saw limitations on free trade as restricting the scope of specialization and, hence, lessening economic prosperity. Smith attacked what he called mercantilism, which in Smith's view impeded the development of competitive markets and the resulting division of labor. David Ricardo stressed that agricultural protection, which raised agricultural rent and reduced the accumulation of capital, was a major impediment to growth. John Stuart Mill also emphasized free trade and production for the market as a source of prosperity. In particular, he saw tenant farms as lowering agricultural productivity and lessening the incentives for rural capital accumulation. To all these writers, development was enhanced and perhaps caused by the extension of isolated markets into a comprehensive market system. This view of the historical importance of markets was highly influential. Almost all contemporary and subsequent scholars concerned with historical explanations of development attempted to explain the rise of markets. Included among these scholars are persons with such diverse viewpoints as Karl Marx and W. W. Rostow.

Marxian Theories

Marx shared the view of the classical economists that the extension of markets was important for economic development. Markets became predominant in capitalism, which is only one of many historical stages. Marx saw not only history but science and nature as an interactive process of tensions that become more intense through time, eventually causing qualitative changes. Marx mentioned three phases through which history had moved and was moving. These stages are primitive communism, feudalism, and capitalism. Believing in progress, Marx believed that a fourth stage – communism – would soon emerge, and he welcomed its emergence. For the most part, he was concerned only with capitalism and the forces that it created which would eventually destroy capitalism. Marx explained these changes in economic order by developing a theory of historical change.

The traditional interpretation of Marx maintains that Marx believed that social, political, cultural, and spiritual aspects of life are conditioned by the mode of production. The mode of production is the sum of the material, productive forces of society. These productive forces include climate and geography as well as the existing technology. It is technology that Marxists view as the chief factor changing the material base of society. The technical nature of production conditions social relationships, and upon these social relationships is built the superstructure of political and legal institutions. These social relationships include the class structure of society and the control of the means of production and exchange.

As productive forces change, new social relationships will develop that are more appropriate to the altered production relationship. New social relationships and social classes will arise and come into conflict with the old. Eventually this conflict brings down the old society and initiates the new. Thus, history is a reflection of the ceaseless struggle between classes that occurs as a result of changes in the productive forces of society.

The rise of capitalism over the ashes of feudalism began with changes in productive forces, both technological and geographical, in that the discovery of the New World resulted in important changes in productive relationships that instituted a series of revolutions in the modes of production and exchange. The economic demands, which occurred because of the discovery of the New World, the development of new markets, and the expansion of trade, placed stress on the feudal economic order. A new commercial and manufacturing class arose in response to the new economic situation. Although this new class eventually transformed society, it initially met resistance from the vested classes of the old order. The extension of markets led to struggles over the political machinery of the state. The new entrepreneurial class ultimately captured political control of the state, and its powers to transform society became complete.

Although Marx believed that capitalism would eventually fail, he had a high regard for the ability of capitalism in general and the capitalist class in particular to revolutionize the means of production. It is in the capitalist stage of history that production and new technology grew very rapidly. He also believed that the need of the capitalist class for a constantly expanding market would drive it to establish itself over the whole surface of the globe. As a result, the less developed nations would also see their economic structures revolutionized as the

> bourgeoisie, by rapid improvement of all instruments of production, by the immensely facilitated means of communication, draws all, even the most barbarian, nations into civilization. The cheap prices of its commodities are the heavy artillery with which it batters down all Chinese walls, with which it forces the barbarians' intensely obstinate hatred of foreigners to capitulate. It compels all nations, on pain of extinction, to adopt the bourgeois mode of production; it compels men to introduce what it calls civilization into their midst, i.e., to become bourgeois themselves. In other words, it creates a world after its own image.[4]

Marx tended to view history as evolutionary in the sense that historical forces lead to progress. Capitalism was a necessary stage in the historical evolution. During this stage, feudalism is destroyed and the production process revolutionized. Thus, there is a period of rapid economic growth and the development of class conflict between capitalist and worker.

A group of scholars within the Marxist tradition has developed a very different perspective. This group, sometimes called *neo-Marxist,* argues that the underdevelopment of Africa, Asia, and Latin America has been a product of the same forces that have led to development in Europe and North America. The integration of backward areas into the world capitalist system is viewed as a major source of underdevelopment. This can be characterized as the development of underdevelopment. One of the major proponents of this view is Paul Baran.[5] He argued that the spread of capitalism into less developed nations resulted in a political amalgam combining the worst features of both capitalism and feudalism that, in a number of ways, effectively blocks all possibilities of economic growth.

To understand Baran's work one must distinguish between a country's actual and potential economic surplus. A country's actual economic surplus is identical with current savings or capital accumulation and is the difference between actual current output and actual current consumption. This is the main factor in promoting rapid economic growth. A country's potential economic surplus is the difference between the output that could be produced and essential consumption.

Within the context of the less developed nations, the actual surplus is much below the potential economic surplus and thus the actual rate of growth is much below the potential rate of growth. This low growth occurs because, when capitalism penetrated the less developed nations, feudalism and its dominant class was not destroyed, as Marx predicted. Instead, an alliance among the foreign capitalists, native capitalists, and feudal overlords is established. Within the context of this alliance much of the potential economic surplus is transferred out of the country by the dominant foreign capitalists. In addition, the native capitalist class and the feudal overlords use much of the potential surplus for luxurious consumption. As a result, the actual economic surplus is meager and the growth rates of these countries are relatively low.

Growth in these nations is further inhibited by other factors. Because wealth and income are concentrated in the hands of a few, the domestic market for industrial goods is not well developed. Hence, there is little incentive to invest and thereby to create productive enterprises supplying these types of goods. In addition, the capitalists have essentially a monopoly position in most of these nations. As a result, they are hesitant to invest in additional activities for fear of generating increased competition. Finally, the infrastructure for servicing a domestic market is also lacking. Indeed infrastructure development is often limited to the servicing of an enclave export section. Thus, few external economies are to be reaped by firms seeking to produce for the domestic market.

Baran is very skeptical concerning the possibilities of increasing the productivity of the agricultural sector. He believes that little additional land is available for agricultural purposes, and what land is available would require significant amounts of investment to cultivate. He doubts that this investment is economical. Thus, the development of industry is the key for Baran. Only through an increase in industrial productivity can agricultural machinery, fertilizer, electrical power, and so forth be made available to the agricultural producer. Only through an expansion of the demand for industrial labor can agricultural wages be increased and a stimulus provided for the modernization of the agricultural economy. Therefore, for Baran, mobilizing the potential economic surplus and using it to promote an unbalanced growth strategy emphasizing industry, is the key to development.

Why do the governments in these countries not take the necessary steps to surmount the obstacles to growth outlined by Baran? These governments, he argued, are not capable of undertaking these steps because the political and social structure of the government in power prevents any resolution of the problem. The alliance of dominant classes controlling the future of most less developed countries cannot be expected to design and carry out measures contrary to their immediate vested interests.

For these countries to experience rapid economic growth, their political framework must be drastically altered. The alliance among landlords, domestic capitalists, and foreign capitalists must be broken. This transition is likely to be abrupt and painful.

Andre Gunder Frank has extended the work of Baran and other modern neo-Marxists. He agrees with Baran that the state of underdevelopment in many poor countries is the result of their contact with and exploitation by the capitalist, developed nations. However, he extends the analysis by concentrating on the role of the city. He believes that the cities incorporate the indigenous population into the economy and serve as an instrument of domination. He refers to this as a metropolis–satellite relationship, which extracts economic surplus from the rural satellite areas and transfers this surplus to the city (metropolis). The extraction of surplus occurs not only at the international level from the less developed, satellite nations to the capitalist, metropolitan nations, it also occurs within nations between metropolitan areas and rural areas. As a result, a whole chain of metropolis and satellites relate all parts of the system from the metropolitan center, in Europe and the United States, to the most distant less developed nation.

Samir Amin also emphasized the idea that the development process of the center retards growth in the periphery.[6] In his analysis, the center economies are characterized by an articulated pattern of accumulation. By this it is meant that productivity increases do not accrue completely to capital, because worker consumption would not grow and thus a market for increased production would lag. Neither do they completely accrue to labor because this would sharply reduce capitalist profit. Instead, productivity gains are split between capital and labor, permitting a dynamic equilibrium to occur among sectors and between production and consumption. However, the underlying tendency of central capitalism is toward underconsumption, and the resulting crisis depresses the rate of profit. State intervention can counteract this tendency through Keynesian-type aggregate demand policies. The social basis for this type of intervention is the presumed social contract between capital and labor. This contract allows the state to manage conflicting wage and profit demands relative to productivity gains. The monopolization of capital and the organization of labor have made this approach possible.

The preceding process represents the internal solution to the maintenance of dynamic equilibrium. An external solution also exists and becomes necessary if the social contract in the center is not sufficiently effective. This solution has the periphery performing two basic functions. These functions are to provide a large market for the output of the center and to increase the rate of profit on the capital of the center.

During the age of competitive capitalism the role of the periphery as a market for the center was most important. During this time period, increases in productivity resulted, according to Amin, in reductions in price, not in increases in wage rates. Thus, underconsumption in the center forced capitalism to use the periphery to absorb the excess production. With the development of monopoly capital and the organization of labor, increases in productivity in the center led to rising wages. Monopolist profits could not be fully utilized in new investment in the center because this would tend to undermine their position in the market. As a result, capital would be exported to the periphery, where labor is relatively cheap. Higher profits could then be earned and repatriated to the center. Of course, this aggravates the center's problem of what to do with this surplus being extracted from the periphery. Internal aggregate demand policies within the center and additional capital exports would become necessary to maintain dynamic equilibrium. In the periphery, the inflow of capital would result in periods of rapid growth for particular sectors of the economy. However, the extraction of surplus via repatriation of profit and unequal trade (the terms of trade turning against the periphery) would create a situation in which long-run development is blocked.

These ideas, in which capitalism (the center) is seen as blocking the development of the periphery, have come under severe criticism from within the Left itself. These criticisms are of both a theoretical nature and empirical nature. Critics argue that a brief examination of the data concerning the development experiences of less developed nations is enough to dispel the notion that these regions have stagnated. For example, the real growth rate of gross domestic product was 79 percent higher in the periphery than in the center for the period 1969–1976. Gross fixed capital formation was 360 percent higher in the periphery than in the center for the same period. Even on a per capita basis, the growth rate was higher in the periphery relative to the center.

There are a number of theoretical criticisms of the development of underdevelopment idea. Only a few will concern us here. First, the development of underdevelopment emphasizes the external factor, surplus extraction by the center, as the prime factor in promoting backwardness. Critics of this view do not deny that the center benefits through the international transfer of the surplus. However, for critics such as Geoffrey Kay, underdevelopment results from an internal class structure that blocks the development of the production process.[7] As a result, the inflow of capital from the center blocks development not because it exploits the less developed countries, but because "it did not exploit it enough." Second, the development of under-development view sees capitalism as being incapable of developing the productive forces of the periphery. Again, critics such as Bill Warren claim that it is absurd to argue that foreign investment leads to stagnation.[8] Finally, the underdevelopment view tends to replace exploitation between social classes with exploitation between geographical areas. The workers of the center have allied themselves with the capitalists via a social contract. Therefore, an objective basis for international workers' solidarity would not exist. Critics, within the Left, vigorously disagree. They argue that the exploitation of labor is greatest within the center and that a basis for international workers' solidarity does exist.

Alain de Janvry attempts to incorporate several aspects of the criticisms just discussed into a modern Marxist perspective.[9] Most of his work is concerned with analyzing the political economy of development in Latin America. He argues that Latin America was transformed into a periphery of the center first through colonization, which integrated the region into the commercial market, and later through efforts by England to destroy the Spanish empire in order to establish free trade. These free trade policies encouraged the development of an economic system based upon the export of primary commodities and the import of manufactured consumption goods. Within this export enclave economy, much of the population earned its living in the traditional sector that had few if any economic links to the modern export sector. Unequal exchange to the benefit of the center is obtained through the maintenance of low agricultural wages through pre-capitalist relations of production. Under these relationships the workers were tied to the land and, consequently, were unable to take advantage of alternative market opportunities. This exploitation produces a deterioration of the external terms of trade to the benefit of the center.

Such deterioration of the terms of trade is the result of a process of unequal exchange, an idea first developed by Arghiri Emmanuel.[10] His argument is developed under the assumptions that capital is perfectly mobile and, thus, rates of profit are equalized between countries. In addition, labor is assumed not to be mobile. If wage rates are lower in the periphery relative to the center, the equalization of profit rates between countries will initially turn the terms of trade against the periphery.

With the rise of national entrepreneurial classes, import substitution strategies were followed in the early 1900s. This, according to de Janvry, induced the traditional landed elites to extend their sectoral control toward the newly rising industries and, also, induced a reverse movement whereby new industrialists sought access to land to gain power over the institutions of society. The industrialization that did occur was aimed at capturing the existing national market for manufactured goods, which was basically for luxury goods. Capital goods necessary for the growth of such industry now became the main import.

The terms of trade between the center and periphery began to further turn against the latter. This deterioration was caused by systematic market distortions imposed by the central economies in taking advantage of the global monopoly, which the technological and capital goods dependency of the periphery conferred upon them. Given the mobility of capital, the cost of the deteriorating terms of trade had to be transferred to the only nontraded factor, unskilled labor. Hence, labor in the periphery serves as only a cost of production and not as a market (source of demand) for industrial goods.

Two means are available to cheapen labor. The first involves the imposition of a repressive labor policy that, according to de Janvry, is limited by the organization and insurgency potential of the working classes. The second is to lower the cost of those items that constitute the bulk of labor's budget. Because food is the major part of labor's budget, this involves turning the internal terms of trade against the agricultural sector. Precapitalist relations of production are gradually replaced as a result of the development of what de Janvry calls a *fundamental dualism*. Labor is separated from the land to form a subsistence sector while a commercial agricultural sector arises. Even though it faces unfavorable terms of trade, commercial agriculture is able to thrive and derive economic compensation by monopolizing such institutional services as credit, technology, and information.

In summary, rural poverty in Latin America is viewed as the logical outcome of a three-level chain of exploitative relations. First, exploitation occurs at the international level between the dominant center and the dependent periphery. Second, exploitation exists at the sectoral level between modern industry, which produces commodities consumed largely by the rich, and the agricultural sector, which produces the food consumed largely by the poor. Third, exploitation comes at the social level between landlords and agricultural labor. Agricultural workers are alienated from the fertile land and forced to bear the burden of the deterioration in both the external and internal terms of trade. This burden is borne in the form of reduced real wage rates.

The pattern of growth that emerges is one in which the alienation of workers from the land creates what de Janvry calls a *marginalized population*, which is becoming increasingly proletarianized. Hence, functional dualism is seen as only a phase in the development of capitalism in the periphery. It is an extended period in which surplus is extracted from the traditional subsistence sector through cheap food and labor policies. Thus the traditional sector gradually decomposes, while sustaining rapid growth in a modern sector that caters to the production of manufactured luxury goods.

De Janvry's approach seeks to integrate the work of the neo-Marxists with that of their critics, whose position is much closer to that originally outlined by Marx. Specifically, in de Janvry's model the periphery experiences rapid growth in the manufacturing sector, not stagnation. However, this growth is fueled, initially, by the impoverishment, stagnation, and destruction of peasants and artisans. Thus, de Janvry contends, the concern of neo-Marxist theorists with stagnation and increasing poverty is correct. However, to argue that this impoverishment represents a stable, self-perpetuating structure is, according to de Janvry, invalid. Instead, it reflects only the dominance of particular class alliances and is only a phase in the development of capitalism in particular areas in the world. Finally, in de Janvry's model, surplus extraction from the periphery to the center does occur. However, this external function does not dominate in the model. Instead, internal and external factors are interrelated. The key to understanding this relationship is thought to be the recognition of the role of classes and the contradictions between them.

Neo-Marxists like Frank and those influenced by this analysis contend that breaking the international economic links will remove a level of exploitation. It is held that breaking these links would result in more of the surplus being kept at home and, hence, would increase the rate of economic growth in satellite nations. Thus, the strategy of development promoted by scholars like Frank would be autarchic in nature. They would have less developed nations turn away from the industrialized nations by limiting trade and capital flows. These recommendations are in sharp contrast to the recommendations that flow from traditional Marxism and the modern critics of the neo-Marxist position. Here the extension of capitalism and markets to backward regions is seen as an engine of growth. It is through the expansion of the capitalist system that the rest of the world is drawn into a situation in which class conflict between capitalist and worker occurs on a worldwide basis.

Culture and Development

Another influential view on the transition from a feudal order to capitalism concerns the role of religion and culture in determining the dynamism of the economic system. Max Weber stressed the role that Protestantism played in the transformation of northern Europe from feudalism to capitalism.[11] Roman Catholicism (and, by extension, many other religions) dampened impulses for accumulating material wealth. Protestantism provided an ethical foundation for wealth accumulation, which was viewed as a sign of God's favor. The person who came by wealth honestly, through work, acumen, and thriftiness, was blessed by God and more likely to be chosen for salvation. Hence, accumulation provided a sense of religious security. The security was incomplete, however, because wealth was only an indicator that one was among the "elect" predestined for salvation. Weber's view, that the acquisitive forces sanctioned by the reformation transformed the economies of northern Europe, is almost the opposite of the Marxist view that changes in productive forces change ethical and religious norms.

A view compatible with Weber was expressed by R. H. Tawney.[12] Tawney's view is more cautious and places more emphasis on the effects of commercial activity on religious beliefs and practices. The rise of commercial activity made some religious doctrines such as the opposition to usury and the condemnation of avarice increasingly anachronistic. At the same time, the rising influence of Protestant beliefs were crucial for the continuing spread of capitalism and the extension of markets into previously nonmarket mechanisms for allocating resources.

The views of Weber and Tawney suggest many areas for further research. First, their views have focused attention on ethical, cultural systems and the conflicts that may occur between parts of these systems and economic development. Second, attention has been directed toward how adaptive people and their cultures are to change in general. Third, the roles played by cultures and cultural conflicts in increasing entrepreneurship has received widespread attention. These three lines of research will be briefly discussed in order.

A casual look at the countries that developed earliest provides apparent support for the Weber–Tawney hypothesis that religion plays a key role in development. The Protestant north is and was generally more prosperous than the rest of the globe. There are, of course, many possible reasons for these differences in prosperity. A reason given, which is directly linked to Weber–Tawney, is that the religious ethical system in poor areas is an overriding impediment to prosperity. Some explanations go far beyond noting that usury prohibitions, employment discrimination against women, and remnants of caste systems are detrimental to economic growth. For example, J. H. Boeke and, later, Allen Sievers stress the irrationality and mysticism of indigenous cultures in Asia and particularly in Indonesia.[13] They contend that economic development is extremely unlikely in these societies, in large part because the people do not respond rationally to economic incentives. Sievers argues that only a strong government, which can destroy the many elements of the culture detrimental to development, can possibly achieve sustained growth and prosperity. Boeke contends that westernization simply succeeds in destroying the traditional culture without replacing it with a coherent culture. Furthermore, this social decay does not lead to development in Boeke's view.

More optimistic views of the prospects for desirable change have been extensively expounded by, among others, Margaret Mead, Charles Erasmas, and Clifford Geertz.[14] Geertz emphasizes that there are a wide variety of cultural systems capable of economic growth. Successful economic planning will incorporate cultural differences in the plans and not try to supplant existing social organizations with drastically different organizations patterned along some predetermined design. Mead emphasizes that people want to be active participants in change rather than merely submit to being changed. They may not be fairly classified as resisting change and clinging to a traditional culture for its own sake. Erasmus insists on the rationality of many decisions in traditional societies. Behavior, which outside experts attribute to resistance to change or irrationality, may result from flaws in the proposed change unperceived by the experts, by lack of appropriate communication about the benefits of the change, or by insufficient funds to undertake a risky venture. Change, in the views of Geertz, Mead, and Erasmus, comes from understanding and working through existing organizations and cultures. It comes from recognizing peoples' desire to participate in their own development. Change does not come from drastically altering social organizations but by recognizing the different situations that people face.

The role that religion and culture play in creating and encouraging entrepreneurship has received much attention since Weber and Tawney. This emphasis on the entrepreneur is also due to the influence of Joseph A. Schumpeter, who made the supply of entrepreneurship the centerpiece of both his theory of development and his business cycle theory.[15] An entrepreneur is a social deviant with the desire to achieve for its own sake. Schumpeter stressed that entrepreneurship is determined by the social climate as well as the level of profits. Long and short waves of economic progress are, in his view, generated by clusters of entrepreneurial activity. Some social institutions encourage more entrepreneurial activity than others and, hence, experience more rapid economic progress. To provide an appropriate climate for entrepreneurship, successful innovation has to be highly rewarded to overcome society's natural resistance to social deviants (i.e., to potential entrepreneurs). Schumpeter doubted that government or business bureaucracies of technocrats could adequately perform an entrepreneurial role. Development was to come through appropriate rewards to entrepreneurship and by resisting the powers of these oligarchies of technocrats.

The supply of entrepreneurship and not the rewards to innovation have been central to the theories of David C. McClelland and Everett E. Hagen.[16] They borrow and extend Schumpeter's notion that an entrepreneur has the need to achieve for achievement's sake. McClelland invents a term, *n-achievement,* to represent the achievement forces in society. The Weber–Tawney thesis of the influence of Protestantism on economic growth is said to be a special case of the argument that societies with high n-achievement have high rates of economic growth. Entrepreneurs are said to be individuals with high n-achievement. McClelland shows little interest in discussing institutions that foster n-achievement. Indeed, the focus of his arguments is on establishing n-achievement as an independent cause of development.

Hagen's views are more comprehensive than McClelland's. Hagen synthesizes elements of Weber, Tawney, Geertz, Schumpeter, and McClelland. Contrary to Mead and Erasmus, he sees traditional society as resisting change. Workers and peasants do not have access to venture capital, and the elite may feel that many enterprises are demeaning. The entrepreneurial class, if it arises, must come from a cohesive group on the fringe of society. Such minority status, however, is not enough to create an entrepreneurial class. The minorities that spawned entrepreneurs also lack status and were looked upon by society's elite as being both inferior and a little odd. At the same time, such minorities regarded the elite as immoral or irreligious. Hence, they felt superior to the elite, which held them in contempt. These groups often turned to the attainment of wealth as a sign of their superiority. Hagen contends that the Protestant dissenters in England were one such group. Rapid economic growth may enhance the supply of entrepreneurship but the latent causes are largely sociological.

For the most part, writers in the Weber–Tawney tradition have been criticized for paying too much attention to sociological or religious factors in economic development. For example, Benjamin Higgins is highly critical of Weber, Tawney, Hagen, Boeke, and especially McClelland. He does not deny that entrepreneurship plays an important role. He does contend that a "big push" on all economic fronts can rapidly overcome traditional reticence to change. Higgins also supports a big push thesis for economic reasons. He contends that the opening of new markets and the discovery of a frontier with easily exploitable resources provided the big push for economic development in much of Europe. This big push occurred with the discovery and exploitation of the New World. The lack of an entrepreneurial class, however, is one of the reasons a big push might be necessary. This concern with the supply of entrepreneurship does, as we will see, influence many specific theories about growth in less developed countries. Concerns about entrepreneurship also play a role in more recent historical theories that attempt to describe stages of development and the forces that lead to a transition from one stage to another. It is to theories of the stages of growth that we now turn our attention.

Stages of Growth

As we saw, Marx classified history in economic epochs or stages. He had a theory of why stages changed. These changes were initiated by changes in the conditions of production. There were competing classifications of economic history developed by Marx's contemporaries, which have been extended by more modern writers such as Allan G. B. Fisher, Colin Clark, and W. W. Rostow.[17] These early theories were proposed by various members of what has become to be known as the *German historical school*. Similar to Marx, writers in this school viewed history as evolutionary in the sense that more advanced economic systems evolved from more primitive systems. An exception to this view was Wilhelm Roscher who likened economic orders to a biological organism, which grows, matures, then decays. Writers in this general tradition also viewed economic forces as eventually leading to cultural changes and, hence, owe a debt to Marx. The stage theorists paid more attention than Marx to cultural and sociological influences in the economy. At least, there was some criticism of others for ignoring these influences. Stage theories retain some influence in formulating and justifying economic and political policy, so a brief discussion of their history will help in understanding their influence.

Stage theorists have used diverse schemes for classifying economic history into epochs. Three such schemes will be considered. One scheme classifies stages by the dominant occupations of an era. For example, Friedrich List divides history into savage, pastoral, agricultural, manufacturing–agricultural, and manufacturing–agricultural–commercial stages. More recently, Clark and Fisher formulated similar schemes. Another scheme classifies epochs according to the dominant exchange system. Bruno Hildebrand organizes history into natural or barter, monetary, and credit stages. The third scheme categorizes economic development by the scope of the economy. Karl Bücher classifies economic development into household, town, and national economies.

Of course, these classification themes are interdependent in many ways. It is, for example, difficult to imagine a pastoral, national, credit economy. Some writers, most notably Werner Sombart, had multiple classificatory schemes. Our attention, however, will be focused on more straightforward taxonomies. First, List and then Bücher will be discussed in more detail. Then, Rostow will be discussed.

Like many stage theorists, List concentrates his attention on more recent stages. Specifically his concern is with the conditions by which the agricultural stage is transformed into the manufacturing–agricultural stage. First, he claims that only nations in the temperate zone are suitable for manufacturing. Other nations will progress more rapidly if they continue to produce agricultural goods and exchange them for the manufactured products of the temperate zone. Thus, free trade should occur between these two types of producers. In addition, those nations of the temperate zone that are not yet prepared for industrialization will advance best by maintaining free trade with the manufacturing nations. However, latecomers, whose regions are suitable for manufacturing, should enact protective tariffs.

The introduction of manufacturing into a temperate region is made possible once the region or nation has achieved a high level of agricultural development. The introduction of manufacturing then changes society both by expanding production and by changing institutions and culture. Thus the main dynamic element in the process of economic growth, according to List, is the introduction of manufacturing. Agriculture grows only as a result of the stimulus of export demand or by its interaction with industrial growth. This view, that industry, not agriculture, is the dynamic factor, does not stem from the notion that industry has superior productive capabilities relative to agriculture. Instead, List emphasizes the association between agriculture and despotism and between manufacturing and both political and personal liberty. Specifically, he believes that societies based primarily upon agriculture will be inhabited by a tradition oriented people who are likely to be dominated by a despot and who lack the spirit of innovation. Whereas, a society dominated by industrial production is likely to be characterized, to a much greater degree, by personal and political freedom and the population would likely be inventive and forward looking. Thus, the superiority of industrial over agricultural production stems from the social and cultural features by which industrial and agricultural societies differ.

A different sort of stage theory was developed in the late 1800s by Karl Bücher. He argues that there were basically three stages in the growth process: the stage of the independent domestic, or household, economy; the stage of the town economy; and the stage of the national economy. The domestic economy is characterized by the absence of exchange and thus production is solely for the consumption of the household. The town economy stage is characterized by exchange, but it is limited to goods that pass directly from producer to consumer; that is, there are no intermediaries. Ideally, all production is directly for the consumer.

The transition from the household to the town economy arises from the dissolution of the household economy and can last a long time. The dissolution of the household economy was, in Europe, related to a peculiar feature of the European city of the middle ages. The city at this time was, according to Bücher, organized for defense; and this required the economic cooperation, through exchange, of its inhabitants.

The national economy is characterized by Bücher as that in which goods are produced for wholesale as well as directly for the consumer. The producer and consumer are generally unknown to each other, and goods generally pass through many stages of production before they finally reach the consumer. The transition from the town economy to the national economy occurs as the result of the rise of the nation state. In other words, the transition is the result of a political reorganization that replaces the particularism of medieval society with the modern unified state. Thus, for Bücher, the process of economic growth and the transition from stage to stage is based on various forms of political and social reorganization.

A major difference between List and Bücher is that List viewed the transition to a new stage as occurring because the level of development in a previous stage had passed some critical level. Cultural, political, and social institutions then changed. Bücher stresses the unintended economic impact of changes in the political system. Bücher also emphasizes the importance of feudalism in Europe for European economic development. Recent historical inquiries have emphasized technological advances in medieval Europe. The invention and implementation of the heavy wheel plow dramatically improved European agriculture from the Roman period.[18] More of these innovations will be considered in Chapter 3.

Rostow, the best known current stage theorist has more in common with List than with Bücher. Rostow stresses that gradual economic changes eventually result in revolutionary changes in economic and political institutions. He posits that all societies pass through five stages in the growth process: the traditional society, the preconditions for takeoff, the takeoff, the drive to maturity, and the age of high mass consumption.

Rostow says little about the traditional society except that it is based on pre-Newtonian science and technology and on pre-Newtonian views of the physical world. He does not view this society as being completely static. Output could be increasing through the expansion of land under cultivation or the spread of a new crop. However, the central fact concerning this type of society is that there is a ceiling on attainable output per head. This ceiling stems from the inaccessibility of modern science. Thus, these societies generally devote a large proportion of their resources to agriculture and are characterized by a hierarchical social structure in which there is little possibility for vertical mobility. The value system that prevails is what Rostow calls a *long-run fatalism*. That is, people view the possibilities open to their children and grandchildren as no different from those available now and in the past. Therefore, there is little or no conception of progress.

The second stage of growth, the preconditions, is that period of time in which the foundations for economic transformation are laid. The insights of modern science are beginning to be translated into increases in productivity for both industry and agriculture. People begin to view the world as dynamic and a place in which economic progress is possible. New types of entrepreneurs appear who are willing to mobilize savings and undertake risk in the establishment of new enterprises. Investment increases and the scope of commerce widens. In terms of political organization, it is during this period that an effective centralized national state begins to emerge.

During the takeoff stage, growth comes to dominate the society. Industry expands rapidly and savings rates rise from 5 to 10 percent of national income. Revolutionary increases occur in agriculture as well as in industry. Urban areas rapidly expand and the urban labor force grows. In a decade or two both the basic structure of the economy and the social and political structure of the society are transformed, so that a steady rate of growth can be maintained.

During the drive to maturity some 10–20 percent of national income is saved and invested. The economy, which during takeoff concentrated on a relatively narrow complex of industry and technology, now extends to new industries and technologies. Thus, maturity is the stage in which an economy demonstrates the ability to diversify beyond those industries that promoted the takeoff and apply new and advanced technology over a wide range of industries.

Finally, a society attains the stage of high mass consumption. The leading sectors of the economy shift to producing durable consumer goods and services. In addition, the society ceases to accept as an overriding goal the development of new technology and rapid economic growth. Instead, additional resources are allocated, through the political process, toward establishing social welfare programs and providing economic security.

The most important stages for development would seem to be the preconditions for takeoff. The preconditions stage is, in essence, the time during which savings and investment rise to a level that regularly exceeds population growth. Much of this investment will be needed to increase the productivity of the agricultural sector. Rostow sees agriculture as performing three important roles. First, it must provide additional food for the increased population as well as for the increasing numbers of people who earn their livings in manufacturing. Second, rising income will lead to increases in the demand for commodities produced by the industrial sector. Thus the expansion of the modern industrial sector will be stimulated. Third, agriculture will have to provide much of the savings necessary to finance the expansion of the modern industrial section.

With respect to the noneconomic side of the preconditions for takeoff, a new elite must emerge and gain the power necessary to construct a modern industrial society. The old land based elite and their control over the resources for growth must be broken. This is likely to involve the establishment of the modern nation state and the development of a nationalist ideology.

The stages of growth theories reviewed here all differ significantly in the types of stages that a nation is hypothesized to pass through. However, a common element that tends to characterize all of these theories is an emphasis on the importance of noneconomic factors in the development process. List argued that promoting manufacturing is the key to growth not because of the economic characteristics of this type of production. Instead, the key is the cultural and social environment that evolves as a result of the establishment of industry. This environment further stimulates growth. With respect to Bücher, political factors play a key role in promoting economic growth. For Rostow, the rise of a new elite and establishment of the nation state are crucial. Thus all these theories stress noneconomic factors in the process of transition from one state to another.

THE CLASSICAL THEORY

Having discussed historical theories of how development occurred, we are ready to turn to specific theories of development. These theories do not necessarily draw insights from historical theories. Indeed, the classical theory that will be sketched in this section was formulated before any comprehensive historical theories of economic development were proposed. Nonetheless, the classical theory draws inspiration from the view that the extension of markets is crucial to what has come to be known as economic development. The classical view of the role of the extension of markets in promoting economic growth and development will be illustrated for a simple exposition of growth based on Ricardian theory. We will later see that variants of this theory are still of interest today within the context of dualistic models of growth. We will also see that the emphasis on market size is important in recently developed neoclassical theories of growth and trade.

The Ricardian model will first be developed for a capitalist agricultural sector.[19] Three key elements of Ricardian theory require a little initial explanation. First, the supply of workers in the long run is determined by the costs of subsistence. In other words,

$$\hat{L} = L(w - w_s), \tag{1.1}$$

where $\hat{L}$ is the rate of growth of the labor supply (i.e., $\hat{L} = (\partial L/\partial t)/L$), w is the real wage rate, and s is the subsistence level of wages. It is usually assumed that $\hat{L} \gtrless 0$ if $(w - w_s) \gtrless 0$, $L(0) = 0$, and $L'(w - w_s) > 0$. In examples, however, labor supply is usually assumed to be perfectly elastic at the subsistence wage rate. Second, wages are advanced to workers, before any production occurs, out of a wages fund. The employer or capitalist earns a return on these funds as one does from every form of investment. In the agricultural sector, capitalists are seen as providing funds for seed, equipment, wages, and perhaps, rent at the beginning of the agricultural season. Revenues, however, are not realized until after the harvest. Third, the quality of land is variable, and the best land is used first. The capitalist might use labor to farm a given plot of land more intensely or to extend cultivation to more land. Ricardo refers to these possibilities as the intensive and extensive margins of production. Having explained these three elements of

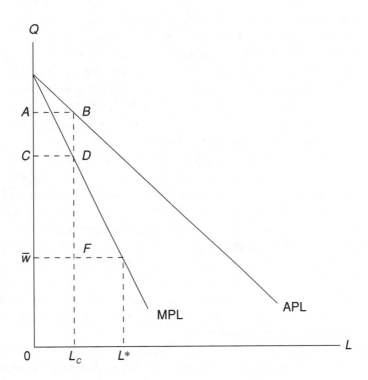

Figure 1.1   The rational choice of the Ricardian capitalist.

Ricardian theory, other characteristics can be explained as the models are developed.

There are (n + 2) factors of production in the simple Ricardian model. They are labor, capital and n types of land. Capital, however, is assumed to be used in direct proportion to labor (i.e., $K = \alpha L$). Hence, on a given plot of land of a given quality, there is only one variable input, labor. The rational choice of the capitalist is illustrated in Figure 1.1. In the figure, $\bar{w}$ is the subsistence wage rate, MPL and APL are the marginal and average products of labor (with its required capital). As can be seen, diminishing returns are assumed for every input combination.

Two types of models are illustrated in Figure 1.1. First, in the neoclassical model as developed in Chapter 2, the firm hires until the real wage rate equals the marginal product of labor. This point is illustrated by L^*. In the classical model, the size of the wages fund, which must be available in advance of production in order to to hire workers, limits the demand for labor. Before discussing the determination of the size of this fund and its dynamics, simply denote E as the fund size. Hence, if $E < \bar{w}L^*$, hiring will be restricted by what will be called the *wages fund constraint*. In Figure 1.1, labor demand is L_c (the subscript is for classical demand) where $L_c = E/\overline{w}$. Note that in the classical model, labor is paid less than its marginal product.

The classical model becomes explicitly dynamic when the determinants of the wages fund are considered. Since the wages fund is available at the beginning of the season, it must come from the previous year's harvest. To illustrate, consider the size of the wages fund for the next year for the capitalist who had hired L_c, in Figure 1.1 in the current year. Total output is $0ABL_c$ of which $CABD$ goes to the landlord as rent, and $0CDL_c$ goes to the capitalist. The amount $0\overline{w}FL_c$ is that paid to workers during the period. In other words, the capitalist could keep the size of the wages fund constant through time by advancing $0\overline{w}FL_c$ to workers at the beginning of each period. This would leave profits of $\overline{w}CDF$ for the capitalists' own consumption. If part of these profits are used to expand production, the wages fund would rise. Hence, employment in the next period would be higher. This process of profit-financed expansion could continue until the size of the labor force reaches L^*. At this point there would be no profits and output would go entirely to landlords as rent and to workers as wages. Hence, L^*, called a *stationary state,* is a point where growth stops in the absence of technical improvements.

The economy might, of course, never reach the stationary state at L^* for numerous reasons. Perhaps most important, the expansion to L^* seems to be based on the assumption of irrationality on the part of the capitalist. Suppose that the capitalist wishes to maximize profits in the stationary state. In other words, employment is expanded until $\partial\pi/\partial L = 0$, where

$$\pi = (MPL) \cdot L - \overline{w}L = (\partial Q/\partial L)L - \overline{w}L \qquad (1.2)$$

are profits. Profits are maximized at

$$\tilde{L} = (\overline{w} - \partial Q/\partial L)/\partial^2 Q/\partial L^2. \qquad (1.3)$$

$\tilde{L}$ is obviously less than L^*. For example, the reader can verify that if MPL $= a + bL$, $a > 0$, $b < 0$, then $\tilde{L} = \dfrac{1}{2}\left(\dfrac{\overline{w} - a}{b}\right)$. Since at L^*, $\overline{w} = a + bL^*$, $L^* = \dfrac{\overline{w} - a}{b}$. Hence, $\tilde{L} = \dfrac{1}{2}L^*$.

When a manufacturing sector is added to the model, however, this apparent irrationality disappears.[20] Ricardo believed, first, that the rate of profits between sectors are equal and, second, that there are constant returns in manufacturing. Hence, for constant output and factor prices, profits and, indeed, the rate of profits would not decline as the manufacturing sector expands. However, the real wage rate would rise because of diminishing

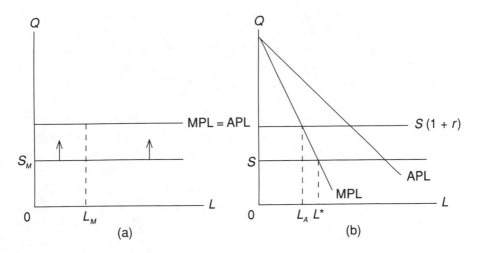

Figure 1.2 The two–sector Ricardian model.

returns in agriculture. Expanding output in manufacturing would reduce the relative price of industrial versus agricultural goods. The real wage rate would rise in the industrial sector, reducing the rate of profits. This in turn would expand agricultural output and reduce the rate of profits in agriculture. This process would continue until profits are zero.

The two–sector Ricardian model is illustrated in Figure 1.2. In Figure 1.2(a), industrial output is shown for the long run where capital is variable. Constant returns mean that the long-run marginal and average products are equal. They are above the subsistence wage rate for manufacturing, S_M. The rate of profits, r, is proportional to $(APL - S_M)/S_M$. However, S_M is not unique. It depends on the relative levels of output of industrial goods and the output of agricultural goods. As the manufacturing sector expands, S_M will rise.

For a given S_M and its implied level of employment, L_M, equilibrium employment in agriculture is L_A, where $S(1 + r) = MPL$. In other words, L_A is the employment level where the rate of profits is equalized between the two sectors. As profits are used to increase the wages fund and expand L_M, the expansion of L_M will raise S_M and lower r. The lower r will in turn lower $S(1 + r)$, expanding L_A until $r = 0$ and $L_A = L^*$. Hence, a stationary state would eventually occur even if capitalists are rational.

The arrival of the stationary state could be postponed in a number of ways. If cheap imported sources of food for workers' consumption could be found, the cost of maintaining workers at subsistence would decline; that is, the wage rate of industrial labor would fall. Alternatively, if technical innovations could be developed and applied to agricultural production, the marginal product curve in agriculture would shift to the right. Both of these would tend to increase profits and thus additional capital accumulation and growth could occur before the final stationary state was attained. Technical improvements in manufacturing would increase both the marginal product of labor in manufacturing and the rate of profits, but again it would merely postpone the final stationary state.

It is not clear how optimistic Ricardo was about the prospects for humankind. He tended to analyze policy for a fixed wage rate identifying progress and improvements in the conditions of workers with expansion of the labor force.[21] Formal Ricardian models, therefore, have an aura of pessimism around them both for the short term and for the stationary state. Clearly something is missing, however, in a model that attempts to make policy recommendations on the basis of which policy will lead to a higher stationary state level of employment.

In the late 1800s marginalism began displacing Ricardian classical economics as the dominant mode of thought. The marginalists replaced the classical concern with the very long-run supply price with a concern over resource allocation and efficiency within a shorter, static framework. Prices and economic behavior were seen as the interaction of supply and demand. It was still possible for the supply of labor to be horizontal in the very long run but the focus of economics was shifted to more immediate concerns. After World War II, economists shifted more attention to long-run problems. At this time a number of economists developed concepts of balanced growth. It was argued that because of indivisibilities in the production function (lumpiness of capital), in demand, and in the supply of savings, a critical minimum effort is necessary to push less developed nations out of their low-level equilibrium traps.[22] It is critical to the success of such a program that the big push must involve a more or less synchronized application of capital to a wide range of different industries; that is, balanced growth.

A number of economists, however, rejected the notion of balanced growth. They argued that it was just not possible for a less developed country to carry out such a program. Two groups of economists argued for unbalanced growth. The group that will concern us in this section developed dualistic models of economic development based on classical theory. These theories provide relevant insights into the balanced versus unbalanced growth debate as well as into the growth process itself. Perhaps the best known modern classical model is that developed by W. Arthur Lewis.[23] Most of the discussion of classical dualistic models of growth that follows is based on his work. The other group, which will be discussed later, is based on the work of John Maynard Keynes. Demand creation in one sector is thought to promote growth by drawing slack resources into supplying this sector. Hence, growth would be stimulated in other sectors as a well. The leading proponent of these Keynesian theories is probably Albert Hirschman.[24] Hirschman further argues that the ability to invest and carry out entrepreneurial activities is the major bottleneck to growth. Therefore, to develop these abilities, growth should be deliberately unbalanced in order to induce entrepreneurs to develop their abilities and carry out investment. In other words, investment should be concentrated in those sectors with extensive links to the rest of the economy. The expansion of these sectors will stimulate investment and entrepreneurial activity in the rest of the economy through such linkages. Although these two groups of theories may be stated in a compatible way, they will be presented separately, with the dualistic models considered here and the Keynsian models in the next section.

In dualistic models, the economy is divided into two sectors called *traditional* and *capitalist*. In the traditional sector, no net savings or capital accumulation occurs. Labor is employed at a subsistence wage, generally greater than its marginal product. In other words, in this sector profit maximization is not a goal of producers. Finally, it is possible, though not required in the theory, for the marginal product of labor to be zero. The capitalist sector is assumed to use capital and labor in the production process. Additional capital can be accumulated as a result of capitalist entrepreneurs saving and investing a part of their profits. Labor is assumed not to save and is employed up to the point where its marginal product equals the real wage rate. Thus, capitalists are profit maximizers. Surplus labor is assumed to exist, meaning that the supply of labor to the modern sector (from the traditional sector) is unlimited at the subsistence wage or a wage slightly above the subsistence wage.

According to Lewis, there are a number of sources of surplus labor in a less developed country, including farmers, petty traders, and retainers; the wives and daughters of the households; and new entrants to the labor force in a rapidly growing population. Note that the concept of surplus labor as used by Lewis does not require the assumption that the marginal product of labor in the traditional sector is zero. This is a misconception that has led to much confusion in the discussion of the Lewis model. All that is required is that labor is supplied to the modern sector at a constant cost.

Figure 1.3 is helpful in discussing the operation of the model. Output of the modern capitalist sector is being measured on the vertical axis and labor along the horizontal axis. MP represents the marginal product of labor, WS is the supply of labor, and $0W$ is the subsistence wage rate. The total output produced by employing $0M$ labor is given by the area $0NSM$. The share of output paid to labor is $0WSM$, and the share received by the capitalist is WNS. The capitalist is assumed to save a proportion of these profits, creating new capital that shifts the marginal product of labor to the right, and hence, additional labor is employed. This process of rapid expansion continues until surplus labor ceases to exist and the wage rate

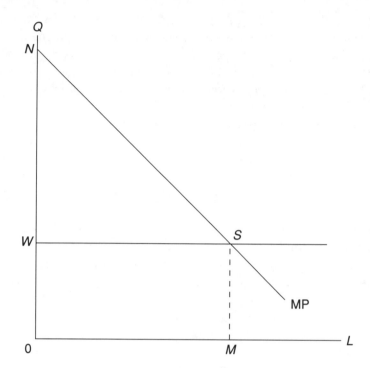

Figure 1.3 The roles of capital and labor in generating rapid economic expansion of the modern sector.

starts to rise. This increasing wage rate reduces profit rates and slows down the rate of economic growth.

Figure 1.3 illustrates the roles of a fixed wage rate and of profits and savings in generating rapid economic expansion of the modern sector. Saving and investment in the modern sector is the key to economic development in Lewis's view. Furthermore, savings and investment occur because capitalists earn profits. Anything that alters the distribution of income in favor of these capitalists would increase savings and investment. This increase in the income of capitalists would, of course, require inequality in the distribution of income, but inequality does not ensure high savings. The income distribution might be highly unequal without a prosperous capitalist class because inequality could be due to high agricultural rents. Thus, according to Lewis, most of the income might initially be going to a traditional landlord class that does little saving. The key to growth is that income must be shifted in favor of the class that saves.

The expansion process can be brought to a halt, before surplus labor is exhausted, by a number of factors. First, if capital accumulation proceeds faster than population growth, the absolute number of people in the subsistence sector will decline and, under certain conditions, average product in that sector will rise. In other words, the availability of goods per person in the traditional sector will rise. To attract additional labor, the modern sector will have to pay a higher wage, and this will slow down capital accumulation. Second, the increase in the size of the modern capitalist sector relative to the traditional sector may turn the terms of trade against the former. If the workers in the modern sector consume the output of the traditional sector (food), the capitalists will have to increase the wage rate of labor, and this will slow down capital formation. Third, the subsistence sector may become more productive, and thus workers there will earn higher incomes. Again, if the modern sector is to attract additional labor it must pay a higher wage, and this reduces capitalist profits. Finally, workers in the capitalist sector may imitate the capitalist way of life and therefore may need more to subsist, leaving the capitalist less to invest.

In summarizing the operation of the Lewis model, it is convenient to assume that the traditional sector is agricultural in nature. Thus, growth in the modern sector is fueled by the savings of the capitalists, which draws surplus labor out of the traditional agricultural sector. Hence, initially we have unbalanced growth. However, stagnation may very well occur as a result of this initial phase of rapid unbalanced growth if technological innovation and investment do not occur in the traditional agricultural sector. The rapid expansion of the modern sector combined with rapid population growth is likely to result in the rapid expansion of the demand for food. This increased demand for food may turn the terms of trade against the modern sector. This deterioration in the terms of trade would slow down the growth of the modern sector.

To ensure the continued rapid growth of the modern sector, investment in new technology and capital for the traditional sector would have to be carried out. Hence, in the long run, growth must be balanced in nature. As a result, the terms of trade might not turn against the modern sector. However, the rise in income in the traditional sector could also threaten further growth, because it could raise rural wage rates and, hence, require higher wages in the modern sector to attract new workers. Thus, balanced long-run growth can be successful only if the benefits of growth in the traditional sector are somehow transferred to the modern sector through, for example, taxation.

The Lewis model represents a modern version of the classical model. In both the Ricardian and Lewis models the supply of labor is infinitely elastic, surplus labor exists, and wages are at subsistence. The capitalist class is the dynamic force promoting growth through their saving and investment activities. Furthermore, in both models the growth process can grind to a halt for similar reasons. In Ricardo's model, the lack of technological innovation allows the law of diminishing returns to operate. Profits in agriculture are reduced by rising rent and fixed subsistence wages. Profits in manufacturing fall as the relative price of food rises. In Lewis's dualistic development model, short-run unbalanced growth in the modern sector could, in the absence of increased productivity in the traditional sector, be halted due to the rising relative cost of food. Within both models, the slowing of growth can be postponed through technological innovation. In addition, the Lewis model implies that in the long run only balanced growth is feasible.

There are also some notable differences between Ricardo and Lewis. Lewis drops the wages fund constraint to hiring. No longer are new workers and new machines assumed to be optimally hired from a competing fund. Instead, savings determine investment. Workers are simply hired up to the point where the marginal product of labor equals the fixed subsistence wage rate. Consequently, the decreasing MPL curve in Figure 1.3 represents short-run marginal product while the constant MPL in Figure 1.2 is for the long run. Diminishing returns come in the agricultural sector in Ricardo's model whereas in Lewis there are numerous assumptions, including constant returns, that could justify the fixed wage rate. It should be evident, however, that in translating the classical model into neoclassical terms many of the basic insights are left intact.

Gustav Ranis and John Fei[25] also developed a classical model of dualistic growth which was based, to a great extent, on the work of Lewis. Their model analyzes the process by which an economy characterized by surplus labor was transformed into a fully commercialized economy. This transformation takes place in three stages. Initially surplus labor exists and the marginal product of labor in the traditional sector (agriculture) is zero. Thus the expansion of the modern sector, through savings and investment on the part of the capitalist class, could occur without any reduction in either agricultural output or the wage rate. In the second stage, the marginal product of labor in agriculture becomes positive. Thus, as labor moves to the modern sector, agricultural output will fall. As a result, the terms of trade will turn against the modern sector if it consumes agricultural commodities from the traditional sector. Consequently, wage rates will begin to rise. These rising wage rates may then pose problems for further expansion. Therefore investment needs to be directed to the traditional sector to increase productivity there and cheapen agricultural commodities. Then the expansion of the modern sector could proceed until the commercialization stage (stage three) is reached, where surplus labor ceases to exist and labor is paid its marginal product.

Again, the similarities between the Ranis–Fei model and the Ricardian model are evident. Unbalanced growth in the short run in the Ranis and Fei model can, due to the lack of productivity growth in the traditional sector, be slowed or stopped. A similar process also occurs in the Lewis model. This period of sluggish growth can be postponed by investment in the traditional sector. Again balanced growth is seen as the only feasible long-run strategy for development.

KEYNESIAN GROWTH MODELS

Keynesian growth models claim inspiration from John Maynard Keynes and his analysis of unemployment. In these models, insufficient aggregate demand limits the prospects for economic growth and development. These models range from the Harrod–Domar growth model, where low investment or savings, combined with limited factor substitutability, prevent the economy from expanding rapidly enough to absorb its labor force, to the import-substitution models of Hirschman. Both of these models will be discussed in this section. Other Keynesian models, such as the Harris–Todaro model and the efficiency wage hypothesis, will be introduced in Chapter 5, when labor markets are considered.

The Harrod–Domar model is constructed on a number of simplifying assumptions.[26] First, savings, S, are assumed to be proportional to income, Y. Specifically, $S = sY$, where s equals the average and marginal propensity to save. The labor force L is assumed to grow at a constant exogenous rate n and therefore $\hat{L} = \dot{L}/L = n$. (Henceforth, $\dot{x}$ will denote $\partial x/\partial t$ and $\hat{x}$ will denote $\dot{x}/x$.) To simplify the exposition, it will be assumed that there is no technical innovation and that capital does not depreciate. The production function is of the fixed proportions type and can be written as

$$Y = \min \left(\frac{K}{v}, \frac{L}{u} \right), \tag{1.4}$$

where u and v are, respectively, the labor to output and capital to output ratios, both of which are assumed to be fixed. Thus output is constrained by either the quantity of labor or the quantity of capital available.

There are two types of capital in the model. There is utilized or required capital, K_r, and total capital, K (utilized plus idle capital). Potential output is given by

$$Q = K/v \tag{1.5}$$

and actual output is given by

$$Y = K_r/v, \tag{1.6}$$

where v is the underlying capital-output ratio defined in equation (1.4). Planned investment as a proportion of income is given by

$$I_p/Y = \dot{K}_r/Y = r \qquad (1.7)$$

where r is assumed constant. The rate of growth of actual income is found by dividing the time derivative of income in equation (1.6) by income, which yields

$$\hat{Y} = \frac{(\dot{K}_r/v)}{Y} = \frac{I_p/Y}{v}. \qquad (1.8)$$

Substituting equation (1.7) into (1.8) yields

$$\hat{Y} = r/v \qquad (1.9)$$

where r/v is called the *actual rate of growth*, G_a.

Another rate of growth, the rate of growth of capacity, $\hat{Q}$, can be found by dividing the time derivative of Q, equation (1.5), by Q yielding

$$\hat{Q} = \frac{\dot{K}/v}{Q}. \qquad (1.10)$$

In a simple Keynesian model, $\dot{K}$ is total investment (planned plus unplanned) and equals total savings. For a constant average propensity to save, s, we have

$$\dot{K} = sY. \qquad (1.11)$$

Substituting equation (1.11) into (1.10) yields

$$\hat{Q} = \frac{sY/v}{Q} = s(Y/Q)/v = s/v_r \qquad (1.12)$$

where $\hat{Q} = G_w$ is the *warranted rate of growth* and v_r is written as

$$v_r = \frac{Q}{Y} v. \qquad (1.13)$$

Dividing Q by Y, equation (1.5) by (1.6), allows (1.13) to be written as

$$v_r = vK/K_r. \qquad (1.14)$$

Before introducing the growth rate of the labor supply n into the model, consider the possibility that $G_a \neq G_w$ and the likely dynamic forces if that is the case. First, suppose r and s are fixed and that initially $Y = Q$ and $v = v_r$. If $r = s$, the economy continues to grow at the equilibrium rate. However, if $r < s$, v_r starts to rise as unplanned investment results in excess capacity in the economy. Although initially $G_a < G_w$, if r and s remain constant, v_r would rise until G_w falls to G_a. This flow equilibrium would not, however, be a stock equilibrium. Facing excess capacity, firms might decrease planned investment, reducing r. Again we would have $G_a < G_w$, which would increase v_r and further reduce r. A similar argument will apply for $G_a > G_w$. Hence, the economy would be unstable. For the economy to be stable, r would have to rise when there is unplanned investment and excess capacity in the economy and fall when demand exceeds capacity.

Interest rates may play a stabilizing role. We would, for example, expect interest rates to fall when savings exceed planned investment. These lower interest rates might stimulate investment enough to equilibrate the economy. Instantaneous interest rate adjustments might be postulated that would keep the economy on the equilibrium path. Once the economy falls off this path, however, it might not return.

Another potential source of disequilibrium arises when the size of the labor source is explicitly entered into the model. Recall that $\hat{L} = n$. Variable n is called the *natural rate of growth*. Even if instantaneous interest rate adjustments equate the actual and warranted rates of growth, there is no reason to assume that they will equal the natural rate. Only if $G_a = G_w = n$ can the equilibrium path be one of full employment. If $G_a = G_w < n$, both savings and planned investment need to be increased to reach the equilibrium path. Here, interest rate adjustments cannot equilibrate the economy. A rise in the interest rate would be required to increase savings and G_w, but this would reduce investment and G_a. Some government action to simultaneously stimulate investment and savings might be required. Alternatively, direct foreign assistance might increase $G_a = G_w$. Before discussing some of these Keynesian growth proposals in general, note that the model can be used by economists concerned with planning growth strategies for less developed nations. Once a country has chosen a target rate of growth, the planners must determine what resources will be needed to achieve this rate of growth. If we have some measure of the overall capital to output ratio, then we can use equation (1.6) to determine the investment (and savings) that will be necessary to achieve the targeted rate of growth. Of course, this sort of analysis can be carried out on a sectoral basis as well as for the entire economy. Hence, part of the Harrod–Domar model has become a rough planning tool for many development economists.

Basically two strategies have been suggested as vehicles for increasing savings and investment. The first strategy is to transfer income away from groups with low marginal propensities to save and invest to groups more amenable to saving and investing. This is a supply oriented strategy, which may imply redistributing income from the poor to the rich. However, this strategy might also imply redistributing income from the indolent aristocracy to the productive middle class. The role of savings will be emphasized in the next section on neoclassical growth. The second strategy is demand oriented and involves creating investment (and savings) opportunities for domestic entrepreneurs. As was mentioned earlier, Hirschman is probably the best known proponent of the demand creation strategy.

Four features of many poor countries and regions are important to Hirschman's view of development. First, there is an inadequacy of entrepreneurship. Second, there is often excess capacity in the economy. In terms of the Harrod–Domar model, r and s are insensitive to interest rates with $r < s$. Furthermore, r is rigid because of the habitual behavior of entrepreneurs, so that the economy is equilibrated by excess capacity (a low v_r). This excess capacity is hidden because much of what appears to be planned investment is really unproductive uses of capital. Third, and largely outside of the model, demand cannot be created by export expansion because the demand for exports is inelastic. Fourth, the reason for slow growth is not a lack of savings. Savings may be more than sufficient to achieve the natural rate of growth. The problem is low investment and a low actual rate of growth. For example, we might have the following situation:

$$r/v = s/v_r < n \leq s/v. \qquad (1.15)$$

The solution is to raise r (lowering v_r) and not to increase s.

Investment opportunities must be created in this demand oriented view by encouraging investment by local producers. There are two ways in which this investment can be encouraged. The first way to encourage investment is through what Hirschman calls *forward linkages*. *Forward linkage* refers to the supply of intermediate inputs of production. For example, electricity is an input to many products. Building a hydroelectric dam (through government spending) could lower the cost of production for many industries and perhaps induce producers to invest in some of these industries by raising r in the Harrod–Domar model. Furthermore, if excess capacity exists through inefficient unproductive capital (i.e., if $v_r > v$), new investment could raise the warranted rate of growth. The second way of increasing investment involves what Hirschman calls *backward linkages*. Backward linkages involve the creation of demand for a final or intermediate good. It is the creation of backward linkages that Hirschman emphasizes most.

One way of creating a market (backward linkages) for a good is to place restrictive tariffs on selected industries in the hope that domestic production will fill the gap. This strategy, called an *import substitution strategy*, has reputedly been widely practiced in poorer nations. Its rationale is that it could stimulate aggregate demand in areas where the economy can respond. The resulting increase in investment would increase r and reduce v, resulting in higher aggregate rates of growth. This success, however, depends on the assumption that the economy is characterized by excess capacity and a lack of entrepreneurship. As long as import substitution increases r for $G_a < s/v$, the import substitution strategy could increase growth rates. Once $r/v = s/v$, however, increased investment in one sector competes directly with investment in other sectors for available savings. At this point, savings would have to be increased to raise the rate of growth (assuming $s/v < n$).

Most criticisms of import substitution have been based on the assumption that the economy is either already at full employment or at least that $r/v = s/v$. They argue against import substitution on the grounds that tariffs distort the economy causing inefficiency. If, however, the economy has excess capacity, as illustrated in a Harrod–Domar growth model, import substitution might result in higher output of all goods by employing unused resources.

It should be pointed out that import substitution is not the only possible way of creating a market. Aggressive marketing by the government of the output of selected industries is an alternative. Again, if $r/v < s/v < n$, investment could be stimulated raising r and the rate of growth. An export oriented growth strategy could be successful as long as $r/v < s/v$. Once resources are fully employed, however, this strategy meets the same difficulties as import substitution. It should be emphasized that export expansion and import substitution are not opposites. They are simply alternate ways of stimulating investment when resources are underutilized. It is perfectly consistent for a country to follow import substitution for some goods and export expansion for others. Both can be justified in terms of backward linkages. If the economy is at full employment, export expansion can also distort the economy causing losses in real income. As we will see in the next section, the assumption of full employment leads to an emphasis on savings and aggregate supply as the important determinants of economic expansion. It is to full employment models that we now turn.

THE NEOCLASSICAL MODEL

There are two ways in which neoclassical growth models differ from Keynesian, Harrod–Domar models. First, the production function allows for unlimited substitution between capital and labor. Consequently, labor can be fully employed for any size of the capital stock. Second, planned investment and savings are assumed to always be equal because of instantaneous price adjustments.[27] Neoclassical models then focus attention on supply. Growth is to be achieved through higher rates of savings and, hence, through higher rates of capital formation. Diminishing returns, however, place severe limits on growth. The neoclassical model will be discussed and then extended in terms of its implications for economic growth and development.

In the neoclassical model, the savings function is the same as that used in the Harrod–Domar model; that is, $S = sY$. Again s represents both the marginal and average propensity to save. For the moment, assume that capital does not depreciate. Hence, investment is simply the rate of increase in the capital stock. Because planned investment is assumed to equal savings we can write

$$I = \dot{K} = sY. \tag{1.16}$$

The labor force is also assumed to grow at the rate of n. Finally, output is assumed to be a function of capital (K) and labor (L). The production function is assumed to be a continuous variable proportions function with constant returns to scale. It can be written as

$$Y = F(K, L)$$

or

$$\frac{Y}{L} = F(K/L, 1) = F(K/L) \tag{1.17}$$

or

$$y = f(k),$$

where y is output per worker and k is the capital to labor ratio. Furthermore, it is assumed that the marginal product of capital is positive for all levels of k but that it diminishes as k rises. Hence,

$$f'(k) > 0$$

and

$$f''(k) < 0. \tag{1.18}$$

To assure the existence of a unique and stable equilibrium, it is often assumed that

$$\lim_{k \to 0} f'(k) = \infty$$

and

$$\lim_{k \to \infty} f'(k) = 0. \tag{1.19}$$

Output or income is defined as consumption plus aggregate investment and, in per worker terms, can be written as

$$\frac{Y}{L} = \frac{C}{L} + \frac{I}{L}$$

or   (1.20)

$$y = f(k) = \frac{C}{L} + \frac{I}{L}.$$

where $I/L = \dot{K}/L$. To derive the fundamental equation for neoclassical growth theory, the determinants of I/L must be analyzed.

To derive the rate of growth of the capital to labor ratio $\hat{k} = \dot{k}/k$, note that

$$\hat{k} = \dot{k}/k = \hat{K} - \hat{L} = \dot{K}/K - \dot{L}/L. \qquad (1.21)$$

Equation (1.21) can be verified by differentiating the natural log of k. Assuming that the labor force grows at a constant rate, $n = \dot{L}/L$, equation (1.21) becomes

$$\hat{k} = \dot{K}/K - n. \qquad (1.22)$$

Multiplying both sides of equation (1.21) by $k = K/L$ we get

$$\dot{k} = \frac{\dot{K}}{L} - nk$$

or   (1.23)

$$\frac{\dot{K}}{L} = \dot{k} + nk.$$

Because I/L in equation (1.20) equals $\dfrac{\dot{K}}{L}$, substituting equation (1.23) into equation (1.20) yields

$$f(k) = \frac{C}{L} + \dot{k} + nk. \qquad (1.24)$$

Equation (1.24) simply states that output per worker goes to consumption, to increasing capital per worker, and to the net investment required to maintain the capital labor ratio as the labor force grows.

Equation (1.24) can be rewritten as

$$\dot{k} = f(k) - C/L - nk$$

or   (1.25)

$$\dot{k} = \frac{Y}{L} - \frac{C}{L} - nk.$$

Because $S = Y - C$ equation (1.25) can be written as

$$\dot{k} = \frac{S}{L} - nk$$

or   (1.26)

$$\dot{k} = sf(k) - nk.$$

Equation (1.26) is called the *fundamental equation* of neoclassical growth theory. Growth in the capital to labor ratio is determined by the difference between the amount of investment per worker that actually occurs and the amount required to keep the capital to labor ratio constant as the population grows.

Figure 1.4 is useful in illustrating the operation of the neoclassical theory of growth. Along the vertical axis output per worker is measured, Y/L, and the capital to labor ratio, k, is measured along the horizontal axis. The $f(k)$ curve shows that output per worker rises at a diminishing rate as k increases, due to the law of diminishing returns. The curve $sf(k)$ represents savings per person and the line nk has a positive slope equal to n. Examining Figure 1.4, k^* and y^* represent the steady state where capital, labor, and output are all growing at the same rate. This occurs where nk intersects $sf(k)$. In other words, when savings or capital accumulation per worker exactly equals the quantity required to keep the capital to labor ratio constant for the growing labor force. Algebraically, k^* is found by setting $\dot{k} = 0$ and solving equation (1.26) for k.

In order to see why k^* is a stable solution, suppose the capital to labor ratio is k_1. The amount of new capital being accumulated per person, $sf(k)$, then exceeds the amount of capital that would be required to keep the capital to labor ratio constant, nk_1. Thus, k and y would increase until k^* is reached. Alternatively, if the capital to labor ratio was k_2 then actual capital accumulation per person would be less than that necessary to keep the capital to labor ratio constant. Thus, y would fall as k fell to k^*. Hence, an equilibrium growth path exists. In addition, this growth path is stable in the sense that if the economy moves away from this path, forces exist that will push the economy back to equilibrium.

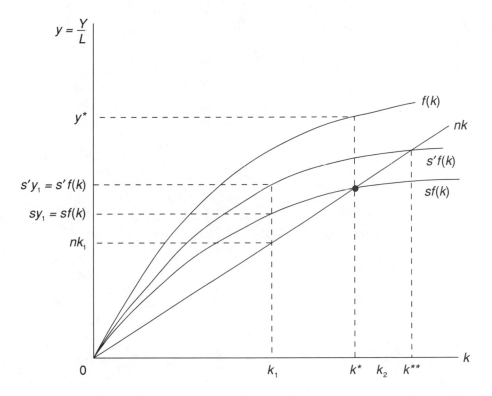

Figure 1.4   The neoclassical theory of growth.

Several interesting implications can be drawn from the neoclassical model both in terms of steady state income and in terms of the rate of growth in general. First, an increase in the marginal propensity to save will increase both steady state income per worker, y^*, and the rate of growth for $k < k^*$. In Figure 1.4, $s' > s$. Hence, at k_1, $\dot{k}_1$ rises from $sy_1 - nk_1$ to $s'y_1 - nk_1$. Eventually income per person rises to $f(k^{**})$ but consumption per worker at k^{**} may either rise or fall, as we will see. Second, a decline in the growth rate of the labor force necessarily increases the steady state, per worker income. The reader can verify this last point by rotating nk down in Figure 1.4.

To verify that an increase in the marginal propensity to save will not necessarily increase consumption per worker is fairly simple. First note that an initial increase in s necessarily lowers current consumption. However, eventually, consumption may rise above what would otherwise have been the case because of the increase in k. The difficulty is that, even in the long-run steady state, consumption per worker might be lower. Note that, if we restrict ourselves to the steady state, a change in s merely changes the point along nk where the economy comes to rest. Steady state consumption is then maximized when the distance $c^* = f(k^*) - nk^*$ is the greatest. By

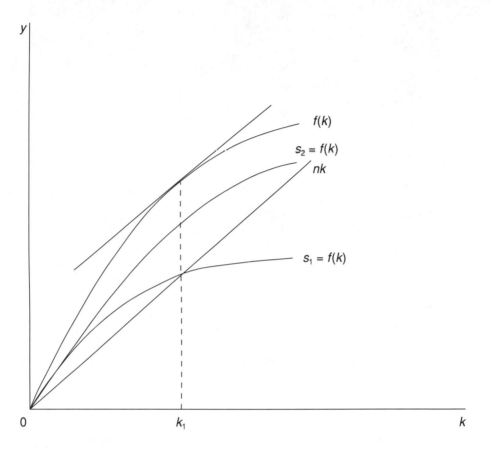

Figure 1.5   Golden rule of accumulation.

differentiating c^* with respect to k^* we have $\partial c^*/\partial k^* = f'(k) - n$. Setting $\partial c/\partial k = 0$ yields maximum steady state consumption

$$f'(k) = n \qquad (1.27)$$

which is illustrated in Figure 1.5. At k_1, $f'(k) = n$ and c^* is maximized. If savings rise from s_1 to s_2, c^* actually declines. Equation (1.27) is called the *golden rule of accumulation*. The implications of the neoclassical growth model for development are simple. Growth in per capita income can be achieved either by increased savings or reduced rates of population growth. These implications will hold when depreciation is allowed in the model. Depreciation can be introduced in several ways. Typically, δk is subtracted from equation (1.24), where δ is the rate of depreciation. The fundamental equation then becomes $\dot{k} = sf(k) - (n + \delta)k$. The line nk in Figure 1.4 is simply relabeled as $(n + \delta)k$.

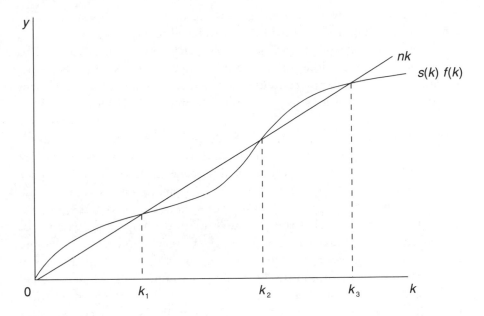

Figure 1.6 Low-level trap.

More interesting extensions involve making s or n endogenous (i.e., functions of other variables in the model). Endogenous population growth will be considered in the next chapter. Some possible implications of making s a function of income will be discussed here. Assume $sf(k)$ takes the shape illustrated in Figure 1.6. Several stories could be told to justify this shape; for example, savings might be a function of wage income and profits with a very low marginal propensity to save out of wages at low levels of wage income per worker. Capital intensity increases for $k < k_1$, and for $k_2 < k < k_3$. However, for $k_1 < k < k_2$ and for $k > k_3$, capital intensity falls. Hence, there are two stationary states. One is at k_1 and the other is at k_3. The economy, however, cannot grow past the low level stationary state because savings do not grow enough with income. It is stuck in this investment–savings trap. Small increases in k will do little good. As we will see in the next chapter, endogenous population growth may also suggest the need for an externally funded "big push."

THE NEW GROWTH ECONOMICS

The neoclassical growth model developed in the last section has been extended in two different ways to better explain actual growth rates. First, exogenous technical change has been introduced to explain why the rate of growth does not converge to zero because of diminishing returns. Second, endogenous technical change has been introduced to explain why per capita income and the rate of growth do not converge for every country. This second group of extensions, called the *new growth theory*, is particularly important for development economics. A central concern of development economics is to explain why per capita income and growth rates differ among countries.

Introducing exogenous technical progress into the model is straightforward. It will explain why a country can grow indefinitely, but it will not give a really satisfactory explanation of differences in growth rates. To see these shortcomings, we will concentrate on the savings rate. We saw in the last section that savings have only a temporary affect on economic growth. Once the economy reaches steady state k or y, the rate of growth is not influenced by the savings rate. For example, if capital depreciates at the rate δ and population grows at the rate n, then output (Y), labor (L), and capital (K) all grow at a rate of n in steady state equilibrium. Thus, k and y remain unchanged in this equilibrium as the rate of per capita economic growth approaches zero. This implication of the model, that growth converges to a rate of zero, is troubling because per capita income has been growing for several centuries in many countries.

The first extension to the neoclassical model will be to introduce exogenous technological progress into the model. Suppose this technological progress is Harrod neutral. *Harrod neutrality* means that technical improvement can be viewed as increasing the effective size of the labor force by making each worker more productive. The labor input can be written as

$$L(t) = e^{\lambda t}N(t) \tag{1.28}$$

where $N(t)$ is the number of workers, which has a growth rate of n, and λ is the constant rate of technical change. The rate of growth of L is then

$$\hat{L} = \lambda + n. \tag{1.29}$$

The neoclassical model can be modified to include Harrod neutral technical progress by replacing n in equation (1.26) with $\lambda + n$. Equation (1.26) becomes

$$\dot{k} = sf(k) - (\lambda + n)k, \tag{1.30}$$

where $\lambda + n$ is the growth rate of the augmented labor force, L. At the steady state, given by

$$sf(k^*) = (\lambda + n)k^*,\qquad (1.31)$$

real output grows at a rate of $\lambda + n$, output per worker grows at a rate of λ, and output per augmented worker is stationary at $f(k^*)$. The rate of growth of per capita income would be exogenous. Hence, long-term growth rates would not depend on savings rates. The introduction of exogenous technical progress explains persistent growth, but it cannot explain the role savings or other variables play in determining technical progress because productivity increases are exogenous to the model.

There are three basic difficulties with the exogenous growth model we have just considered. First, it implies convergence, in that the growth rates of countries with high and low savings rates will converge with time. Such convergence seems to be slow at best. Second, with free international trade or capital mobility, differences in per capita income should disappear, convergence in living standards should occur. Third, even if we assume initial differences in the rate of technical innovation between nations, a different kind of convergence should occur. First, each growth rate should converge to the long-run equilibrium, which is equal to the rate of technical change. Furthermore, if technical knowledge flows between nations, we would expect the rate of technical progress to converge. Hence, the growth rates should converge. The difficulty here is that such convergence is not occurring in the world or is occurring for only limited subsets of the world's countries.

Three different approaches have been developed that address the problems discussed previously. These approaches have collectively been called *new growth theories* or *endogenous growth theories*. In all these approaches it is assumed that each individual firm or entity faces a constant returns to scale production function but that external increasing returns exist for various reasons. These external returns are interpreted as though they were technical improvements. The three approaches emphasize technical improvements as resulting from the rate of investment, the size of the capital stock, and the stock of human capital. Each approach adds its own insights to development economics.[28]

The approach that can be most directly incorporated into the neoclassical model views technical progress as being a result of the rate of investment.[29] In other words,

$$\lambda = a + b(\dot{K}/Y),\qquad (1.32)$$

where λ now has an exogenous component, a, and an endogenous component, $b(\dot{K}/Y)$. If the savings rate is exogenous $\dot{K}/Y = s$, λ can be substituted into equation (1.31), yielding

$$sf(k^*) = (a + bs + n)k^*. \tag{1.33}$$

Per worker income would then grow at the rate $\lambda = a + bs$. A higher savings rate would clearly lead to a permanently higher growth rate. Hence, the growth rate would not converge.

There are numerous reasons to suppose that investment is a source of technical progress. If investing merely consists of the reduplication of existing capital, then investment does not represent innovation and is not a source of technical progress. However, investment may represent innovation in that firms invest to solve problems the firm faces, which are partly unique. If the investment is successful, other firms will seek to adapt the successful investment to their own needs. Thus, investing may represent a sequence of innovations with each innovation building upon previous innovations. This type of technical progress has been called *learning by watching*. Externalities, resulting from learning by watching, are seen as a key to development. Policies that increase investment should be pursued. These policies should be pursued even if savings are endogenous. Because the public returns to investment exceed the private returns, optimal savings, from the viewpoint of individuals, will be too low.

The remaining two approaches to endogenous growth differ from the learning by watching models in two basic ways. First and most important, they assume that only certain types of investment generate technical progress. Investment in human capital, research and development, and capital for a new, monopolistically competitive firm and not general investment are assumed to be the source of technical progress. Second, savings are exclusively treated as endogenous. For example, infinitely lived individuals are assumed to maximize the present value of consumption.

The first approach we will consider assumes that investment in human capital is the only type of investment generating externalities. This approach was developed by Uzawa and Lucas.[30] Labor can be devoted either to production or to the accumulation of human capital. Human capital, accumulated by the individual worker, will both make that worker more productive and increase the productivity of capital and other workers in the economy. Let e be the proportion of labor directly devoted to production and H be human capital. Output becomes

$$Y = AK^a(HeL)^{1-a}, \tag{1.34}$$

where the technical coefficient, $A = H^b$, represents the external effect of human capital on the Cobb–Douglas production function. Since H is a function of labor, per worker output can be found as a function of capital and labor. Each firm faces constant returns to scale, but there are increasing returns for the economy as a whole.[31]

Arrow and Romer have considered an approach where the size of the capital stock generates externalities.[32] Arrow introduced the concept of "learning by doing," and Romer has developed such a model where the size of the capital stock and research and development play crucial roles. Market size, interpreted as the amount of capital, determines the number of new goods introduced in monopolistically competitive markets. The technological index, A, represents the number of designs for new goods that are available. The research and development by firms can be represented as

$$\dot{A} = \delta H_A A, \tag{1.35}$$

where H_A is human capital employed in research, A is the existing number of designs, and δ represents the productivity of such research. An intermediate goods sector uses these designs together with foregone output to produce new producer durable goods available for use in final production. In the last sector, labor, human capital, and the set of available producer durables generates final output. The development of new intermediate goods is justified by the fact that decreasing returns in intermediate goods utilization in final goods production are assumed. Therefore, the only additional source of profit is through the creation of new intermediate goods.

The external increasing returns stem from the linking of the availability of new designs and the number of intermediate inputs. Each individual firm makes its decision concerning the allocation of resources to research, H_A, based on its effect on the number of new designs that will directly result. However, the new designs one firm generates increase the stock of knowledge available to all other firms. A will be larger in equation (1.35), making for more rapid innovation in all other firms (an externality).

The new growth theory has a number of interesting implications. Convergence of per capita growth rates can, in the environment of new growth theory, no longer be expected to occur. The external increasing returns to the accumulation of capital (this concept includes human capital) implies that the rate of return to investment will not fall in developed relative to less developed nations. Indeed, one might expect the rate of return to capital in capital abundant nations to exceed that in capital scarce nations, and capital need not flow from rich to poor nations, but actually just the reverse. Even if capital is not mobile between nations, Krugman has shown that trade between two countries can result in uneven development with manufacturing concentrated in the center and agricultural production in the periphery. This will naturally occur if manufacturing is subject to external increasing returns while agriculture is characterized by constant returns to scale.

The implication for government policy is also quite important. Neoclassical theory has recently argued that shrinking the size and influence of the state will markedly improve the economic performance of less developed countries. However, new growth theory indicates that private provision of human capital and investment in technological research will be too low given the existence of external increasing returns. Thus increases in overall growth can be achieved through appropriate government policy.

CONCLUSION

Theories of growth and development range from historical theories to specific theories of production and growth. Historical theories attempt to explain current conditions in terms of sequences of interconnected historical events. The historian then gathers detailed information to describe these salient events and support the historical story. This story is then generalized to make statements about development in general. Theories of production and growth explain current conditions in terms of current factor proportions and economic institutions. The exact sequence of events that led to the present state of the economy is not thought to be important to understanding the economy and how it will grow and perhaps evolve in the future. The growth theorist specifies production relationships, estimates the parameters of these relationships based on current or past data, and projects the path of the economy into the near future. Each approach has obvious strengths and weaknesses that will be discussed in turn.

Historical theories of growth focus attention on the interaction of events, culture, and economic institutions. Economic changes are viewed as a consequence and a cause of this interaction. Because changing culture and economic institutions are undeniably important in determining differences between economies, the historical approach has a valuable role to play in describing these factors. However, the seeming divergence of cultures and institutions make historical theories, which take account of this diversity, difficult to generalize. The generalizations risk being meaningless as a result of their attempt to be relevant to all regions or so specific that they are largely irrelevant to many regions. However, at a minimum, historical theories provide insights as to important institutional features to incorporate into specific models of production and growth.

Specific growth theories rigorously show the impact of key parameters on current production and growth. The relationships between key economic variables are derived through time for these (perhaps changing) parameters. To derive these relationships, the model has to be kept fairly simple. It will hold for only a few assumptions about institutions and economic relationships. These theories risk becoming irrelevant to an explanation of most actual behavior or intractable if they attempt to explain too much behavior. At a minimum, specific theories force us to be rigorous in our reasoning. If A is thought to cause B, the growth models make us rigorously state the intervening mechanism and tell a logically consistent story.

Elements of both types of theories add to our understanding of the development process. It is our contention that an economist who fails to incorporate both types of theories into explanations of the current economy will have more than the usual difficulty saying anything of relevance to the problems of less developed nations.

NOTES

1. For a comprehensive treatment of many development theories see W. W. Rostow, *Theorists of Economic Growth from David Hume to the Present with a Perspective on the Next Century* (Oxford: Oxford University Press, 1990).

2. For a detailed treatment of List, Bücher, and others in the German historical school, see Bert F. Hoselitz, "Theories of Stages of Economic Growth," in *Theories of Economic Growth*, ed. B. F. Hoselitz (New York: Free Press of Glencoe, 1960), pp. 193–238. For a treatment of Marx, see A. James Gregor, *A Survey of Marxism: Problems in Philosophy and the Theory of History* (New York: Random House, 1965), pp. 139–170. See also W. W. Rostow, *The Stages of Economic Growth: A Non-Communist Manifesto* (Cambridge: Cambridge University Press, 1961); and Andre Gunder Frank, "The Development of Underdevelopment," *Monthly Review* 18 (September 1966): 17–31.

3. See W. Arthur Lewis, "Economic Development with Unlimited Supplies of Labor," *Manchester School* 2 (May 1954): 139–191; and J. C. H. Fei and G. Ranis, *Development of the Labor Surplus Economy* (Homewood, Ill.: Irwin, 1964).

4. Karl Marx and Friedrich Engels, *The Communist Manifesto* (Baltimore: Penguin Books, 1972), p. 84.

5. Paul Baran, *The Political Economy of Growth* (New York: Monthly Review Press, 1957).

6. Samir Amin, *Accumulation on a World Scale: A Critique of the Theory of Underdevelopment*, 2 vols. (New York: Monthly Review Press, 1974). See also Ronald H. Chilcote, *Theories of Development and Underdevelopment* (Boulder, Colo.: Westview Press, 1984) for a review of neo-Marxist theories of development.

7. Geoffrey Kay, *Development and Underdevelopment: A Marxist Analysis* (New York: St. Martins Press, 1975).

8. Bill Warren, "The Postwar Economic Experience in the Third World," in *The Political Economy of Development and Underdevelopment*, ed. Charles Wilber (New York: Random House, 1984), pp. 109–133.

9. Alain de Janvry, *The Agrarian Question and Reformism in Latin America* (Baltimore: Johns Hopkins University Press, 1981).

10. Arghiri Emmanuel, *Unequal Exchange: A Study of the Imperialism of Trade* (New York: Monthly Review Press, 1972).

11. Max Weber, *The Protestant Ethic and the Spirit of Capitalism* (London: Allen and Unwin, 1983).

12. R. H. Tawney, *Religion and the Rise of Capitalism* (New York: New American Library of World Literature, 1955).

13. J. H. Boeke, *Economics and Economic Policy of Dual Societies* (New York: Institute of Pacific Relations, 1953) and Allen M. Sievers, *The Mystical World of Indonesia* (Baltimore: Johns Hopkins University Press, 1974).

14. For a summary of these contributions and the relevant bibliography, see Benjamin Higgins, *Economic Development: Principles, Problems and Policies*, rev. ed. (New York: W. W. Norton, 1968). We are highly indebted to Higgins for his treatment.

15. Joseph Schumpeter, *The Theory of Economic Development* (New York: Oxford University Press, 1961).

16. Everett E. Hagen, *On the Theory of Social Change* (Homewood, Ill.: Dorsey Press, 1962); David C. McClelland, *The Achieving Society* (Princeton, N.J.: D. Van Nostrand Co., 1961).

17. For a discussion of their views, see Hoselitz, "Theories of Stages."

18. See Rondo Cameron, *A Concise Economic History of the World: From Paleolithic Times to Present*, 2nd ed. (New York: Oxford University Press, 1993), pp. 44–77.

19. David Ricardo, *The Principles of Political Economy and Taxation* (London: Aldine Press, 1965; originally published in 1821).

20. See R. Grabowski and M. P. Shields, "Lewis and Ricardo: A Reinterpretation," *World Development* (February 1980): 193–197.

21. See Frederic Kolb, "The Stationary State of Ricardo and Malthus: Neither Pessimistic nor Prophetic," *Intermountain Economic Review* 3 (Spring 1972): 17–30.

22. See P. N. Rosenstein-Rodan, "Problems of Industrialization of Eastern and Southeastern Europe," *Economic Journal* 53 (June–September 1943): 202–211; and Ragnar Nurkse, *Problems of Capital Development in Underdeveloped Countries* (New York: Oxford University Press, 1953).

23. W. Arthur Lewis, "Economic Development with Unlimited Supplies of Labour," *The Manchester School* 22 (May 1954): 139–191.

24. A. O. Hirschman, *The Strategy of Economic Development* (New Haven, Conn.: Yale University Press, 1958). See also, Hirschman, "The Rise and Decline of Development Economics," in *The Theory and Experience of Economic Development*, ed. Mark Gersovitz, Carlos F. Diaz-Alejandro, Gustav Ranis, and Mark R. Rosenzweig (London: George Allen and Unwin, 1982), pp. 372–339.

25. John Fei and Gustav Ranis, "A Theory of Economic Development," *American Economic Review* 51 (September 1961): 533–565.

26. See R. F. Harrod, "An Essay in Dynamic Theory," *The Economic Journal* (March 1939): 14–33; and Evsey Domar, "Capital Expansion, Rate of Growth and Employment," *Econometrica* 14 (April 1946): 137–147.

27. For a similar treatment, see Hywel G. Jones, *An Introduction to Modern Theories of Economic Growth* (New York: McGraw-Hill, 1976), pp. 66–94.

28. See A. R. Barros, "Some Implications of New Growth Theory for Economic Development," *Journal of International Development* 5 (1993): 531–558; and Elhavan Helpman, "Endogenous Macroeconomic Growth Theory," *European Economic Review* 36 (1992): 236–267.

29. For more on investment as a source of technical progress, see Maurice Scott, "A New Theory of Endogenous Economic Growth," *Oxford Review of Economic Policy* 8 (Winter 1992): 29–42; Scott, *A New View of Economic Growth* (Oxford: Clarendon Press, 1989); and Mervyn A. King and Mark H. Robson, "Investment and Technical Progress," *Oxford Review of Economic Policy* 8 (Winter 1992): 43–56.

30. R. Lucas, "On the Mechanics of Economic Development," *Journal of Monetary Economics* 22 (1988): 3–42; and Hirofumi Uzawa, "Technical Change and the Aggregate Model of Economics Growth," *International Economic Review* 6 (1965): 18–31.

31. See King and Robson, "Investment and Technical Progress," p. 45; and Sergio Rebelo, "Long-Run Policy Analysis and Long-Run Growth," *Journal of Political Economy* 99 (June 1991): 500–521.

32. Kenneth J. Arrow, "The Economic Implications of Learning by Doing," *Review of Economic Studies* 29 (1962): 155–173; and Paul M. Romer, "Increasing Returns and Long-Run Growth," *Journal of Political Economy* 94 (1986): 1002–1037.

2

A Unifying Theme

There was much diversity in the theories of growth and development reviewed in the first chapter. The various theories seem to represent a welter of various views often contradictory and thus confusing. Furthermore, these views do not seem to be integrated into the main body of economic theory. Despite this diversity, an underlying theme can be found that provides a unifying framework for the study of development theory and integrates development theory with the rest of economic theory.[1]

The source of the unifying theme is found in the microeconomics of household and firm choice. Households and firms in less developed nations will be viewed as making choices in the same manner as households and firms in developed countries. Therefore a distinguishing characteristic of households and firms in poor nations is not to be found in terms of the process by which choices are made, but in terms of the context in which those choices are made. Explanations of behavioral differences will be sought, not in terms of differences in how choices are made but in terms of constraints on the choices that can be made. The rest of this chapter will be divided into two broad sections. First, a discussion of microeconomic choice theory is presented. Second, the context within which such choice is made in a less developed nation is explored. In this setting the distinguishing characteristics of a less developed economy are highlighted.

Economists assume rational behavior and yet irrational behavior is seemingly everywhere. Introspection and casual observation suggest that much of our own behavior and the behavior of others appears to be erratic, compulsive, or perverse. We behave irrationally out of anger, habit, whim, ignorance, laziness, fear, or lust. Indeed, we may take pleasure in our perceived irrationality because total rationality may imply a lack of creativity, spontaneity, or passion. In considering other cultures, as we must in development economics, rational behavior seems less likely. Rationality, after all, is often associated with modern, scientific modes of thought. Fleeting images of ritualistic behavior and mystical modes of thought pass through our minds as we imagine societies in economically backward areas of the world. Yet, the assumption that behavior is rational is rarely questioned or defended by economists. In choice theory, the meaning of rationality is explored in terms of the ways in which choice is structured. Furthermore, the implications of these choices in terms of their interactions are often the starting point for applied and theoretical work in other fields of economics. A discussion of rationality will help to explain and clarify the attractiveness of rationality assumptions for economists despite the seeming abundance of irrational behavior.

We will consider three concepts of rationality: strong rationality, rationality, and market rationality. First, an individual may actually calculate the pleasures and pains derived from alternative courses of action and choose to act in a way that maximizes net pleasures. Such behavior is called *strong rationality*. Second, *rationality* can be defined as behavior consistent with optimizing behavior. Households that act as if they are optimizing will be said to be behaving rationally. Hence, rationality as opposed to strong rationality is not a psychological assumption about the internal workings of the minds of individuals. Individuals, households, or firms are not assumed to calculate and then select an optimum. It is merely assumed that their behavior can be explained in terms of purposeful action. Although some behavior cannot be thought of as rational, otherwise the notion of rationality would be tautological in the most trivial sense (i.e., behavior is behavior), much behavior can be explained in terms of optimizing behavior. For example, in experimental economics animal behavior is analyzed as though it were rational. Even perverse behavior may be rational. A household that always selects its least preferred option is rational because such behavior is consistent with rationality.

Within the context of the second definition of *rationality*, it is not difficult to think of examples of individual behavior that is irrational. Whimsical, arbitrary behavior is irrational. An individual who chooses options at random is irrational in the sense that his or her choices cannot be explained as the result of optimization. For example, suppose our individual can choose either A or B and chooses, at random, A. Next, suppose the choice is restructured so that the person can choose B or C and chooses, at random, B. The individual is acting as if the alternatives are ranked A, B, C. Yet, suppose the individual, when allowed to choose between A and C picks, at random, C. There is then no clear choice and the individual would be behaving in an irrational manner in the sense of both strong rationality and rationality. However, the average behavior of such individuals may not be irrational.

The third concept of rationality, *market rationality*, will now be considered. Market rationality exists if market behavior is consistent with the optimizing

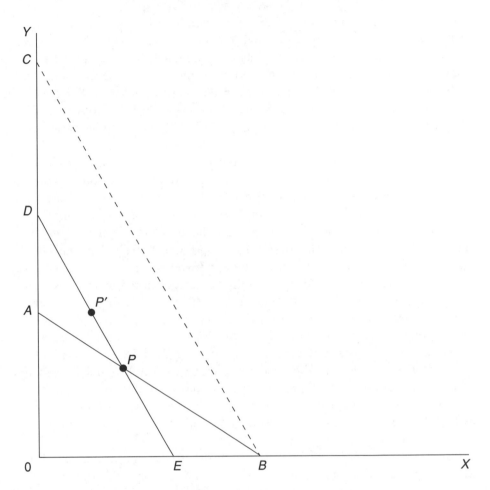

Figure 2.1 Budget set.

behavior of representative individuals and firms. Many types of behavior that are irrational at the level of individuals are rational for their aggregate behavior in the market. Consider the example of random choice, which is irrational for an individual. Suppose each individual is allowed to choose from a budget set defined by $M = P_x X + P_y Y$, where M is some maximum amount of expenditures, P_x is the price of good X, and P_y is the price of good Y. This set is illustrated in Figure 2.1. Each individual chooses a goods vector (X, Y) within the set. The maximum possible purchase of X is $B = M/P_x$ and the maximum possible purchase of Y is $A = M/P_y$. Random choice of points within the budget set can be used to derive market demand curves, which could have been derived from utility maximization subject to a budget constraint, if we add the assumption that individuals are on the budget line.

Individuals will be on the budget line if we define unspent income as a good called *savings* (either good X or good Y could be called *savings*).

Let point P be the amount of X and Y purchased. For example, if each person's choice of X is completely random in the sense that every point on AB has an equal probability of being selected, P will consist of $X = M/2P_x$ and $Y = M/2P_y$. If there are a large number of individuals, the observed (X, Y) vector will be very close to $(M/2P_y, M/2P_x)$. Now consider what will happen if P_y falls.

As we will see in the next section, a testable implication of choice theory is that compensated demand curves are downward sloping. In other words, if there are only two goods, a reduction in P_y will always cause a decrease in X demanded and an increase in Y demanded if M is simultaneously reduced to a point where the original bundle of goods (P) could just be purchased. In our example, the budget constraint initially becomes BC, where $C = M/P_y'$ and where P_y' is the new, lower price of Y. If income is reduced enough, the new budget constraint can be shifted to the left until it becomes DE, where $E = M'/P_x$ and $D = M'/P_y'$. M' is the new income level just necessary to purchase the original (X, Y) vector P. The new average amount purchased becomes $P' = (M'/2P_x, M'/2P_y')$. To see that X is lower and Y is higher at P' simply note that $M'/2P_x < M/2P_x$, because $M' < M$. Hence, X is lower. Y must then be higher, because P and P' are on the same straight line. Hence, consistent with optimization theory, the market behaves in this example as if it were a collection of rational consumers even when the behavior of each individual in the market is actually irrational, in the sense that it is random.[2]

Because rational behavior is behavior consistent with optimizing behavior, a full appraisal of rationality assumptions will have to await a formal treatment of optimization. Two points concerning the meaning of rationality should be made before beginning our treatment of choice theory. First, rationality is not a direct statement about how the ends of human action are valued. Rationality merely says that whenever ends are selected by a decision maker, means are also chosen that will achieve the ends. This is not to say that the decision maker is never mistaken about the relationship between means and ends. The decision maker is, however, assumed not to be perverse in the selection of means. Max Weber puts this realization, that the achievement of ends depends upon the behavior of decision makers, as an important element in economic development.[3] If ends and means are interdependent in the sense that the objectives of decision makers change with their behavior, the meaning of *rationality* becomes more complicated.[4] Second, the focus of choice theory is on the interaction of individuals through markets. If individual choices interact directly, the analysis is again complicated.[5] In choice theory, tastes are generally assumed to be constant but this assumption can be relaxed to accommodate these two complications. Before considering the direct interdependence of choices, we will first consider individual choice and household choice, holding tastes constant.

RATIONALITY: INDIVIDUAL CHOICE

Rationality, within the context of static demand theory, has been formalized in terms of assumptions about the choice between pairs of vectors of goods (or services). The amount of the ith good consumed is X_i and the vector is denoted as $X = (X_1, X_2, \ldots, X_n)$. Assumptions are made about the ordering of vectors of goods that yield a well-behaved utility function $U(X)$. Consumers are assumed to maximize utility subject to a budget constraint. For our purposes, it will be sufficient to begin with the utility function and the constraint. After describing the properties of a utility function, rationality can be formalized in terms of the effect of changes in budget constraints on the utility maximizing vector of goods.

Consider the standard problem where the consumer wishes to maximize

$$U = U(X)$$

subject to (2.1)

$$B = \sum_{i=1}^{n} P_i X_i,$$

where B is the income or budget available to the consumer and P_i is the price of the ith good. The consumer may not be able to purchase the vector of X, which maximizes $U(X)$ subject to the constraint, because some goods may not be available (i.e., the price vector P may not be an equilibrium price vector). It is, however, implicitly assumed that there are no other restrictions on the freedom of the consumer to choose any vector X that satisfies the budget constraint.

The optimal purchases for a consumer are graphically represented in Figure 2.2. The budget constraint is the straight line $B = P_1 X_1 + P_2 X_2$ and gives the maximum combinations of goods that could be purchased. Each indifference curve, denoted as U_1, U_2, and U_3, gives combinations of goods that yield the same utility. Indifference curves to the northeast are associated with higher utility. Hence, $U_3 > U_2 > U_1$. Furthermore, the indifference curves are drawn so that they are convex and do not intersect. The rational consumer chooses the bundle of goods with the highest obtainable level of utility (i.e., on the highest indifference curve). Utility maximization occurs when the budget constraint is tangent to an indifference curve. In Figure 2.2,

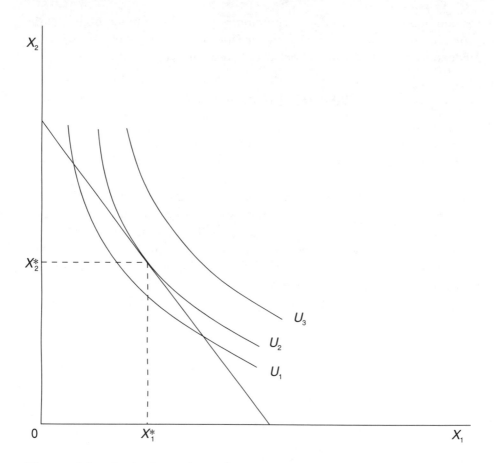

Figure 2.2 Optimal purchases for a consumer.

utility is maximized at point (X_1^*, X_2^*). Two conditions are satisfied. First, $P_1X_1^* + P_2X_2^* = B$, so that we are on the budget constraint. Second, the slope of the budget constraint, $-P_1/P_2$, equals the slope of the indifference curve passing through (X_1^*, X_2^*).

Rationality assumes utility maximization subject to a budget constraint (equation (2.1)). The solution, henceforth, can be more formally represented by considering the solution to the related problem of maximizing

$$Z = U(X) + \lambda(B - \sum_{i=1}^{n} P_iX_i), \qquad (2.2)$$

where $\lambda > 0$ is a yet to be defined constant. (Note that because $B = \Sigma P_iX_i$, we have $Z = U(X)$). A solution to (2.2), henceforth denoted as X^*, exists and is unique if two conditions are satisfied. The first condition is that partial derivatives of Z with respect to every X_i and with respect to λ are zero at X^*. The second condition is that the utility function is strictly quasiconcave. In the graphical example, this condition was interpreted in terms of indifference curves that do not cross and are convex.

Elasticities

Having found an optimum, X^*, which depends on prices, P, and the budget, B, the implications of rational decision making can be explored in terms of the responses of X^* to changes in P or B. For example, a change in the budget B influences both the level of utility and the quantity of goods desired. It can be shown that

$$\partial U^*/\partial B = \lambda^*, \tag{2.3}$$

or that λ^* is the marginal utility of income. Furthermore,

$$E_{X_i,B} = \frac{\partial X_i^*/\partial B}{X_i^*/B} \tag{2.4}$$

is the income elasticity of the demand for X_i. If $E_{X_i,B} > 0$, X_i is a normal good and its demand rises as income rises. For $E_{X_i,B} < 0$, X_i is an inferior good and less of the good is demanded if income increases. In Figure 2.3, optimal consumption (X_1^*, X_2^*) is shown for different budgets B_i, where both X_1 and X_2 are normal goods. Hence, the consumption of both X_1 and X_2 rises as B increases. The curve that traces out combinations of (X_1^*, X_2^*) as B rises is called the *income consumption curve* (the I.C.C.). The I.C.C. is positively sloped for normal goods and negatively sloped if one of the goods is inferior.

Income elasticities obviously play an important role in determining rational production plans in a growing economy. Estimated income elasticities have also raised important theoretical issues. For example, family size (the number of children in a family) and fertility in general tends to fall as income rises. If children are thought to be economic goods, they appear to be inferior goods. Yet, inferior goods are low cost replacements for some good that is both more expensive and has more desirable properties. The difficulty in conceptualizing such a high quality substitute for children has added support to skepticism about the applicability of choice theory to analyzing fertility and has led to theoretical innovations in fertility theory.

Price elasticities and cross-price elasticities are defined as

$$E_{X_i,P_i} = \frac{\partial X_i^*/\partial P_i}{X_i/P_i}$$

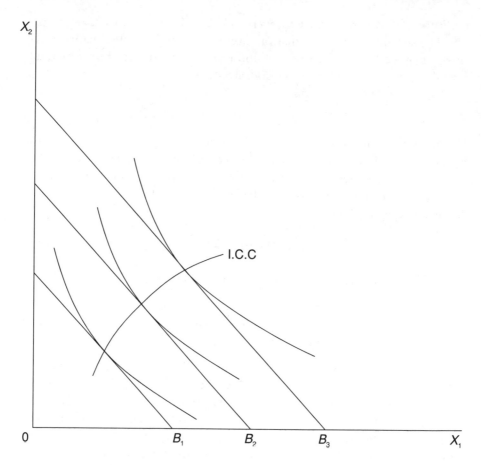

Figure 2.3   The income consumption curve.

and   (2.5)

$$E_{X_i, P_j} = \frac{\partial X_i^* / \partial P_j}{X_i / P_j}.$$

Again, the size of these elasticities is important for formulating production plans. There is no restriction on the sign of either E_{X_i, P_i} or E_{X_i, P_j}. However, examples of a Giffen good, where $E_{X_i, P_i} > 0$, may not exist. Discussing the theoretical possibility of such a good will both serve to further explore the meaning of rationality and be useful for some later applications. Note, that if P_i falls, the consumer may be able to purchase more of every good, because, in a sense, real income has risen. Similar to the last section, Figure 2.1, income could be reduced (B could be cut) until the consumer could just

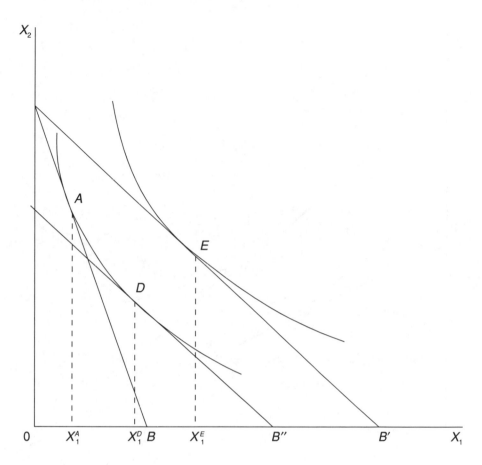

Figure 2.4 Substitution and income effects.

attain the original indifference curve. $B(P_1, P_2)$ is the original budget constraint, $B'(P_1', P_2)$ the new budget constraint, and $B''(P_1', P_2)$ the new compensated budget constraint. The consumer purchases, as a result of the new
price, $P_1' < P_1$, at point E. The reduction in income would result in consumption at D. X_1^A would then increase to X_1^D solely because of the compensated
fall in P_1 and from X_1^D to X_1^E because of the rise in real income. The change
in demand of $(X_1^D - X_1^A)$ is called the *substitution effect*, and $(X_1^E - X_1^D)$ is called
the *income effect*. The convexity of indifference curves implies that the substitution effect is positive but the income effect can be negative (i.e., the
income effect is negative if $\partial X_i^* / \partial B < 0$). If the negative income effect,
$\partial X_i^* / \partial B$, is large enough, $\partial X_i^* / \partial P_i$ can be positive. Recall from the last
section that random behavior also resulted in a positive substitution effect for
a representative consumer, and hence, such a consumer behaves as if he or
she were rational.

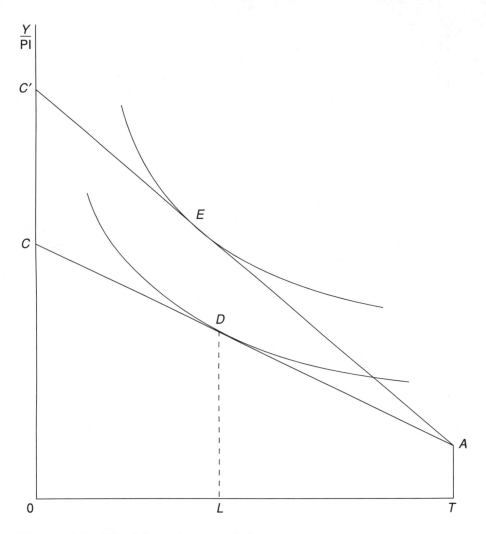

Figure 2.5   The leisure–income choice.

Labor Supply Decisions

We can now consider a choice about which there has been considerable concern in the development literature. It has at times been claimed that workers are not rational in their labor supply decisions. To see the meaning of rationality in this context, let T be the total time available to the household during a given period and $(T - L)$ be the number of hours worked at a wage rate W, where L is the number of leisure hours from which the consumer derives pleasure. If no direct pleasure or displeasure is attached to work, the individual maximizes

$$U = U(X_1, X_2, \ldots, X_n, L)$$

subject to   (2.6)

$$B + W(T-L) = \sum_{i=1}^{n} P_i X_i,$$

where B represents nonwage income.

The observed income is now a matter of choice, where income is given by

$$Y = B + W(T - L) = B + WN,   \qquad (2.7)$$

and where N is the number of hours worked. The sign of $\partial N^*/\partial W$ has been a focus for political controversy. If $\partial N^*/\partial W < 0$, then increases in the wage rate will reduce hours worked and the supply of labor is "backward bending." The possibility of a backward bending supply curve of labor has been used as an argument for trying to keep wages low. If $\partial N^*/\partial W > 0$, then taxes on wages may reduce work effort. Consequently, a positively sloped supply curve of labor has been used as an argument for low taxes.

The leisure–income choice is illustrated in Figure 2.5. Y is an index of goods that can be purchased and L is leisure. The kink at point A exists because the individual can consume real nonwage income of TA while maximizing leisure (i.e., $L = T$). A change in the price index PI will both rotate the budget AC and change the height TA. A change in W will merely rotate AC. In Figure 2.5 AC' shows the effect of an increase in W on the budget constraint. In this example, the consumer moves from point D to point E as the wage rate rises. More goods and less leisure is consumed in this example. Consequently, the supply of labor $(T - L)$ increases as W increases. Hence $\partial N^*/\partial W > 0$. Of course, the indifference curves could easily be drawn so that $\partial N^*/\partial W < 0$.

RATIONALITY: HOUSEHOLD CHOICE

In the previous section rationality was viewed from the perspective of individual decision making. In this section, the analysis of rationality will be extended from the individual to the household. Households are seen as being composed of more than just one member. The simplest household decision models start with the assumption that there exists a continuous, strictly quasi-concave utility function that is dependent upon goods consumed by the household and the leisure of each household member. More

complicated models consider game theoretical solutions, where each individual has his or her own utility function and where each utility function
is dependent upon the utility of other household members. Another type of
household model starts with a household utility function but incorporates
time into the model through its input into a household production function.
The models developed and compared in this section are those that begin
with a household utility function. First, we will consider the introduction
of the leisure of both husband and wife into a household utility function.
Then we will consider household production.

In the traditional theory of household choice, leisure is introduced into
the household utility function and budget constraint so that the rational
household maximizes

$$U = U(X_1, X_2, \ldots, X_n, L_w, L_h)$$

subject to   (2.8)

$$B + W_w(T - L_w) + W_h(T - L_h) = \sum_{i=1}^{n} P_i X_i,$$

where W_w and W_h are the wage rates of the wife and husband, and L_w and
L_h are their leisure time. The model focuses on the tradeoff between the
labor market decisions of husband and wife and has additional applications
to household decisions in locational preference (migration), fertility, and
dualistic development models where the household produces agricultural
products.

A related model of household choice begins with a household production
function, where time is an input into the production of household activities
and is not entered directly into the utility function. In household production
models, the family derives no utility directly from the consumption of goods
but from their contribution to the production of household activities (or
commodities). Commodities are produced with inputs of both time and
goods (purchased in the market). The household technology is written as

$$Z_i = F^i(X_1, X_2, \ldots, X_n, t_h, t_w)$$

$$\text{for } i = 1, 2, \ldots, k,$$

(2.9)

where Z_i is a given commodity, $F^i(X_i, t)$ is the household production
function for that commodity, and t_w and t_h are the time of the husband and
wife used in the production of that commodity. The household maximizes

$$V = V(Z_1, Z_2, \ldots, Z_k)$$

subject to

$$Z_i = F^i(X_1, X_2, \ldots, X_n, t_h, t_w) \text{ for all } i = 1, 2, \ldots, k \qquad (2.10)$$

and

$$Y = B + W_w(T - t_w) + W_h(T - t_h) = \sum_{i=1}^{n} P_i X_i.$$

For example, the commodity "eating dinner" is produced with time used to buy and prepare food, various market goods purchased by the household, time for eating, and time used cleaning up after dinner.

There are many similarities between the household production approach, equations (2.10), and the more traditional formulation of household choice, equations (2.8). The budget constraint for goods is the same, and time is shared between employment and household activities. Indeed, the utility function in (2.10) can be written in terms of goods by substituting the production functions for each Z_i into $V(Z_1, Z_2, \ldots, Z_k)$ and collecting terms yielding

$$U(X_1, X_2, \ldots, X_n, L_h, L_w) = V(Z_1, Z_2, \ldots, Z_k). \qquad (2.11)$$

Hence, in principle the two formulations are equivalent.

A major disadvantage with the formulation in equation (2.10) is that we cannot directly specify the demand for commodities. Commodities do have implicit costs or prices. These implicit prices depend upon the household production functions, the prices of goods, and the wage rates. If these implicit commodity prices are constant, then the family can be viewed as maximizing

$$V(Z_1, Z_2, \ldots, Z_k)$$

subject to the constraint $\qquad\qquad\qquad\qquad\qquad\qquad\qquad (2.12)$

$$I = \sum_{i=1}^{k} \pi_i Z_i,$$

where $I = B + W_w T + W_h T$ is the implicit, full income, of the household and π_i are the implicit prices (shadow prices).

Before discussing the formulation in equations (2.12), we need to consider when the shadow prices, π_i, will be constant. Constant shadow prices can be found if the household production functions have constant returns to scale (doubling all inputs doubles output), if there is no joint production, and if time is used in both household production and employment. For example, for Cobb–Douglas production function with two goods and one time input, $Z = AX_1^\alpha X_2^\beta t^{1-\alpha-\beta}$, the shadow price of Z is

$$\pi = W/A(1 - \alpha - \beta)[(W/P_1)(\alpha/(1 - \alpha - \beta))]^\alpha$$
$$[(W/P_2)(\beta/(1 - \alpha - \beta))]^\beta.$$

Here π is constant in that it depends only on parameters of the production function, prices, and the wage rate, and π does not depend on Z.[6] If $\pi_i = \pi^i(Z)$, then we cannot describe the solution to equations (2.12) in terms of standard choice theory. If π_i is given, then equations (2.12) can be rewritten as maximize

$$L = V(Z_1, Z_2, \ldots, Z_k) + \lambda(I - \sum_{i=1}^{k}\pi_i Z_i). \qquad (2.13)$$

The rational household will then produce and consume a commodity where

$$\partial V/\partial Z_i - \lambda\pi_i = 0 \text{ for all } i,$$

and   (2.14)

$$I = \sum_{i=1}^{k}\pi_i Z_i.$$

Hence, a rational household's behavior can be described in the same terms in which a rational individual's behavior was described with the additional complication that we need to at least speculate concerning the impact of prices and wage rates on full income and shadow prices. For example, an increase in the wife's wage rate will cause an increase in the shadow prices of time intensive commodities relative to the shadow prices of goods intensive commodities. Hence, the household would shift its consumption toward the more goods intensive commodities. Consequently, the household production model has implications for the demand for goods as income rises. Goods are substituted for time. As we will see, the household production model has been used in population economics and labor economics to describe fertility and migration in addition to analyzing labor supply.

To illustrate the differences between the traditional theory of household choice and household production theory, consider the impact of a change of wage rates on household choice. In the traditional approach attention is focused on the supply of labor. In the household production model, changes in wage rates are seen as influencing both the demand for commodities and the way in which these commodities are produced. First consider the emphasis of the traditional approach. For simplicity, assume the husband's working hours are fixed but that the wife is free to vary her income. Figure 2.5 can be used for illustration. TA is real nonwage income plus the husband's (exogenous) real wage income. The slope of the budget constraint will, in this example, depend upon the wife's real wage rate. Changes in the husband's wage rate will change the height of A but not the slope of the budget constraint. Hence, if leisure (the wife's leisure in this example) is a normal good, an increase in the husband's wage rate will, by definition of a normal good, increase leisure and reduce (the wife's) working hours. An increase in the wife's wage rate may decrease (as drawn in Figure 2.5) leisure or increase leisure. Leisure becomes more expensive causing a substitution of goods for leisure. Simultaneously, income rises, which, if leisure is a normal good, causes a rise in leisure. If this income effect is stronger than the substitution effect, the supply of labor $N^* = T - L^*$ is reduced and leisure L^* is increased. When more than one good is considered, little can be said about the sign and size of $\partial X_i^*/\partial W_w$. The sign is determined largely by preferences so that we would be directly speculating about the shape of the utility function.

In the household production model, attention is focused on the effect of changed wage rates on the consumption of commodities. Changes in an income variable such as the wife's or husband's wage rate will change the implicit budget constraint $I = \pi_1 Z_1 + \pi_2 Z_2$ by changing I, π_1 and π_2. This linear budget constraint for commodities is shown in Figure 2.6. An increase in the wife's wage rate will increase full income (I) and change relative prices. The prices of time intensive commodities will rise relative to the prices of goods intensive commodities. For example, the household might substitute food, which is already partially prepared (Z_2) for more time intensive meals (Z_1) as income rises. The change in the slope of the implicit budget constraint causes the goods intensive commodity to be substituted for the time intensive commodity.

This model has a number of interesting implications for economic development. First, it points to the important role that the opportunity cost of women's time can play in determining fertility rates. Children or the satisfactions obtained by caring for children are certainly time intensive activities. Therefore, if development should open up opportunities for women for employment outside the home, one would expect families to substitute goods intensive commodities for time intensive commodities such as child care. Thus fertility rates seem likely to decline with the expansion of opportunities for women.

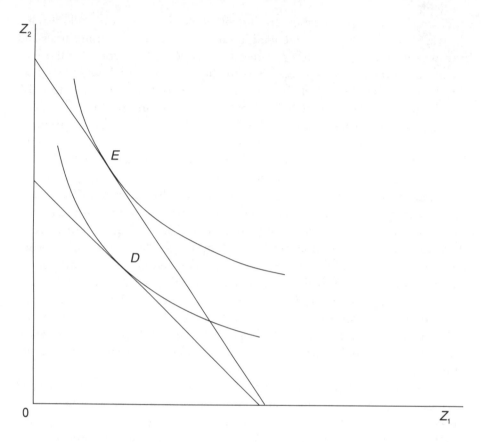

Figure 2.6 The linear budget constraint for commodities.

A second implication of such models is even more interesting. In much of the Third World women undertake a myriad of activities in the home, producing such things as clothing, processed agricultural goods, and so forth. This is all part of the subsistence orientation one finds in such households. Economic development involves the transformation of such households through participation and exchange in the market. Thus, instead of all these commodities being provided within the home, they will be purchased via the market. Development that fails to provide alternative employment opportunities for women is likely to reinforce the subsistence orientation of households and prevent or hinder market participation. Alternatively, employment opportunities for women will raise the cost of home production of a number of goods. Hence, these production activities will be forced, via increased cost, out of the home and into the market. Thus, by viewing rational decision making within households, valuable insights into the development process can be generated.

EXTENSIONS OF RATIONALITY: A SOCIOLOGY OF CHOICE

The description of rational behavior, whether individual or household, becomes more complicated if there is limited knowledge or if choices are affected by past choices, by the choices of others, or by generally acceptable modes of behavior. These difficulties have generated considerable attention. For example, Alfred Marshall was concerned with the impact of behavior on preferences. Rising income and consumption may increase people's desires for material goods. "Speaking broadly, therefore, although it is man's wants in the earliest stages of his development that give rise to his activities, yet afterwards each new step upwards is to be regarded as the development of new activities giving rise to new wants, rather than new wants giving rise to new activities."[7] This dynamic systems approach has been explored by Talcott Parsons and Gunnar Myrdal, who tend to formulate development questions in terms of circular, reinforcing causal cycles.[8]

This dynamic interrelationship of ends and means is difficult to incorporate into choice theory. A related dependency is easier to handle. People's tastes might be influenced by the consumption of others. For example, the demand for video recorders might be expected to rise as people become more familiar with video recorders through knowing more people who have purchased them. Consequently, the utility of a consumer might be written as $U(X_1, X_2, \ldots, X_n, L; \overline{X}_1, \overline{X}_2, \ldots, \overline{X}_n, \overline{L})$ where $\overline{X}_i$ is the average quantity of good i purchased by others. Note that $\overline{X}_i$ does not depend directly on the individual's own purchases. However, each individual's own purchases will affect the purchases of others and indirectly influence $\overline{X}_i$. This noncooperative, indirect effect will be minimal in the short run and difficult to measure in the long run. For simplicity, assume that each individual assumes that the purchases of others will be independent of his or her own purchases.

Consider the question raised by Marshall concerning the influence of increased prosperity on a person's wants. The individual maximizes

$$U = U(X_1, X_2, \ldots, X_n, L; \overline{X}_1, \overline{X}_2, \ldots, \overline{X}_n, \overline{L})$$

subject to

(2.15)

$$B + W(N) = \sum_{i=1}^{n} P_i X_i,$$

where $N = T - L$ is the supply of labor. The optimal consumption, X_1^*, $X_2^*, \ldots, X_n^*$ and leisure L^* can be derived for a given vector $(\overline{X}_1, \overline{X}_2, \ldots, \overline{X}_n, \overline{L})$. Optimal choices will now change both as prices (P and W) change and as average consumption changes. Consequently, it is possible to have

$\partial N^*/\partial W < 0$ for a given $(\overline{X}_1, \overline{X}_2, \ldots, \overline{X}_n, \overline{L})$ but for N^* to rise if average consumption rises. Average consumption of normal goods will, of course, rise as W rises, which may create an outward shift in the demand for each good. However, individuals may also wish to increase L^* if $\overline{L}$ increases so the net effect is far from determinate. Consequently, a demonstration effect does not guarantee a positively sloped supply of labor in the long run.

The effect that the consumption of others has on utility can be interpreted in terms of social norms. Sociologists stress that social norms are properties of groups and are not simply another term for utility, preferences, or even values — all of which are properties of individuals. Social norms may influence choice by changing utility or by changing the budget constraint. To the extent that these norms are represented by the average consumption of others, entering $\overline{X}_i$ incorporates social norms into utility functions. The more complicated effects of social norms on individual choice involve changes in constraints. Appropriate social behavior may be reinforced by penalties attached to deviant behavior. Because many of these penalties may involve a very complicated social accounting system, their direct incorporation into models of individual choice might be difficult. Indeed, social scientists in general and economists in particular may not be well suited by training or by inclination to enhance our understanding of the impact of complicated social systems on individual choice. It is much easier to quantify and test relationships at a given level of discourse than to try partial integrations of differing levels. The introspective insights of novelists and some anthropologists perhaps provide the best framework for posing and understanding the impact of social pressures on the behavior of individuals. The more modest and less descriptive approach of economists is, with few exceptions, to assume these social pressures to be already reflected in individual utility. Although tastes may vary with many socioeconomic variables such as income, education, age, occupation, location, and so forth, economists usually are skeptical about explaining differences in behavior in terms of differences in tastes. Economists usually prefer to explain changes in behavior as reactions to differences in the budget constraint, which is presumably measurable whereas tastes are not measurable.[9]

LIMITATIONS OF RATIONALITY

As we have seen, the assumption of rationality implies very little about preferences. Many economic applications such as compensated (market or individual) demand curves being negatively sloped may be more a property of the budget set than of preferences. Rationality is a vehicle that facilitates the study of how changing constraints affect behavior. The strength of rationality is its generality in that it allows us to model many diverse patterns of behavior. A stronger rationality assumption is needed for many applications in welfare economics and public finance. For example, consider the question of whether a voluntary exchange of goods or services can make either party worse off.[10] The usual assumption is that, given each person's preferences, income, and information at the time of the trade, both parties become better off. One person might, of course, be deceived about the nature of the exchange or undergo a subsequent change in preferences. Such a person might then regret the exchange. However, the voluntary exchange would not take place unless that trade was believed by both parties, assuming they are rational, to improve their own welfare. Note that the term *rational* is no longer taken to mean that individuals act *as if* they are maximizing utility. They are assumed to be actually maximizing utility. Otherwise, there is no reason to suppose voluntary transactions make either party better off. Hence, unless we are willing to accept rationality as a psychological statement, we are limited in the statements of economic welfare that can properly be made. However, the weaker notion of *as if* rationality may be sufficient to guide empirical research.

It is possible to suggest many additional limitations to the application of various concepts of rationality, but only three will be discussed here. First, individual rationality may lead to undesirable results for both the individual and society. Second, individuals or firms may be inefficient (and, hence, not rational from society's perspective). The removal of these inefficiencies are an important part of public policy and the development process. Third, the extension of the rationality assumption to groups such as firms, families, or government bureaucracies presents additional problems. The allocation and distribution of resources within these institutions may take place outside the market mechanism. Consequently, implicit prices and implicit income enter the budget constraint, which further strains the notion of rationality. Each of these limitations will be explained in turn.

To illustrate the first limitation, that irrationality may be preferable to rationality, consider examples of commitment to a cause where this commitment leads to action that is not in the person's self-interest.[11] Voting, volunteer activities, monetary contributions, or even the sacrifice of one's life are actions that may be beneficial but are not necessarily in a person's best interest. Citizens vote perhaps not because it gives them satisfaction to vote but because they feel obligated. To illustrate the role of these obligations consider an example, familiar to many students, where two roommates have to keep some semblance of order in their housekeeping. Each roommate is deciding whether or not to clean the house. The choices are illustrated in the payoff matrix shown in Figure 2.7. In outcome *y*, for example, person B cleans the house without A's help. Suppose A ranks the outcomes

B

A	Clean	Do not clean
Clean	*w*	*x*
Do not clean	*y*	*z*

Figure 2.7 Payoff matrix.

$y > w > z > x$. Hence, A cares little about B's feelings and places a high priority on leisure. If B has the similar ranking of $x > w > z > y$, each roommate is better off not cleaning regardless of what the other person does. Hence, z is the outcome resulting from rational behavior. Outcome z is an illustration of a Nash equilibrium. Note that if both roommates were obligated for some reason to clean the apartment, the outcome w would occur and both persons would be better off than at z. Hence, irrational behavior could result in higher utility for everyone. This is of course the famous prisoners' dilemma situation drawn from game theory.

There are, of course, other possible outcomes to this game. A, B, or both could value cleanliness more highly ranking the outcomes $y > w > x > z$ or $x > w > y > z$, respectively. Alternatively, the game might be repeated an indefinite number of times. As long as the number of times the game is played is unknown, there is an incentive to clean the room. Finally, the players may have some notion of fairness that leads them to act in a way that seems rational from a social but not an individual perspective. Person A may get satisfaction from a clean apartment and displeasure from work but pleasure from doing his or her share. Indeed, some sense of satisfaction from fulfilling obligations may be necessary if the two are to remain roommates. Altruism, or a sense of commitment to behavior that is not strictly in the person's best interest, may be essential for a society to work smoothly. Some suggest that a sense of commitment may be the result of a Darwinian mechanism.[12] Groups whose members are altruistic may prosper over aggregates of narrowly self-interested individuals. Furthermore, individuals with strong commitments to some types of nonself-interested behavior may be better off. Indeed, much of parenting consists of instilling values in children that the parents believe will help them lead happier and more prosperous lives.

Another way in which the rationality assumption might block our efforts at understanding decisions concerns the possibilities of inefficiencies. Specifically, firms may be technically or allocatively inefficient. A firm is technically inefficient if more output could have been produced than is being produced with the same or fewer inputs. Allocative inefficiency occurs when the firm chooses an inappropriate input or output combination. An example of allocative inefficiency is found in first year economics texts, where it is stressed that a monopolist does not expand production to a point where price equals marginal cost, as would occur in competition. The monopolist uses too few inputs and is allocatively inefficient. The existence of allocative inefficiency implies that firms are, to some extent, behaving irrationally from society's perspective, although rationally from their own. This may be due to constraints placed upon their behavior by their environment. Therefore, increases in output may be obtainable by making changes in the environment to allow firms to become more technically and allocatively efficient.

The final limit of rationality concerns the allocation of resources within institutions such as the family, firms, government, and religious or social organizations. Nonmarket mechanisms often allocate and distribute resources within these organizations. Included among these mechanisms are force, intimidation, tradition, professional ethics, and a general sense of obligation. Rationality could be evoked when considering the interaction of these organizations. For example, earlier in this chapter, the family was treated in much the same way that individuals were treated in the section on individual choice. It was simply assumed that the family maximized utility subject to constraints. The preferences of family members were not directly considered. The family was assumed to be simply a cohesive, rational, decision-making unit. This assumption may be useful when considering how external forces change the observable behavior of families. The cohesive family assumption might be less useful if our concern shifts to the allocation and distribution of resources within a family.

One reason for going beyond the assumption of the cohesive family is that we may be explicitly interested in the welfare of individuals within the family. For example, compulsory schooling laws are enacted partly in the belief that some parents or guardians will, in the absence of these laws, underallocate family resources devoted to their children's education. Other examples where there has been some state intervention include child abuse laws and direct feeding programs such as school lunch programs in the United States. An area of continuing concern is the possibility that families do not allocate enough resources to females. Policies to intervene in the allocation of resources within families are based partly on the notion that family decisions are not rational in the sense that they reflect the rational choices of family members.[13]

There are three basic difficulties with applying the concept of rationality to resource allocation within a family. First, parents wish to teach their children appropriate behavior and develop their children's attitudes and tastes in appropriate ways. Although it may be true that children are rational, few would accept the tastes of their children as sovereign. Hence, the family utility function should not necessarily be viewed as a sort of social welfare function with its arguments being the utility of individual family members. Second, possibilities of undesirable equilibria abound. Recall that, in the roommate example, the undesirable equilibrium of an uncleaned apartment could be prevented if each person felt obliged to perform a task and, in a sense, behave irrationally. Such irrational behavior may be important for the survival of a family. Third, the constraints to behavior that do not involve markets are often unobservable. The family can be viewed as a miniature economy, where rational individuals interact in a market where prices and income are implicitly defined by their optimal behavior. Such an approach forgoes one of the strengths of the rationality assumption and choice theory in general. The "as if" defense of rationality is not as persuasive because rationality is defined in terms of implicit prices, which are, in turn, defined by optimal behavior. Furthermore, because the constraints are unobservable, it can no longer be argued that the rationality assumption is simply a useful vehicle for describing and predicting the relationship between one observable variable (such as a price) and another observable variable (like the quantity of a good purchased).

THE DEVELOPMENT PROCESS

In this chapter, we indicated that the unifying theme, in the analysis of the problems of less developed countries, of this book will be the assumption of rationality. However, what then will distinguish development economics from being merely a straightforward application of microeconomic theory? The answer is given partly by the discussion of the three limitations to the concept of rationality discussed in the previous section.

If a less developed country is separated into a modern sector and traditional sector, as most dual economy theorists do, then it becomes obvious that limitations to the application of the rationality assumption are of less concern for activities in the modern sector. This sector is generally characterized by production and sale for the market because the supporting institutional infrastructure for market activity already exists. Therefore, little economic activity occurs within the household (for subsistence) and most choice, with respect to resource allocation and production, occurs within a market context where constraints can be observed. Thus, the household's economic activity can be relatively easily analyzed, applying principles of microeconomic theory.

Furthermore, extensive development of markets in the modern sector implies that most producing firms face similar relative prices for inputs and outputs and have access to similar technologies. If, in addition, the modern sector is open to international trade, economic activity in this sector is likely to be highly competitive. Hence one would expect firms to be relatively efficient both in an allocative and technical sense. The main source of inefficiency would then likely be government policies that distort relative prices and inhibit entrepreneurial activity. Thus assuming that firms behave as if they were optimizing subject to constraints is likely to shed light on both firm behavior and the effects of government induced distortions.

Finally, in the previous section it was argued that, in many situations, the pursuit of what is individually rational results in an undesirable situation for society. Analyzing these kinds of situations under the rationality assumption may not shed much light on human behavior in these situations. This sort of problem certainly would arise in the modern sector. However, with respect to exchange through markets this problem has been solved in this sector. Specifically, before exchange through markets can occur an institutional infrastructure supporting such activities must be created. It is optimal from society's perspective (the group) that resources and efforts be directed to establishing such an infrastructure. However, no single individual has an incentive to contribute resources to the construction of such institutions. This lack of incentives is the heart of what is called *free riding*. This conflict has been largely resolved in the modern sector, where markets have been established.

It is with respect to economic activity in the traditional sector that the limitations to the rationality assumption must always be kept in mind. The characterization of the traditional sector varies from author to author. Some assume that agriculture is by definition a traditional activity, some that *traditional* is defined in terms of the primitiveness of technology, others define *traditional* in terms of decision making that is *not* guided by profit maximization. In this book a slightly different distinction is made. Families and their household production activities are much less market oriented than in the modern sector. So one might view the traditional sector as being represented by a number of islands of economic activity. Each island is relatively isolated from others because of the lack of market development. Thus much economic activity occurs within the family (subsistence activities). Those activities oriented toward the market involve choices that are made within an environment of observable constraints and therefore can be analyzed using standard microeconomic principles. However, much of the activity occurring within the family is not so easily explained by assuming optimizing behavior. The economic activities within each island are likely to be efficiently conducted, given the prices and technology available to that island. However, a variety of prices and technologies are likely to exist throughout the traditional sector, implying that if the isolated islands could be linked via markets significant increases in output could be obtained (eliminating sector inefficiency).

The lack of development of markets is thus the key characteristic of the traditional sector. This sector has, of yet, not been able to create the institutional infrastructure necessary for the development of an integrated market system. Therefore, the conflict between what is rational, from the perspective of the individual, and what is socially optimal has been resolved to only a limited extent. It follows then that markets function only locally and family production activities occur in relative isolation. This fragmentation is what distinguishes the traditional sector from the modern sector and what makes development distinctive from applied microeconomics. Rationality as a methodology for analyzing individual behavior is very useful and forms the underlying basis of this book. However, the development process itself is crucially dependent upon solving the conflict between what is individually rational and what is socially optimal in the traditional sector. Development involves the transformation of the traditional sector by creating the institutional infrastructure, within which this conflict can be productively solved.

CONCLUSION

Economists often assume rationality upon the part of decision makers. However, they usually spend little time explaining what *rationality* means. This chapter has discussed rationality. Optimal choice by individuals as well as households was explored to illustrate the use of this notion. It was also pointed out that understanding behavior by assuming that people make choices as if they were optimizing becomes much more difficult within the context of the traditional sector. In particular, decision making carried on within families is difficult to analyze in this way, because many of the constraints cannot be easily measured and parents often seek to teach their children appropriate patterns of behavior (norms and rules). Also, in the traditional sector much behavior that is individually rational is not socially rational. Finally, it is difficult to understand how allocative and technical inefficiency can exist if individuals and firms are rational.

Given the preceding points, it was argued that the development process is intimately connected with these limitations. That is, the traditional sector is represented by islands of economic activity that are only very loosely, if at all, connected to each other via markets. As a result, much economic activity is subsistence oriented (production in the household), significant technical and allocative efficiency exists if one views the traditional sector as a whole, and the creation of an extensive market system is limited by the clash between what is individually rational and what is socially optimal. Development therefore involves the transformation of the traditional sector through linking these various island economies via the market. Thus more and more production becomes market oriented. As a result, decisions that are rational from the individual perspective and society's perspective become more coincident, and allocative and technical inefficiencies are exploited for their potential increased output.

This transformation process is the subject matter of the rest of this book. Throughout we will analyze individual behavior as if individuals are making optimal choices, always keeping in mind the limitations of this methodology when dealing with the transformation of the traditional sector.

NOTES

1. For more on this possible integration of development theory with economic theory in general, see Pranab Bardhan, "Economics of Development and the Development of Economics," *Journal of Economic Perspectives* (Spring 1993): 129–142.

2. The example comes from Gary S. Becker, "Irrational Behavior and Economic Theory," in *The Economic Approach to Human Behavior*, ed. Gary S. Becker, pp. 153–168 (Chicago: University of Chicago Press, 1976). See also Angus Deaton and John Muellbauer, *Economics and Consumer Behavior* (Cambridge: Cambridge University Press, 1983), for this example and a discussion of the restrictions linear budget constraints place on observed consumer behavior.

3. Max Weber, *The Protestant Ethic and the Spirit of Capitalism* (London: G. Allen and Unwin, 1930).

4. See Jon Elster, *Ulysses and the Sirens: Studies in Rationality and Irrationality* (New York: Cambridge University Press, 1979).

5. An example of interdependent preferences and rational behavior is the literature on Becker's "rotten kid" theorem. See Theodore Bergstrom, "A Fresh Look at the Rotten Kid Theorem – and Other Household Mysteries," *Journal of Political Economy* 97 (October 1989): 1138–1159.

6. See M. P. Shields and Gail M. Shields, "A Theoretical and Empirical Analysis of Family Migration and Household Production: U.S. 1980–1985," *Southern Economic Journal* 4 (April 1993): 768–782 for a derivation of shadow prices and see Deaton and Muellbauer, *Economics and Consumer Behavior*, Chapter 10, for a review of household production theory.

7. Alfred Marshall, *Principles of Economics*, 8th ed. (London: Macmillan, 1920), p. 89.

8. See Gunnar Myrdal, *An American Dilemma: The Negro Problem and Modern Democracy* (New York: Harper and Row, 1944); and Talcott Parsons, *The Structure of Social Action*, vol. 1 (New York: Macmillan, 1937).

9. This methodology is strongly stated and defended in George J. Stigler and Gary S. Becker. "De Gustibus non est Disputandum," *American Economic Review* 67 (March 1977): 76–90.

10. See Amartya Sen, "Rational Fools," *Philosophy and Public Affairs* (Summer 1977): 317–344. For a discussion of the importance of some types of irrationality in making voluntary market transactions work, see Kanshik Basu, *The Less Developed Economy: A Critique of Contemporary Theory* (Oxford: Basil Blackwell, 1984).

11. In particular, see Howard Margolis, *Selfishness, Altruism, and Rational Behavior: A Theory of Social Choice* (Cambridge: Cambridge University Press, 1982).

12. See George Akerlof, "Loyalty Filters," *American Economic Review* 73 (March 1983).

13. See Amartya Sen, "Economics and the Family," *Asian Development Review* (1983): 14–26.

3

The Traditional Sector and Development

Upon visiting a less developed country for the first time, the traveler is often struck by the coexistence of things that appear to be modern and things that appear to be backward. Modern hotels and office buildings may tower above dilapidated one story structures. Sleek automobiles and horsedrawn carts may share the same roadway. This coexistence of the modern and the backward has long been formalized in the dualistic models of development introduced in Chapter 1. In these models, the transfer of resources from the traditional sector to the modern sector is the key to economic development. Thus, the emphasis in these dualistic models is on understanding the modern sector and how it can grow more rapidly. The traditional sector in many treatments is only briefly described as the agricultural sector or as the nonrational sector. In this chapter we will turn our attention toward the traditional sector and theories that place traditional sector development as the key to economic development and sustained economic growth. First, we will briefly describe the notion of a traditional sector that fits in well with the discussion of limits to rationality in Chapter 2. Then, we will discuss the role of transactions costs in creating the traditional sector. Third, some reasons why dualistic development of the modern sector may not work are presented. Fourth, the dynamics of how traditional sector development might proceed are sketched. The fifth section turns to historical evidence supporting the view that traditional sector development might work. The remainder of the chapter turns to theoretical work on the traditional sector. Land tenure and technological change in agriculture are discussed first. Then traditional sector manufacturing is analyzed. Next to last, economic interests and how they may distort traditional sector development through their influence over government policy are dealt with. Some brief conclusions are then drawn.

THE TRADITIONAL SECTOR

The term the *traditional sector* will be applied to both agricultural and non-agricultural activities. The key distinction between traditional and modern will be the extent to which producers are integrated via the market system. That is, in the modern sector consumption and production are presupposed to be closely linked through markets. Producers and consumers face similar prices for inputs and outputs and competition is likely to be intense. As we saw in Chapter 1, the expansion of market activities is the key to both classical and Marxist views of development.

The traditional sector can be viewed as containing many islands of economic activities that are partially isolated from one another due to the lack of market development. Thus, within each of these islands of activity, there is much competition. However, there is limited interaction between islands, limited exchange of information and technology, and limited exchange of goods and services. The implication is that significant increases in output could be generated if inputs could be obtained from other regions at favorable prices, if new technology could be effectively borrowed from other regions, and if markets in other regions could be effectively exploited.

The main distinction to be made between traditional and modern activities is then the extent to which economic activities are linked via the market. Linkage, of course, is a matter of degree, and we can view the degree to which economic activities are linked through markets as being measured along a scale. Those at the traditional end of the scale are less integrated through markets than those at the modern end of the scale.

MARKET INTEGRATION AND TRANSACTIONS COSTS

The limited development of markets and their supporting institutions is related to the problem of high transactions costs.[1] Transactions costs can be classified based on the different phases of the exchange process. The first step in the exchange process requires that the parties seeking to exchange must search out each other, and this is certainly a costly process. Once the parties have found each other, information concerning exchange possibilities must be shared. This search and information exchange will require resources. If a large number of individuals are involved, additional costs are incurred in coordinating the plans of individuals and costly bargaining will be necessary to determine the terms of trade. After a bargain has been struck, it must be monitored and enforced to ensure that the stipulated obligations are carried out. In summary, there are search costs, bargaining and decision costs, and policing and enforcement costs. Correspondingly, there must be a set of rules limiting the types of behavior that will be allowed to occur in the search, bargaining, and enforcement phases. The set of rules represents the institutional structure.

Perhaps a simpler way of looking at this process is to understand that dealing with uncertainty concerning what can be expected about the behavior of others is the underlying problem of human relations. This uncertainty makes exchange costly, and as a result, institutional rules must be developed that limit individual behavior to create an environment in which one can, with some assurance, predict the behavior or range of behavior likely to occur. Markets and their supporting organizations represent rules, which reduce transaction costs and, thus, allow exchange to occur. However, it must also be kept in mind that organizing a system of institutional rules will be subject to the same sort of transactions costs discussed previously. Thus, exchange may fail to take place or occur only to a limited extent because of the lack of a set of institutional rules that creates assurance. These institutions themselves do not exist or exist only incompletely because of the high transactions costs of organization.

The institutional rules governing production and exchange extend throughout the modern sector, resulting in a process of exchange that links all producers and consumers into a network. This institutional infrastructure is lacking in the traditional sector, which consequently may be fragmented into islands of isolated economic activity. Within each island the rules of exchange are agreed upon by the vast majority of participants. However, there is little communication and a lack of transport facilities between these islands, which makes long distance exchange riskier, more time consuming, and thus more costly. Also the mechanisms for engaging in exchange and enforcing contracts often differ between island regions. Therefore, individuals in one region often lack assurance as to whether individuals in other regions will abide by the terms of any particular agreement. Due to the costliness of exchange, the linkage between the various economic islands is tenuous at best. In other words, market failure occurs, markets fail to develop.[2]

The implication of the preceding is that the traditional sector must be transformed. This transformation can occur through development of the traditional sector or through displacement of the traditional sector by the modern sector. Most of this chapter, in focusing on the traditional sector itself, is concerned with traditional sector development. We will first need to consider dual economy models, which argue that this transformation must occur by absorbing the traditional sector into the modern sector and that it is not necessary to directly transform the traditional sector.

An example of displacement can be found in the Lewis model, discussed in the first chapter, where the modern sector expands through savings and capital accumulation, which draws labor out of the traditional sector. Eventually, the wage rate in the traditional sector is brought into equality with the marginal product of labor, surplus labor is eliminated, and the traditional sector becomes modernized. Thus development is seen to be the result of the absorption of the labor force of the traditional sector into the modern sector. Hence, the dynamism for this development process originates mainly within the modern sector. Ranis and Fei do see a positive role for the traditional sector to play. That is, if productivity in the traditional sector can be increased, then the expansion of the modern sector is easier and the transformation process can occur that much more rapidly.

In essence, this view of the transformation process sees development as the creation of capital in the modern sector, which transfers labor from the traditional sector to the modern sector. Thus, over time the traditional sector becomes displaced by the modern sector. It follows then that development does not occur as a result of the creation of market links within the traditional sector, but by the displacement of this sector by the already existing modern sector. Henry Bruton has labeled this process *development by displacement*.[3]

DEVELOPMENT BY DISPLACEMENT

A criticism of development by displacement of the traditional sector, as outlined in Chapter 1, is that it may not lead to a transformation of the traditional sector. Instead, it may result mainly in the relocation of this sector to urban areas with few links to the modern sector. That is, as the modern sector expands, families are likely to be drawn to the cities by the relatively higher wages offered in the modern sector and may even find jobs in modern sector economic activity. However, for the most part these families will still remain as part of the traditional sector, unconnected to the rest of the economy via markets. Economic growth, increased output, may occur, but economic development has not. Economic development in part means that the traditional sector has been transformed by linking the islands of economic activity together via the market. In fact, this process of displacing the traditional sector may actually retard development (transformation).

To understand this point, we must take a closer view of economic activity in the traditional sector. Much of this activity occurs within the context of the family. The family is both the production unit and the consumption unit. Most likely the family will farm and spend a large share of its labor in agricultural activities. In addition, handicraft and cottage-type production activities also take place using female labor and seasonally available male labor. These nonagricultural activities produce a variety of products for use by the family as well as for sale. The relative importance of agricultural relative to nonagricultural activities varies from family to family.

The exchange between families in a particular region make up the local island of economic activity referred to earlier. Competition is generally vigorous and, given the relative supplies of factors of production and the local technology, production is generally efficient.[4] Institutions have evolved for standardizing the exchange process within these economic islands. That is, norms and rules governing conduct in economic exchange have developed such that each individual family can be reasonably sure about the types of behavior to expect when engaging in exchange. In addition, a variety of village institutions are aimed at facilitating exchange, enforcing agreements, and punishing individuals who fail to obey the community's rules.

Note, in the previous paragraph, the introduction of the word *community*. Within a community most of the relationships are of the face to face variety. The community is generally bound together through intricate rules and norms that govern behavior. The enforcement of such rules and norms usually involves social sanctions as well as explicit punishments. The rules and norms, as well as the various forms of enforcement, have the sanction of the community at large. That is, they are regarded as legitimate and provide assurance as to what individuals can expect in everyday economic activity.

This institutional network is limited to the area surrounding the community, which we have labeled an *economic island*. Thus the rules and norms (institutions) are applicable and legitimate only within that region. Each region is only loosely connected with others as the result of poor communication and transport networks. It follows then that the specialization process has not proceeded very far, and a significant amount of economic activity is subsistence oriented.

The modern sector in most less developed nations generally consists of economic activities involving manufacturing or large scale commercial agriculture. The technologies utilized have frequently been imported from the developed nations and are generally technically sophisticated and capital intensive in nature. There has been much previous work on the appropriateness of this technology for less developed nations, which are generally labor abundant. It has been argued that the importation and utilization of such technology is inefficient from society's perspective, resulting in increased unemployment, balance of payments difficulties, and slower growth in the long run.

The institutions, which serve as the infrastructure for the development of the modern sector, are also, for the most part, imported from developed nations. That is, the form of the business organizations sanctioned by the state, the judicial system, the political organization of the state itself, and most of the rules and norms concerning work hours, appropriate worker behavior, and so forth are generally imported. Thus, the modern sector represents a grafting of not only imported technology but also an imported institutional infrastructure on the indigenous, traditional economy.

As the modern sector expands, it draws resources and labor from the traditional sector by displacing the latter. Individuals and families are drawn out of a social environment in which the rules and norms guiding behavior are well known and regarded as legitimate and are thrust into an alien environment. In this new environment many of the rules and norms are strange and lack legitimacy. As a result, problems arising from a clash between what is rational from the individual's point of view and what is rational from society's perspective (see the last section of Chapter 2) become more numerous and severe.

It must be noted that there are many instances in which the pursuit of individual interests clash with those of society. For example, workers often have an individual incentive to shirk their duties. This is especially so if the costs of monitoring work effort are exceedingly high. Consider a landlord who hires labor to farm his land. If the work effort of each individual worker could be costlessly monitored, then shirking could be eliminated. However, if the costs of monitoring work effort are high, then individual laborers have an incentive to shirk. After all, an individual who works very hard will often receive the same reward as one who shirks. Thus, if each individual worker cannot be assured that the other workers will not shirk, then it is individually rational for each worker to shirk. The pursuit of individual interests results in less output for the society as a whole. It should be pointed out that the same kind of logic can be applied to individuals who manage resources for absentee owners. Shirking and its implications for labor markets will be considered in detail in Chapter 5, when efficiency wage models are introduced.

Institutions generally provide that sense of assurance as to what individuals who are involved in economic activities can expect from others. In the traditional village (economic island), individuals who work a landowner's land are less likely to shirk because the existing institutions operate to effectively punish the shirker. Often this punishment involves social and economic ostracism for the individual who breaks the rules. It follows that each individual is assured that his or her fellow workers will work with a given, socially acceptable level of diligence. Thus individual interests and those of society are made coincident, and less of what is called *free riding* behavior occurs. Institutions, in this instance, restrain individual interests in light of the interests of the group (society).

However, as the traditional sector is displaced, the old rules and norms are rejected, and a set of imported rules and norms are substituted. Individuals from the traditional sector are not likely to understand this new institutional infrastructure, let alone regard it as legitimate. As a result, individuals will not be assured as to what they can expect from others in economic production and exchange activities. Shirking or free riding behavior would then occur more frequently. The clash between the interests of individuals and society would become more prevalent and more intense.

In other words, as economic activity in the modern sector expands, problems of economic and social organization are likely to grow. Firms in the modern sector would operate at a very low level of productivity, not only because of the inappropriateness of the imported technology but also because of the inappropriateness of the institutional infrastructure. As a consequence, the modern sector would have to significantly expand its institutional structure to attempt to deal with the increased free riding activity. Specifically, the educational system will have to be expanded to try to inculculate individuals displaced from the traditional sector with the new norms and rules. The police and judicial systems will also have to be expanded to increase the intensity of the enforcement effort. New institutional forms for monitoring individual effort will have to be introduced to ensure that a socially acceptable level of labor effort (by managers and workers) will be attained.

All of the activities discussed in the previous paragraph will involve the expenditure of large amounts of resources. The GNP as conventionally calculated will of course expand, but much of this expansion represents the expenditure of resources in an attempt to restrain individual behavior in the interests of the welfare of society; that is, to restrain free riding behavior. As a result, the actual standard of living of individuals in the modern sector may increase very little if at all, once these "costs of displacing the traditional sector" are subtracted from the social product. This may well account for much of the dissatisfaction many people in developing nations feel with the whole process of modern economic growth.[5]

In summary, development by displacement involves substituting imported technology and institutions for traditional, indigenous ones. As this occurs, significant inefficiencies may arise in two ways. In many instances the imported technology is not appropriate for the conditions found in developing nations. Thus, in the long run, growth may be retarded. Second, the replacement of traditional institutions by imported institutions could lead to social breakdown or disorganization. That is, individuals from the traditional sector will not regard these new rules and norms as legitimate and will not be assured as to what to expect from others involved in economic activity. Productivity would decline and a significant amount of society's resources would be devoted to enforcing the imported institutional structure that makes up the modern sector.

TRADITIONAL SECTOR DEVELOPMENT

As an alternative to development by the displacement of the traditional sector, the traditional sector could serve as the center of the development process. In other words, instead of attempting to generate development by imposing an imported institutional structure onto the traditional sector, the traditional sector itself can serve as the dynamic force for expansion. This would involve significant investment in traditional sector economic activities. We will now consider how traditional sector development might occur.

The development process outlined in the previous paragraph would be based upon the existing indigenous institutional structure of the traditional sector. This does not mean that the institutional structures within the island economies of the traditional sector would remain unchanged. The institutional structure would have to adapt and evolve as growth occurs and the traditional islands become more closely linked through the market. The key, however, is that these rules and norms would continue to be regarded as legitimate because they have evolved within the context of the traditional sector itself. Thus, the interests of the individual would be constrained where they clash with the interests of society, and the social disorganization, which comes from growth through displacement of the traditional sector, will not likely occur.[6]

The contrast between growth by displacement and development through expansion of the traditional sector is illustrated in Figure 3.1. In diagram (a) the society initially begins with most of its resources in the traditional sector and operating inside the production possibilities curve at point B. The latter is due to the lack of market development in the traditional sector resulting in isolated islands of economic activity. Investment is concentrated in the modern sector (M) so that the production possibilities curve shifts from PP to $P'P$. Also, society is moving from point B to point C. In this illustration, the society is operating even further inside their production possibilities due to the social disorganization generated by the displacement of the traditional sector institutional structure with that of the modern sector. It is not possible to determine whether there has actually been an improvement in living standards.

Contrast this with the process of traditional sector development envisioned in diagram (b). As investment is concentrated in the traditional sector, not only does the production possibilities curve shift out from PP to PP', but the society has moved from within the curve to a point on the curve, point B to point C. This occurs because the existing institutional structure is utilized as the basis for organizing the economic expansion. It should be further emphasized that the development envisioned here is not so much the result of technical change or capital accumulation as much as the linking together of the isolated economic islands of the traditional sector via the extension of connecting markets based upon the indigenous institutional structure. Therefore, increased output will result from increased specialization in production and exchange and the diffusion of already existing techniques of

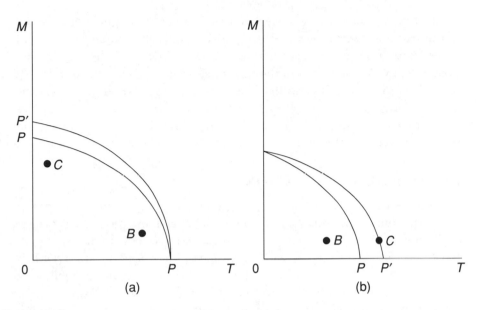

Figure 3.1 Growth by displacement (a) versus development through expansion (b) of the traditional sector.

production throughout the traditional sector, as well as the development of new technology.

For most less developed nations agriculture makes up a significant share of traditional sector activity. Hence, a traditional sector strategy of development will involve significant investment in peasant agricultural production. Economists have recently realized the important place that agriculture has in the development process. However, economists have tended to view investment in agriculture as a means to an end. That is, they see agriculture as a source of a number of factors critical to the overall expansion of the modern sector.[7] Specifically, agriculture must serve as the supplier of labor as well as food to the modern (industrial sector). That is, the workers to staff the modern sector must come out of agriculture and must be provided with the food necessary to sustain them in the production of modern sector goods. In addition, the agricultural sector is seen as serving as a market for the produce of the modern industrial sector, as well as an earner of foreign exchange, which can be utilized to purchase the foreign capital needed to expand industry. Finally and, for many, most important, agriculture may also serve as the main source of the savings necessary to finance the expansion of the modern sector. Again, all of this analysis views the traditional sector, in this case, agriculture, as a means to an end, the creation of a modern sector.

The development process as viewed here does not view agricultural activity in the traditional sector as a means to an end but an end in and of itself. In other words, investment in agriculture is aimed at increasing the productivity of agriculture. As the islands of the traditional sector expand, the institutional structure will evolve, linking the islands closer and closer together via the market. However, the purpose is not to then extract resources from this sector to finance the modern sector but to allow the resources to remain within the traditional sector to fuel its continued expansion and evolution.

HISTORICAL ILLUSTRATIONS

The preceding discussion indicates that significant increases in the output of the agricultural traditional sector can be obtained by promoting market development through the creation of the necessary institutional structure. However, the case of what we call *traditional sector agricultural development* must rest on much more than the mere existence of this possibility of development. There should be historical examples, where traditional sector agricultural development occurred. In fact such development occurred both in Europe and Japan. Both cases will be briefly examined here.

The English experience has often been interpreted as supporting the dualist model's view of development as displacement. Specifically, the elimination of the Corn Laws in England in 1846 has often been seen as a mechanism by which the state shifted the terms of trade against the agricultural sector. This extraction of surplus from the latter sector is seen as having promoted the rapid expansion of the modern industrial sector. However, as Bates[8] has pointed out, this is a basic misinterpretation of historical experience.

The policy of the British government towards agriculture is summarized by Bates as follows:

$$\max(P_d, P_w), \tag{3.1}$$

where P_d is the price of grain on the domestic market and P_w the price on the world market. Under the Corn Laws, if the world price was higher than the domestic price, then farmers were allowed to export grain. Alternatively, when the international price was lower than the domestic price, imports were prohibited. Thus the Corn Laws were geared to providing high prices to British farmers. The Corn Laws were a subsidy provided to the agricultural sector. This subsidy had been in place in England since 1688. The repeal of the Corn Laws therefore represented a repeal of a subsidy.

There was throughout the period prior to 1846 a slow, steady growth of productivity on all British farms, whether they were enclosed or open field, large or small. How can this slow but steady increase in productivity be explained? Bates suggests several reasons based upon historical analysis

		Seller II	
		A	B
Buyer I	A	5,5 (6,6)	0,7
	B	7,0	−1,−1

Figure 3.2 Potential exchanges between buyers and sellers.

of British agriculture. Part of the increase is surely attributable to biological improvements stemming from improved seed and plant varieties. However, a common theme in many explanations is the growth of the market. This perspective argues that it was in England that a broad national market first developed. As a result, specialization in agricultural production began to evolve. Some areas specialized in the production of wool; others, near cities, specialized in truck farming. Those who worked the heavier soils generally shifted into the production of livestock. Along with such specialization, of course, came the productivity increases that characterized English agriculture.

Indeed, this discussion illustrates the arguments presented earlier. The development of a market system within the traditional sector led to traditional sector growth and development. Although the direct investment by the English government in agriculture was limited, the Corn Laws acted as an indirect method for promoting the growth of the agricultural sector. It achieved this goal mainly by promoting the development of the rurally based national market discussed previously. The development of this market involved the creation of an atmosphere where beneficial exchange was possible and expected.

One can understand this process of market creation by viewing potential exchange by buyers and sellers as a prisoners' dilemma game, as discussed earlier in Chapter 2 and illustrated in Figure 3.2. Buyer I and seller II can both gain by choosing to cooperate (strategy A) and engage in a good faith exchange of goods and services.[9] However, each is tempted to cheat in the exchange process by choosing to be uncooperative (strategy B) when the other is choosing to be cooperative (strategy A).[10] This cheating can involve the seller providing a poor quality product or perhaps even failing to deliver the product. The buyer may choose to steal the product or refuse to pay after delivery or pay with counterfeit money, and so on. If both distrust each other, then both will choose uncooperative strategies and the worst result will emerge, both lose. In this kind of situation markets will fail to function due to mutual distrust.

Of course, the question becomes one of how the trust necessary for market creation can come about. One can visualize this as occurring as the result of repeated interactions between buyer and seller. In the game theory context, one must allow for repeated play of the game in which the end of the game is unknown or it is played an infinite number of times. If the same players are involved in each replay of the game, then the possibility of a cooperative solution emerges. In this context each player must weigh the gains from noncooperative behavior today against the possible losses in the future resulting from such behavior.

Let us assume that a buyer will choose to be cooperative with (trust) a seller as long as the seller is honest (chooses strategy A). However, the moment the seller cheats, the buyer will choose to punish the former by choosing to cheat from that point on in all future plays of the game. In this situation, the seller must weigh the short-run gains from cheating against the long-term losses that result from retaliation. The same sort of logic prevails for a buyer thinking of cheating a seller. As long as the discount rate is low enough, cooperation now becomes a possible equilibrium solution. Even if the same players, buyers and sellers, do not interact over time, cooperation can also emerge if the information concerning an individual's previous choices is widely know. In this context a person's reputation in such exchanges is widely known. Any individual who chooses to be non-cooperative risks damaging this reputation and, thus, losing benefits that could result from future market exchanges. The conclusion to be drawn from this is that trust, which allows market exchange to succeed, must be built through continuous interaction by buyers and sellers. Thus, such trust is slowly accrued through this interaction process.

The Corn Laws played an important role in fostering such interaction. Sellers, representing domestic grain producers, found that these laws raised the return to cooperative (trust enhancing) choices relative to noncooperative choices. For buyers, the taxes on foreign produced grain effectively precluded them from interacting with foreign suppliers. Instead, it raised the relative return to interacting with domestic producers. Thus, by raising the returns to cooperation between domestic buyers and sellers (the new returns to buyers and sellers are given by the numbers in parentheses), the Corn Laws enhanced the likelihood that trust building interaction would occur. This laid the foundation for the national market, which, in turn, stimulated specialization and the resulting increases in productivity.

It must be emphasized that the Corn Laws did not guarantee the development of a domestic market. The state generally must provide some external enforcement mechanisms to strengthen the expansion of the market system. These involved the establishment of property rights systems and enforcement procedures for contracts and agreements. However, the point

to be made is that the Corn Laws served as an important factor in stimulating market development.

As it turns out, a similar process was at work in Japan during the Tokugawa
(1600–1868) and Meiji (1868–1912) periods. During the former period
Japanese social, political, and economic relationships were formulated within
a feudalistic structure dominated by the Tokugawa Shogunate and a series
of lesser warlords. Within this structure, rice for the warlords was extracted
from the countryside in the form of a tax in kind on land. Producers in the
countryside did not have to worry about foreign produced rice from foreign
countries being imported because Japan was basically closed off from the
outside world.

Within this context the feudal lords were most interested in maximizing
the extraction of rice from peasant farmers, leaving them only with enough
to survive. However, in the early part of the 17th century the warrior class
(Samurai) had been moved from the countryside to the castle towns. This
was done to reduce the ability of the warriors to cause trouble in the
countryside and thus strengthen the hand of the dominant warlord. The
Samurai were given stipends by the Tokugawa Shogunate (dominant warlord family) and the latter took over the power of taxation. The dependence
of the warriors on the Shogunate provided the foundation for a relatively
long period of internal peace.[11]

The Tokugawa Shogunate was now faced with a significant increase in
its financial liabilities. Specifically, it had to pay the stipends to the warriors,
and the latter were no longer connected to the countryside. A new mechanism
for collecting the rice tax had to be created. The tax itself was not levied
on individuals but on whole villages. In other words, it was the group's
(village) responsibility to collect the rice tax and make it available to the
central authority.[12] However, Thomas Smith documents that the Shogunate
had increasing difficulty in extracting this rice tax. In particular, from 1650
to 1850 neither the assessed yields nor the tax rate could be increased. Thus
any increases in the productivity of raising rice remained in the countryside.

One can examine this process within the context of a two sector model,
where the sectors are peasant farming and an urban sector made up of
warriors, a feudal elite, and others. Rice is extracted from peasant farmers
via a land tax, in return for which the feudal elite provides protection of life
and property. The terms of trade between the two sectors is represented by
the proportion of total tax collected by the feudal elite. A decline in this
proportion represents the terms of trade turning in agriculture's favor. Thus
agriculture is, in a sense, being protected.[13]

The protection stimulated the expansion in rice markets by raising the
return to cooperative, trust building behavior. Farmers were increasingly
rewarded for the production and marketing of rice while feudal landlords,

warriors, and so forth had to increasingly rely upon markets to purchase the rice they needed.

This process of protecting agriculture continued into the Meiji period as well. Japan was now somewhat open to trade and within a little over 20 years would become a net importer of rice. However, there was intense pressure to impose a tariff on imported rice and such a tariff (15 percent ad valorem) was imposed at the beginning of the Russian–Japanese War (1904–1905). This tariff was made permanent in 1906. Eventually, imports of rice from Taiwan and Korea (Japanese colonies) were allowed. However, the domestic price of rice in Japan continued to be well above the international price up to the World War II period. Once again this stimulated the development of a rural based market system by raising the return to producers of selling in the marketplace and by tilting incentives for buyers so as to lead them to interact with domestic sellers. Thus, once again, the trust foundations necessary for market development were augmented.[14]

The protection of the agricultural sector just discussed had an indirect, but powerful, effect in market formation. However, the new government that came to power in 1868 engaged in a number of policies aimed directly at promoting market development, and these resulted in significant increases in agricultural productivity. Nationwide communication was facilitated with the introduction of a modern postal service and railroads. This certainly reduced transaction costs and spurred market development. A motivating factor for this reform was the realization of Japan's relative economic backwardness compared to the West following Commodore Perry's arrival in 1853.

One of the most important sets of reforms carried out by the new government involved the land tax and property rights. Prior to the restoration, although property rights were not well developed, feudal lords owned all agricultural land in their domains and collected taxes on this land. During the Tokugawa period a sub-ruling class with land ownership evolved, in which some well-to-do farmers gained landholdings by foreclosing on defaulted loans to poorer peasants. Technically, however, the richer peasants did not own the land, and hence their activities were dependent on the whim of the feudal lord. Thus, richer peasants faced an unstable situation in which property rights with respect to land were highly uncertain. Therefore, improvements in productivity were limited and farm operators tended to be subsistence oriented. The new government recognized peasant holders as the rightful owners and gave them the authority to buy and sell land as well.[15] Thus, property rights were assured, and this in itself not only promoted innovation and productivity increases but also the development of a land market.

The land tax previously discussed was levied in kind, although sometimes it was actually paid partly in money, especially on land planted to cash crops. In 1873 the new government began to calculate the value of all of the agricultural land in Japan and set an annual tax of 4 percent of the assessment, 3 percent for national and 1 percent for local taxes, to be paid in the national currency. The impact of the tax was twofold. First, it seems to have reduced the tax burden for traditional farmers. It has been estimated that late Tokugama feudal revenues were 103 million yen per year, on the basis of 1878–1880 rice prices. Alternatively, the Meiji government's annual national and local tax revenues were 71.4 million yen. In addition, in January 1877 the national and local tax rates were lowered to 2.5 percent and .5 percent.[16] Thus the Meiji tax left a larger share of the output of the traditional farms in the hands of the farmers themselves. This additional revenue was then used to increase consumption levels and finance increased market purchases. The second impact of the tax was linked to the payment of the tax in money not in kind. Therefore, farmers were compelled to market a larger share of their crops to pay the taxes.

Both of the impacts of the tax created incentives for the creation and expansion of markets. Traditional sector farmers had greater incentives to market their crops, and benefits were to be gained by establishing new markets and integrating already established ones. The result was a rapid intrusion of commerce into the countryside, which led to the integration of local markets, to the gradual establishment of interregional crop prices, and to the allocation of resources nationwide. This, in turn, allowed farmers to gauge their returns more accurately and thus encouraged them to invest time and money in improving managerial and cultivating techniques.

The government also took an active role in promoting the establishment and extension of other markets. For example,[17] in much of rural Japan, credit markets were not well developed until, in 1897, the government established the Japan Hypothec Bank, whose purpose was to advance long-term credit for land infrastructure investments. As a supplement, the government also established the Banks of Agriculture and Industry, one of which was located in every prefecture. Later, the government advanced credit from funds mobilized from postal savings banks for land improvement projects through the Hypothec Bank and the prefectural Banks of Agriculture and Industry.

At the time of the Meiji restoration, a variety of very productive agricultural techniques were available that were not being effectively utilized. Many of these practices, such as the use of saltwater in seed selection, improved management of nursing beds, and check row planting, were discovered by the farmers. The government promoted the diffusion of these techniques by selecting the best farmers from various regions and having them travel from village to village. Of course, many of these comparative techniques tended to be quite location specific, implying that some modification would be required before the techniques could be successfully transferred. Therefore, an experimental station system was established that utilized relatively simple comparative tests to screen the various techniques, in this way reducing greatly the cost of technical information for farmers.

Although nearly 100 percent of the paddy field area in Japan was already irrigated at the beginning of the Meiji era, in many areas the water supply was insufficient and drainage facilities were lacking. In response, the government sought to promote the establishment of cooperatives and associations whose aim was to bring about land improvements. In fact, in 1899 the Arable Land Reclamation law was enacted. By this law, participation in land improvement projects was made compulsory and legal person status was given to associations and cooperatives involved in these improvement projects. As a result of this institutional innovation, these associations and cooperatives became eligible for the credit becoming available as a result of government efforts to promote the development of a credit market.

In summary, the English and Japanese experiences illustrate some similarities in the development of rural market systems. In both cases, the protection of agriculture seems to have stimulated the development of specialization on a national scale, which in turn increased productivity. In the Japanese case the state, especially during the Meiji period, took even more direct steps aimed at the promotion of a rural market system through development of the traditional sector. It must be emphasized that the resulting productivity changes were not completely the result of rapid technological change. Instead, they were often the result of utilizing already existing technologies, moving from a point within to a point on the production possibilities curve. This possibility also exists for many of today's less developed nations. The rapid development of new biochemical technologies in the last two decades have not been effectively exploited by today's less developed countries. Most of these technologies will have to be modified to be compatible with local environments, but a significant technology backlog exists.

Before closing this section, one additional point should be made. It has been assumed that the transformation of the traditional sector would be led by growth in agricultural productivity. The fundamental rationale for this assumption is ultimately based upon the idea that many less developed nations possess a potential comparative advantage in agricultural production. That is, with significant investment in agriculture productivity, this sector will grow faster than if investment resources had been allocated to other lines of production.

The assumption that agriculture has a potential comparative advantage is based upon two circumstances. First, there is a substantial backlog of agricultural technologies that, with some adaptation, can be utilized by most less developed countries. Second, it has been argued here that, comparing the traditional sector to the modern sector, market failures are more likely to be the case in the traditional sector. Therefore, the divergence between the social rate of return and the private rate of return is likely to be higher in the traditional sector.

With respect to the second argument one must, of course, remember that the traditional sector is made up of manufacturing as well as agriculture. Hence, it is possible that, although the potential comparative advantage does lie within the traditional sector, it may lie with investment in and production of manufactured goods rather than agricultural goods. In this case, traditional sector manufacturing activities would form the leading sector in the transformation process, and agriculture would play a secondary role. Further discussion of traditional sector manufacturing will be presented later in this chapter. However, much of the discussion in this chapter is based upon the notion of agriculture possessing a potential comparative advantage.

LAND TENANCY

Up to this point, the discussion of improvements in agricultural productivity has ignored the issue of land tenancy. There is some reason to believe that low agricultural productivity may be related to the way land utilization is organized. Specifically, much of the land in less developed nations is farmed under some form of a share contract whereas in developed countries the land is usually farmed by its owner or on a fixed rent basis. We will now consider reasons for the prevalence of share contracts in poor regions, whether the contract results in significant inefficiency, and how traditional sector development will change agricultural property rights.

Before agricultural production can take place to any significant extent, property rights with respect to the use of land must be developed. If property rights are not developed, arbitrary confiscation or other activities inimical to the application of effort to the land will prevent productive cultivation. For example, if an individual or group can be excluded from consuming the output of cultivated land, there is little incentive for such individuals or families or groups to cultivate the land.

With the formation of communal property rights the principle of exclusion is applied to individuals who are not members of the community. Thus, only those individuals who are community members can partake of the output resulting from cultivating the land. The free rider problem still arises within the community. However, community social sanctions may work as effective deterrents to free riding behavior, and thus the free rider problem may be avoided. We will not discuss, in any great detail, farming systems based upon communal property rights systems. Instead, our attention will be confined, for the most part, to situations in which private property rights in

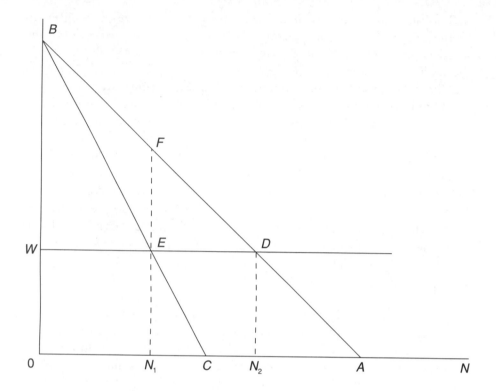

Figure 3.3   Sharecropping example.

land prevail. One may think that in such a situation the free rider problem
is avoided; however, as will be seen, this is not necessarily the case.

Within the context of private property rights in land, land could be
farmed under a variety of contractual arrangements. An individual may farm
the land through the use of family or hired labor. Alternatively, one could
rent the land to others through the use of a share tenancy contract or a fixed
rent leasehold.[18] Of the latter two, it has traditionally been thought that the
sharecropping contract was extremely inefficient. We shall begin our analysis
of contractual forms by reviewing the traditional arguments concerning
sharecropping.

The traditional view concerning sharecropping is that it leads to reduced
output. This view can easily be presented with the use of Figure 3.3. Assume
that there are only two inputs, land and labor, and land is fixed in quantity.
Labor is provided by the tenant whereas the land is owned by the landowner. Tenant labor N is measured along the horizontal axis, with output
being measured along the vertical axis. AB represents the marginal product
of tenant labor and CB represents $(\partial Q/\partial N)(1 - r)$, where $\partial Q/\partial N$ is the
marginal product of tenant labor and r is the landlord's share of output,

which was agreed upon in advance. Thus $(1 - r)(\partial Q/\partial N)$ represents the share of marginal product going to the tenant.[19] The horizontal line drawn at distance $0W$ from the horizontal axis represents the opportunity cost of tenant labor.

If the landowner is a profit maximizer and hires labor to farm the land, $0N_2$ units of labor will be hired. Labor will be employed up to the point where the marginal product of labor is equal to the opportunity cost. The total wage bill would be $0WDN_2$ and the total return to the landlord would be BWD. The same result would occur if the landowner were a profit maximizer and farmed the land with his or her own labor. Finally, the same result would occur if the landowner leased the land out on a fixed rent basis. If the rental market were competitive, the tenant would apply labor up to $0N_2$ and pay BWD to the landlord.

With respect to share tenancy, the result, according to the traditional view, is much different. Because the tenant receives only a share of his marginal product, $(1 - r)(\partial Q/\partial N)$, the rational tenant will apply labor only up to N_1, where the tenants net marginal product is just equal to the opportunity cost of labor. The tenant would therefore receive $0BEN_1$ in payment, with the landlord receiving rent equal to BFE. Thus, allocative inefficiency would result from the farming of land under a share tenancy contract.

This view has been questioned. The most well known and often cited critique is provided by Steven N. S. Cheung. He argued that if perfect competition is assumed the situation outlined in Figure 3.3 could not be one of equilibrium. Obviously, in Figure 3.3, the tenant is earning a return greater than his opportunity cost; that is, $0BEN_1 > 0WEN_1$. Conversely, the landlords return must be below his or her opportunity cost, what one could earn from a fixed rent contract or from farming the land oneself ($BFE < WBFE$).

Given the preceding, the landlord can stipulate that the tenant work up to $0N_2$ rather than $0N_1$ and manipulate the rental rate to ensure that the tenant earned only his or her opportunity cost and no more. If the tenant should refuse, the landlord could easily replace the tenant with one willing to accept the tenant labor's opportunity cost as payment. Indeed, in a perfectly competitive land market, the landlord need not even understand or know the details of farming the land. If the tenant would apply less than the efficient quantity of labor, or any other input in the multiple input case, or grow a less valuable crop, in a multiple output case, the landowner could make the proper adjustments by leasing the land to a different tenant, choosing a different contractual arrangement, or selling the ownership outright.

The conclusion to be drawn from the analysis is that a more complete analysis of sharecropping shows that under perfect competition all contractual forms (fixed rent lease, hired labor, owner operation, and share tenancy) could be equally efficient. If so, then how can one account for the fact that in certain regions the dominant contractual mode is sharecropping whereas in others it is a fixed rent lease?

To answer the question raised at the end of the last paragraph, it must be remembered that underlying Cheung's analysis is the notion that perfect competition prevails. Specifically, perfect knowledge exists, there is no risk, and, most important, the institutions that underlay markets and their effective operation exist. However, as discussed previously, in the traditional sector none of these assumptions is likely to be appropriate.

In the traditional sector, markets for credit, fertilizers, and other inputs are often not well developed. Thus a farmer may not be able to independently purchase these items. As a result, farmers will need to rely upon landlords to supply many inputs. The question then becomes, under what contractual form should these inputs be provided by the landlord? It is only natural to think that the relationship between landlord and tenant would be, as anthropologists call it, multiplex in nature. That is, an individual plays not one but a variety of roles in interacting with fellow members of the community. Therefore, the landlord not only provides land to the tenant but also fertilizer, credit, and so on.[20]

Within this context, one important factor in determining the type of contract that will evolve is risk. Within the traditional sector few mechanisms are available to the tenant farmer to deal with risk. Markets for crop insurance do not exist, and diversification of sources of income as a hedge against risk is also not available due to the lack of market development, in particular the labor market. One could argue that peasants, given their precarious living standards, are more risk averse than landowners. With a fixed rent lease, the tenant bears, at least theoretically, all of the risk. With the share tenancy contract, risk is shared by the landlord and the tenant. Finally, one would think that wage labor would be most preferred by risk averse tenants, because the landlord would bear all the risk. However, labor demand in agricultural production is highly uncertain due to weather and other ecological conditions, and it follows that employment opportunities and wage levels also may be highly uncertain. Hence, risk averse tenants are likely to prefer share tenancy contracts in regions where output variability, risk, is high. For the landlord, the risk would be greatest with hiring wage labor, least with fixed rent contracts, with share contracts taking the intermediate position. Thus share tenancy may be the choice that minimizes the conflict between the objectives of the tenant and landlord.[21]

A number of individuals[22] have argued that risk cannot be the factor to explain the choice of contract by both landlord and tenant. This is because the same degree of risk derived from sharecropping can be achieved by an appropriate combination of fixed-rent land lease and fixed-wage labor contracts. However, if the tenant's entrepreneurial and managerial ability is indivisible, it would become inefficient for the tenant to allocate his time among wage employment and fixed rent leasehold contracts. The inefficiency becomes even worse if the tenant owned other indivisible resources such as family labor and draft animals for which markets are inactive.[23]

In addition, one must remember that transaction costs are involved in the creation and enforcement of these contracts that these costs may depend upon the type of contract. These costs arise because information is not perfect and freely available; that is, it is costly. Specifically, the terms of the contract must be developed, and then they must be enforced. The enforcement is costly because the landlord must gather information concerning the intensity with which the tenant is applying labor to the land. From the landlord's perspective, the fixed rent tenancy contract is best because, theoretically, all the landlord need be concerned with is setting the optimum fixed rent. The tenant receives his or her marginal product and thus has an incentive to apply the efficient quantity of labor. With respect to the use of wage labor, the costs of gathering information concerning the intensity of work effort would be great, to try to prevent shirking on the part of labor. Sharecropping represents the middle ground in that there are information and enforcement costs for the landlord. The landlord must find out whether the tenant is living up to the terms of the agreement and is correctly representing the output level being produced. However, the share agreement does provide more incentive than a fixed wage contract to apply tenant labor to production.[24]

Another factor likely to play a role in the choice of a contract is the opportunity for the tenant to exercise entrepreneurial ability in dealing with disequilibrium. From this perspective the fixed rent leasehold is the most attractive form of contract because rent is a fixed cost in the short run. Thus, any increase in the productivity of land goes to the tenant. From this perspective, the wage contract is least attractive, because the benefits of productivity increase either go to the landlord or merely increase the quantity of labor the landlord will hire. Again share tenancy occupies the middle ground.[25]

The actual choice of contract will be determined at "a saddle point of conflicting preference orderings between tenant and landlord."[26] Consider a traditional economy in a stationary state. In such an economy there is little technological innovation and markets are not well developed. In addition, such a society is likely to be characterized by a social structure that ties individuals tightly together through expectational bonds. In other words, tenants have certain duties that people in the community expect them to perform for the landlord and vice versa. An individual who violates these exceptional bonds may be penalized by the society at large, say, through social ostracism.

In such a traditional society, risk is likely to be an important factor in the decision–making process of the tenant, given the tenant's exceedingly low level of living. In addition, because technological change does not occur, the tenant can gain little from entrepreneurial ability. The landlord is better able to bear risk because of a relatively high standard of living and the wide availability of knowledge about tenants. Finally, with respect to information and enforcement costs, it would seem relatively easy for the landlord to obtain and evaluate information concerning the best techniques and likely output on the land. Given the tight social structure likely to exist in such a village society, the cost of shirking is likely to be high for the tenant. Thus, the pervasive choice of sharecropping contracts, which is generally found in traditional societies, seems to represent a "saddle point between the tenants strong risk aversion and the landlords calculation of enforcement and information costs."[27] Therefore, share cropping would seem to be an institutional adaptation to an environment in which market development is limited.

A strategy of development aimed at creating those missing markets and the institutional structure necessary to support them is likely to dramatically alter the tenancy situation. New technologies would become available to the village or region via expanded interaction with the rest of the traditional sector. Such changes would dramatically increase the gains to entrepreneurial ability to the tenant. Also the degree of risk is likely to increase because the technologies are new and subject to some uncertainty as to their outcome if adopted. Many new seed varieties and cultivating techniques provide higher average yields, but at the expense of a significant increase in the variability of those yields. At the same time, the information and enforcement costs of the landlord are likely to increase. This is due to the landlord's lack of experience with new ways of doing things. Thus there is a substantial increase in the difficulty of knowing the correct intensity of tenants' labor input and the likely resulting output. Also, the social structure of the village is likely to be undergoing significant transformation. The exceptional bonds linking individuals in the society are likely to weaken. This weakening of bonds will also increase informational and enforcement costs to the landlord.[28]

As a result of these factors, it is highly unlikely that sharecropping will remain the dominant form of contracting. The rising enforcement and informational costs are likely to lead the landlord to prefer fixed rent contracts. Wealthier tenants, who are better able to gain access to the technology and to bear risks, are also likely to prefer fixed rent contracts. Those tenants, who have trouble gaining access to the new technology and lack a cushion against increased risk, may prefer wage labor. Landlords will likely agree to wage contracts if they are able to limit their dependence on hired labor through the use of machinery or because of other factors such as technological change.

Up to this point, it has been assumed that the main input provided by the tenant is labor and that, except for land, no other inputs are involved. Obviously there are numerous inputs. Contracts concerning the provision of these inputs will, under certain circumstances, be necessary. Obviously, if the landowner rents the land on a fixed rent basis, the tenant makes the decision concerning quantities of other inputs to be used. In owner operation or operation through hired labor, the landowner makes the decision. Under share tenancy contracts, the costs of other inputs can be shared between the landlord and tenant. Given equilibrium, as the degree of input sharing rises, so will the rental rate charged by the landlord. The larger the share of input costs borne by the landlord, the higher the rental rate will likely be and vice versa.

In summary, the widespread occurrence of sharecropping in the agricultural sectors of many less developed nations may be a reflection of the traditional character of agricultural production. That is, in situations where markets are not widespread, it is extremely difficult for a tenant farmer to gain access to the inputs necessary to effectively farm. In addition, the lack of well-developed markets implies that the tenant farmer will lack adequate opportunities to insure against risk by purchasing insurance, by finding opportunities for wage employment, and so forth. If the tenant is risk averse, then sharecropping may be explained because it is a mechanism for sharing risk with the landowner. The landowner is willing to bear this risk if he or she can make sure that the land is used productively. Thus, the landlord wants to be assured that the tenant will not shirk. The fixed rent contract provides the tenant farmer with the greatest incentive not to shirk. However, in a tightly knit village atmosphere there may be little difference between share and fixed rent contracts in terms of preventing shirking. Therefore, share contracting is the result of the interaction between tenant and owner within the context of a traditional society.

The analysis also indicates that economic changes within the traditional sector, brought about by the development and integration of markets, may spur a shift in the type of contracts used to organize the production process. Specifically, change within the traditional sector may lead to a switch from share to fixed rent contracts. This type of process is an example of what has been called induced *institutional innovation*. This view of institutional innovation stems from the work of a number of theorists such as North and Thomas,[29] Feeny,[30] and Hayami and Ruttan.[31] The basic notion is that one can understand institutional innovation in terms of changes in exogenous economic variables. Given a specific set of rules and norms (institutions), the

existing technology, input prices, and output prices, certain types of economic activities are likely to be profitable. Changes in relative prices or
technology will create new opportunities for profit. The pursuit of some of
the opportunities may be restrained by some of the existing rules or norms
(institutions). This creates incentives for political and social entrepreneurs to
organize in order to bring about institutional innovation. The implication is
that, as the traditional sector becomes dynamic, the institutional structure of
this sector will be induced to evolve in new directions.

TECHNOLOGICAL CHANGE

Up until now the discussion has focused on how the creation of markets and
the necessary institutional infrastructure for such markets can lead to significant productivity improvements. These changes will in turn induce changes
in the structure of land tenancy institutions. However, if such productivity
increases are to be sustained, persistent technological innovation must occur.
Several nations including Japan, Taiwan, and Korea have all recently succeeded in rapidly increasing the productivity of traditional agriculture. Total
factor productivity studies reveal that much of this increase in productivity
is attributable to technological change.

Technological change can be viewed from the perspective of an increase
in output obtainable from a given set of inputs or, equivalently, the decrease
in inputs necessary to produce a given level of output. This can be illustrated
as an inward shift of an isoquant representing a particular level of output or
an upward shift in the production function. Of course, technological change
is not likely to effect all factor inputs in the same manner. In other words,
technological change is likely to be biased. To grasp the concept of biased
innovation, we will refer to Figure 3.4. Inputs, x_1 and x_2, are measured along
the vertical and horizontal axis. I_0 is an isoquant representing a particular
level of output.

PP is the isocost line and thus the initial equilibrium, prior to technological
change, is at point A. I_1, I_2, and I_3 are isoquants representing the same level
of output after technological innovation has occurred. All of these innovations will result in this output being produced at the same cost. Consequently, we might choose any of the technological innovations. Suppose the
new technology is given by I_1, then the new equilibrium would be given
by point B. In this situation, the technical change saves both inputs in the
same proportion maintaining the input ratio given by $0X$. This is what is
known as a *Hick's neutral technical change*.[32]

Alternatively, technical change may be biased. For example, assume that
technical change results in isoquant I_2 in Figure 3.4. Given unchanged input
prices, the new equilibrium would be given by point C. As can be seen, this

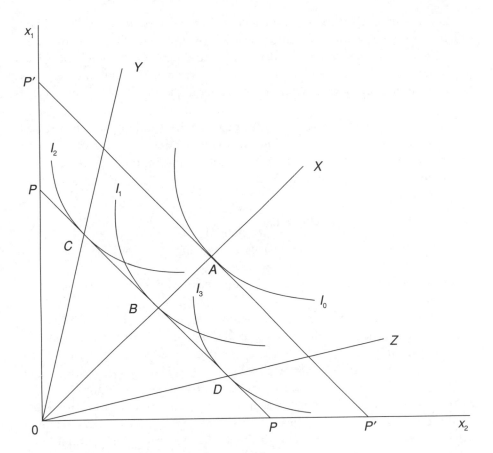

Figure 3.4 Technological change and output.

technical innovation saves both inputs. However, it saves proportionately more of x_2 than x_1. This results, given input prices, in a rise in the equilibrium input ratio from $0X$ to $0Y$. Thus this technical innovation is said to be relatively x_2 saving (x_1 using). It follows then that a technological innovation such as that given by isoquant I_3 would be characterized as x_1 saving (x_2 using), with the input ratio falling from $0X$ to $0Z$.

An alternative specification of neutrality and bias in technological innovation is often used. In this approach, input prices are no longer held constant, instead the input or factor ratio is held constant. Thus, neutrality of an innovation occurs when the marginal productivity of each input increases proportionately. If the marginal productivity of x_1 grows faster than that for x_2, holding the input ratio constant, then the innovation is said to be x_1 using and x_2 saving. Firms would then seek to use more of x_1 and relatively less of x_2, which would, of course, raise the price of x_1 relative to x_2. The reverse holds if the marginal productivity of x_2 grows faster than that for x_1.

A final approach is based on the idea of factor shares. Specifically, holding factor prices constant, if an innovation is x_1 using, x_2 saving then the ratio of x_1's share to that of x_2 would increase. Alternatively, holding the factor ratio constant, an innovation that is x_1 using, x_2 saving would raise the price of x_1 relative to x_2. Again, x_1's factor share would tend to rise relative to that of x_2.

All three approaches result in the same division of innovations into x_1 and x_2 using and saving categories. The advantage of the factor shares approach is that it can be easily generalized to handle many inputs. Technically, the definition of bias can be written as

$$\frac{dS_i}{dt} \cdot \frac{1}{S_i} \begin{array}{l} > 0 \text{ factor } i \text{ using} \\ = 0 \text{ neutral} \\ < \text{ factor } i \text{ saving,} \end{array} \tag{3.2}$$

where S_i is the share of factor i in total costs and factor prices are held constant.[33]

Economic explanations of the rate and bias of technical change have, until recently, been most prominent in the study of economic history. Habakkuk[34] and Rothbarth[35] have both sought to examine and compare the development of British and American technology in the 19th century. The higher labor productivity in the United States is attributed to the greater use of labor saving machinery, which was in turn induced by the relatively higher industrial wage rate in the United States. The higher industrial wage rate in the United States is attributable to the higher returns to agricultural labor due to the relative abundance of land.

A different perspective on the development of new technologies is provided by Nathan Rosenberg.[36] He argues that bottlenecks, labor problems, and obvious and compelling needs stimulate the development of specific types of technology.[37]

These ideas have slowly come to be formulated into what is known as the *theory of induced technical change*. Hicks played an early role in the development of these ideas when he suggested that there are two distinct types of inventions.[38] First, there are inventions that are induced by changes in the relative prices of the factors of production, and second there are innovations that are autonomous. Hicks saw no reason for supposing that autonomous inventions would be biased in any direction and therefore assumed a random dispersion. As a result, the bias of technical change would be determined by the bias of the induced innovations. Hicks argued that technical progress has been labor saving and that this bias must be the result of the rapid increase in capital relative to labor that has marked European history during the last few centuries.

Ahmad formalized these ideas through the use of what he calls a *historical innovation possibility curve*.[39] This curve is simply an envelope of all the alternative isoquants, each representing a given output on various production functions, that the entrepreneur expects to develop with the use of the available amount of innovating skill and time. Ahmad assumes that these innovation possibilities curves are neutral and that the cost and time involved in moving from one isoquant to another, both belonging to the innovation possibility curve of the current period, is equal to that required for moving to the innovation possibility curve of the next period. Because this latter curve is always nearer the origin than the innovation possibility curve of the current period, it must be concluded that all of the isoquants belonging to a particular innovation possibility curve, except the one actually chosen, become irrelevant for economic decisions after the choice is actually made.

An analysis of Ahmad's model can be clarified by considering Figure 3.5. C_{n-1} and C_n represent the innovation possibilities curves for periods n and $n - 1$. If P_{n-1} represents the ratio of factor prices in time period $n - 1$ then, as can be seen, the firm will choose to develop and use the technology represented by isoquant I_{n-1}. If this price ratio remains unchanged into period n, the firm will then make use of the technology represented by isoquant I_n. If, however, wages rise relative to interest rates so that the slope of the budget line changes to that of P_n, it would follow that the firm would, in period n, choose to use the innovation represented by isoquant I_n'. From this analysis we can conclude that a rise in the price of labor relative to capital will result in firms making use of a new innovation that is labor saving in character. In other words, relative factor scarcities stimulate the development of innovations that save the relatively scarce factor by making greater use of the more abundant factors of production.

Although Ahmad's analysis provides insight into the adoption of new technologies, it has several limitations. It is applicable only to technology that is costless to adopt. Furthermore, nothing is said about the research process that generates the new technology. Presumably firms will engage in research that will have the potential of saving on expensive inputs if they can capture the gains from that research. Therefore Ahmad provides little insight into research carried out by public research groups. This distinction between private and public innovation is important in understanding technical innovation in agriculture because of the characteristics of the agricultural technology itself. Therefore, before proceeding, some time will be spent identifying the characteristics of this technology.

Technology in agriculture is generally divided into two types: mechanical and biochemical. Mechanical technology is designed to facilitate the substitution of power and machinery for labor. In addition, mechanization usually involves the substitution of land for labor because the resulting higher

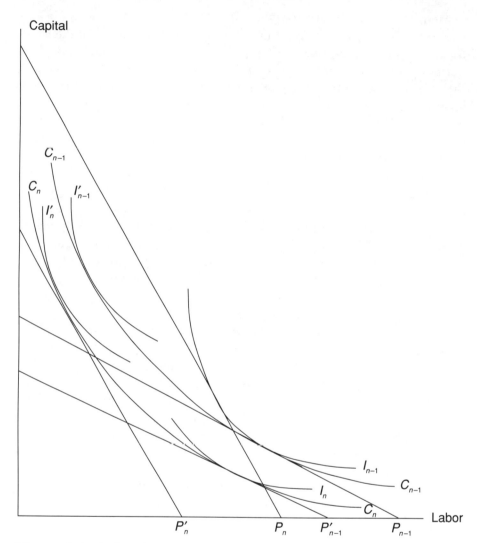

Figure 3.5   Induced innovation.
Provided by The Royal Economic Society

output per worker usually requires cultivating a larger land area per worker. Mechanical technology is generally developed by private sector firms because the returns to research are largely embodied in the machines themselves. Hence, there are incentives to private research and development.

The second type of agricultural technology is biochemical in nature. It is generally designed to facilitate the substitution of labor and industrial inputs for land. This substitution may occur through increased recycling of soil fertility by more labor-intensive cultivation systems, an increased use of chemical fertilizers through better husbandry practices, and better manage-

ment systems using inputs more efficiently. Irrigation combined with increased usage of chemical fertilizers and fertilizer responsive seed varieties
represents the typical package of inputs characterized as biochemical technology. This type of technology is not, however, generally developed as the
result of the research activities of individual private firms. The technology
is not embodied in expensive machinery and it can be easily imitated. The
development of biochemical technology then may require public research
activities.

Biochemical technology possesses many of the characteristics of a public
good. Public goods are generally defined in terms of their being nonrival and
nonexclusionary in nature. That is, a public good is nonrival in the sense
that its consumption by one individual does not affect its availability to
others. A public good is nonexclusionary in the sense that if one individual
has access to the good, others cannot be prevented from using it. Both
mechanical and biochemical technologies represent new knowledge that is
basically nonrival in nature. If farmer A uses a new piece of knowledge, that
use does not prevent farmer B from also utilizing it. However, mechanical
technologies can be made exclusive with respect to their use, although this
is extremely difficult for biochemical technologies.

Mechanical technologies are exclusive in the sense that the new knowledge
can be used only when the machine is purchased. The developer of a
mechanical innovation can obtain patent protection for the innovation, and
others can make use of the knowledge only after paying a fee. Many biochemical techniques are, however, nonexclusionary. Those who develop the
new knowledge cannot prevent others from utilizing it at little or no cost
because of the difficulty in establishing and enforcing property rights with
respect to biochemical techniques. For example, it is hard to patent a new
husbandry technique. Thus property rights cannot be established or enforced, and the new technique can be copied, at little or no cost, by others.
The difficulty here is not so much that such property rights could not be
established but that the information and enforcement costs of making such
a system work would indeed be extremely high.

Because of the nonexcludability characteristic of biochemical technology,
private firms will not spend enough resources on the research necessary to
develop such techniques. In other words, market failure would occur, and
if no public research effort were made, it would be natural to expect the
private development of mechanical technologies only.

Hayami and Ruttan recognized that the public sector had been largely
ignored in the literature on induced innovation. They took the theory as
developed by Hicks and Ahmad and extended it to allow for public sector
research. In the following few paragraphs their theory will be discussed
and analyzed. In general, their theory is important because it suggests that

research and innovation in the public and private sectors can be treated in a similar way.

Hayami and Ruttan[40] argue that, as the demand for agricultural production increases, due to growth in population and income, the prices of the inputs for which supply is less elastic will rise relative to the prices of inputs for which the supply is more elastic. In the same manner, as the supply of certain inputs increases faster than others, the prices of these inputs will fall relative to the prices of other factors of production. As a result, technical innovations, which save factors of production that are relatively scarce, will become more and more profitable for agricultural producers. This would, according to Hayami and Ruttan, induce farmers to search for technical alternatives that save the increasingly scarce factors of production.

Up to this point the analysis is almost identical of that of Ahmad. However, Hayami and Ruttan extend the analysis by arguing that farmers will press the public research institutions and agricultural supply firms to develop new techniques and new inputs that allow the substitution of those factors of production in abundant supply for those that are scarce. Perceptive scientists would respond to these demands by developing and making available these sorts of new techniques and inputs.

The crucial link in the inducement mechanism presented above is the response of public research scientists and administrators. It is not necessary, according to Hayami and Ruttan, to assume that scientists and administrators respond directly to the demands of farmers in the selection of research goals. It is only necessary that there exists an effective incentive system to reward administrators and researchers, materially or by prestige, for their contributions to the solution of significant problems in the society. If one accepts these ideas, then the inducement mechanism developed by Hicks and refined by Ahmad can be directly related to the experience of less developed nations.

Hayami and Ruttan attempt to support their induced innovation models by analyzing the historical experiences of agricultural development in the United States and Japan for the period 1880–1960. The experiences of these two nations would, they believe, have important implications for two groups of nations; countries of the new continents that have a favorable human–land ratio and countries in Asia that have an unfavorable human–land ratio. The problems of those nations faced with unfavorable human–land ratios can be explained by considering their analysis of Japanese agriculture.

Hayami and Ruttan's analysis of Japanese agricultural development can be easily understood through the use of Figure 3.6. The quantity of land is measured on the upper half of the vertical axis, the use of new biological inputs is measured along the bottom half of the vertical axis, and the quantity of fertilizer along the horizontal axis. In the top half of the diagram, V represents the innovation possibility curve and V_0 and V_1 represent specific

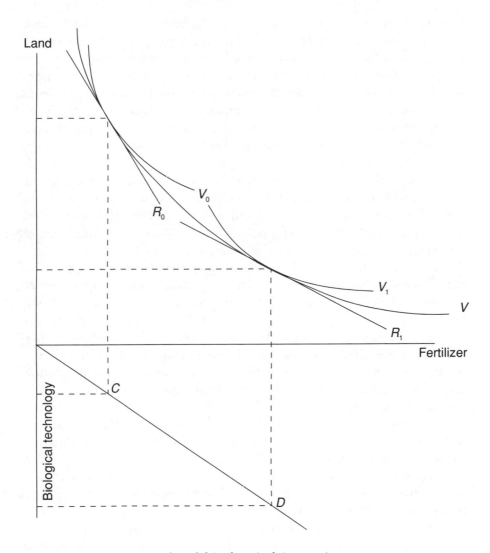

Figure 3.6 Mechanical and biochemical innovations.
Reprinted by permission of the Johns Hopkins University Press

technologies that could be used. In the bottom half, line $0CD$ represents the
assumption that fertilizer and new biological inputs (seeds, husbandry techniques,
etc.) are complements. As can be seen, if the price of fertilizer falls relative to the
price of land, R_0 to R_1, it would be profitable for the farmer to use a technology
that substituted fertilizer for land. According to the Hayami–Ruttan inducement
model, farmers would press private and public research organizations to produce
such technology. These organizations would respond by developing new types
of seed that allow the substitution of fertilizers for scarce land.

In Japan during the period 1880–1960 the price of land tended to rise relative to the wage rate of labor. Therefore, it was not profitable to substitute land for labor through the use of new mechanical inputs. However, the price of fertilizer fell relative to land between 1880 and 1960, which would, according to the induced innovation hypothesis, lead to the development of biochemical technologies. Hayami and Ruttan argue that this was indeed what happened. They support this conclusion by arguing that the substitution of commercial fertilizer for land was too great to be explained by mere factor substitution.

The tests of the induced innovation hypothesis used by Hayami and Ruttan could not distinguish between the effects of technical change and simple factor substitution. However, other studies differentiated between the effects of technical change and factor substitution. Most of these studies tend, on balance, to offer support for the induced innovation hypothesis.[41]

Binswanger[42] has expanded the analysis of Hayami and Ruttan to incorporate supply as well as demand. That is, Hayami and Ruttan's analysis basically dealt with factors that influence the demand for innovation including factor input prices and product demand. They did not include supply factors, including the size of research budgets and the costs of undertaking alternative lines of research. Binswanger developed a theoretical structure in which the goal is to maximize the discounted present value of the profit function, subject to a variable research and development budget. His results show that any rise in the expected present value of the total cost of a factor will lead to an increased allocation of resources to the research activity that most saves that factor. In addition, a rise in the cost of research that saves a particular factor or a decline in the productivity of that research will bias technical innovation in the direction of other factors. Finally, with no budget constraint on research, a rise in the value of output will increase the research budget and the rate of productivity growth.

The Hayami–Ruttan theory of induced innovation depends on two crucial assumptions about agriculture. First, farmers are assumed to convey their needs to public research organizations through some sort of institutional network linking the two. If this institutional network does not exist, then the whole process breaks down. Second, even if such institutional links exist, farmers might have diverse interests, so that the form these links take and the groups that they serve will significantly influence existing research activities. Political power instead of economic merit may thus influence the type of research undertaken. More will be said later concerning political power. For now, the discussion will be restricted to the institutional network.

As already outlined, if the induced technical innovation process is to occur, an institutional network composed of research organizations that are linked to farmers' interests must exist. In the traditional sector of most less developed nations this institutional network is missing, and as a result the development and diffusion of new technologies is often retarded or non-existent. If the traditional sector is to be made dynamic, then such an institutional network must be created. Furthermore, given the public good nature of much agricultural research, the government will have to play an important role. Hayami and Ruttan argue further that such a research system needs to be decentralized in nature because conditions such as climate and soil type vary from region to region. Therefore, technologies developed for one region are often not appropriate for another. Hence, research institutions must be aware of local conditions and local needs. Decentralization of research stations and extension services allows local farmers to convey their problems and needs to the research network.

TRADITIONAL SECTOR: MANUFACTURING

Up to this point, the discussion of the traditional sector has been limited mainly to agriculture. Although it is obvious that in most less developed countries the vast majority of the population earns its living in the traditional sector, part of the traditional sector in many countries has already moved to urban areas, partly as a result of development by displacement. In addition, in the off-season many family farms engage in household manufacturing. A small number devote most of their time to small-scale manufacturing, which comprises the typical village industries: smiths, shoemakers, garment makers, handicrafts, masons, and various crop processing activities. For the most part, these traditional activities involve the use of family labor. Much of the manufacturing is geared to provide rudimentary inputs and processing services to agriculture as well as to provide for the nonfood needs of the large rural population. Finally, the production techniques used tend to be very labor intensive.

Some development economists have argued and predicted that such nonfarm manufacturing activities in rural areas will decline with economic development.[43] However, much of the evidence indicates otherwise. Anderson argues that in the course of economic growth manufacturing activities appear to pass through three phases.[44] First is a phase in which household manufacturing is predominant in both output and employment terms. Second is a phase in which small workshops and factories emerge at a rapid rate and displace household manufacturing in some sectors. Third is a phase in which large scale production becomes predominant, displacing the remaining household manufacturing and a large share of workshop and small factory production. This phase is partly a product of the previous one in that many of the large firms will evolve from small workshops and factories. However, many large firms, because of economies of scale, are originally established as large operations and grow even larger through time.

The declining importance of household manufacturing is not surprising, but the large role played by small workshops and factories is worth emphasizing. Much of the empirical evidence indicates that small workshops and factories grow rapidly during the second stage. This trend is surprising in light of the preference given to large, capital intensive industry by most less developed nations. This preference has manifested itself in various policies subsidizing large scale industry at the expense of small workshops and factories.

One might wonder why small workshops and factories are able to grow in importance even in the face of policies inimical to their operation. Three reasons are generally put forward. First, this process takes place while the majority of the labor force still resides in rural areas and villages. As rural incomes rise and thus create new markets, these markets are highly dispersed. Given the poor infrastructure and transport services in these regions, the cost of providing consumer and capital goods to these dispersed markets poses a substantial barrier to large firms seeking to market their goods in rural areas. Staley and Morse[45] argue that many industries may hold advantages of location for small scale production as long as transportation costs remain high. These industries include the processing of a dispersed raw material where transport costs are reduced by reducing the bulk, weight, and handling difficulty at the source; the production of other bulky and heavy goods; the production of perishable goods that must be refrigerated, transported quickly, or consumed locally; and the service and repair industries.[46]

The question that immediately arises with the preceding discussion is why large firms do not set up local branches to compete with local producers. They eventually do, but only after an extended period of time. This difficulty in setting up local branches is due to a lack knowledge of the local markets and the high cost of training local labor. The key here would seem to be that the small workshops and factories are part and parcel of the traditional sector, governed by its system of values and mores. Thus, employment and operation practices reflect local conditions and accepted ways of doing things. Laborers are often family members or members of the local village who are tied both to each other and to the local owners through a web of cultural and social relationships that prevent shirking.

A second reason for the rapid growth of small workshops and factories concerns the types of goods produced. Often these goods are highly differentiated and have low economies of scale. Some researchers have labeled these sorts of goods as *small scale culture goods*.[47] This is because they are often peculiar to the particular culture involved, are often produced by artisans, and require significant handwork (handicrafts). Because of their differentiated nature, labor intensity, and lack of scale economies, large firms are prevented from taking advantage of these markets. Again, it should be stressed that the compatibility of the products and techniques with the existing culture partly accounts for the success of small, family run firms in producing them. In addition, small firms may be more labor intensive and better able to take advantage of existing factor proportions.

Finally, the third factor accounting for the emergence and growth of small firms is the practice of subcontracting. This involves large firms contracting out to small factories and workshops the responsibility to supply particular parts and components. The production of these parts and components is not likely to be characterized by scale economies. As has been pointed out by Kazuo Sato,[48] the success of such relationships depends on the reliability of the smaller firms and workshops to produce high quality parts. In Japan, for instance, subcontracting has been and still is an important feature of the Japanese economy. The subcontracting relationship there often becomes semi-permanent in nature, and this allows the larger parent firms to provide technical advice and promote improved quality. This, according to Sato, most likely reflects the emphasis in Japanese society and culture on long-term relationships, which may go back to the goningumi (household team in rural villages) concept in the Tokugawa period or the apprenticeship system in the Meiji period.

In summary, the success and growth of small workshops and firms in the development process would seem to be due, in large part, to the fact that they evolved from the traditional sector and consequently seek to serve its needs, and they mold their employment and business practices to reflect traditional ways of doing things. Hence, they are generally labor intensive in nature and are likely to be more efficient, from a social perspective, for labor abundant societies. However, the evolution of traditional sector manufacturing is likely to be closely connected to the development of the agricultural sector. Economists refer to these connections as *linkages*, and linkages are generally categorized as backward, forward, and consumption. Linkages were introduced in Chapter 1.

Recall that backward production linkages exist when the expansion of one production sector requires inputs produced in another sector; as agriculture expands, it often requires machinery, machinery repair, fertilizers, seeds, and so on. These inputs may be provided by firms located in rural areas or small market towns. Forward linkages exist when the expansion of production in one sector provides materials that can be further processed through activities in another production sector; as food production expands, it enhances the opportunity for rural based firms to process such materials into finished products. The third category concerns consumption linkages. As income is generated through production in one sector, that income or part of it is spent on output produced in another sector. As agricultural incomes rise, consumption expenditures for goods produced by rural based firms will expand thus stimulating the expansion of traditional sector manufacturing.

Empirical estimates of the relative sizes of these linkages indicate that the consumption linkage is by far the largest.[49] However, this perspective tends to neglect linkages that might run from traditional sector manufacturing to agricultural production. Ranis and Stewart[50] have pointed to three such possible linkages: demand, supply, and motivation related. As rural based manufacturing expands, it stimulates the development of markets for agricultural production, and as these markets expand they allow agricultural producers to diversify into nonfood agricultural production as specialization occurs. Second, production of manufactured goods in the traditional sector will often provide the supply of inputs necessary to increase agricultural production.

The final linkage is motivation related. Farmers in rural areas are often willing to trust only family members, and thus investment of savings in far off urban areas is likely to be seen as fraught with risk and uncertainty. Hence, there is little incentive to intensify agricultural production effort to generate surpluses for such investment. Rural based opportunities for manufacturing are more familiar and less risky for farmers. Thus they are likely to intensify production efforts and increase agricultural productivity to provide the resources for investment in rural based nonagricultural activities.

There is another important avenue by which traditional sector manufacturing can foster agricultural growth. Farmers in less developed nations can raise their incomes in a variety of ways. They can change their crop mix by choosing to grow crops with a higher market value. On the input side they can choose to buy more land and purchase additional inputs. In combination with additional inputs, farmers can choose to market a larger proportion of their crop. All of these activities represent behavioral changes requiring greater market participation, and this generally imposes considerable risk upon the farmer. Low income farmers, who are likely to be risk averse, are likely to be reluctant to engage in such innovative behavior.

In situations in which insurance and credit markets either do not exist or are limited, income diversification upon the part of farmers can dramatically reduce the risk associated with innovation. One mechanism for income diversification is provided via traditional sector manufacturing activity. Under these conditions farm households will be much more willing to undertake innovative changes in behavior.

The interactive process just outlined sees manufacturing and agriculture in the traditional sector locked in a virtuous circle of income expansion[51] and market expansion. This seems to contradict the conventional view of the industrial revolution in Europe and Japan, which views this process as structural change in which both population and economic activities were urbanized.

However, it seems, in the early stages of the establishment of a market system in Japan, that a movement of manufacturing into the countryside did indeed occur. Thomas Smith has shown that during the 18th century towns generally stagnated and lost population, with the heaviest losses occurring in regions with growing economies.

In analyzing the reasons for such a decline, Smith[52] finds that most contemporaries blamed the development of trade and industry in the countryside. The state sought to limit this movement of manufacturing into the countryside. As long as such activity remained in urban areas, it was easy to regulate and tax. As these activities moved into the countryside, this was difficult to do, and thus laws were designed to prevent the development of traditional sector manufacturing. However, these laws failed, and this failure was linked to the fact that the enforcement of the laws was in the hands of rural village authorities, who were likely to be directly involved in such activities.

Jan de Vries[53] finds the experiences of Europe and Japan to be very similar. Urban areas in Europe did grow but this growth was concentrated among the largest of Europe's cities, with the smaller cities characterized by experiences similar to those of Japan. The decline of cities in Europe was similar in its causes as well, with industrial production migrating into the countryside and the rise of villages and market towns.

Mendels[54] has labeled the process just outlined *proto-industrialization*. This was marked by the growth of "traditionally organized, but market oriented, principally rural industry."[55] These activities utilized labor that was, at certain parts of the growing season, in surplus and allowed capital to accumulate in the hands of merchant entrepreneurs. The growth of the traditional manufacturing sector is thought to have provided a market for agricultural output and thus led to increased specialization in agriculture, resulting in growing productivity.

In summary, traditional sector manufacturing and agricultural production are linked to each other via a variety of channels. Through interaction via these channels a virtuous circle of traditional sector development can arise.

DISTORTED DEVELOPMENT

Up until now the traditional sector strategy of development has emphasized two types of institutional innovation: direct and indirect. That is, the government can directly play a role by seeking to establish the institutions necessary for the diffusion of technology and the creation of markets. Examples of this are provided by the Japanese government's attempts to foster the development of a rural credit market and the establishment of research and extension networks. Indirect institutional innovation occurs when such innovations are induced to occur as the result of government policy. For example, the land tax reform in Meiji Japan induced the commercialization of agriculture and the spread of markets. Rapid technological change in agriculture is likely to lead to the substitution of fixed rent for share contracts. The former is likely to promote greater specialization and the extension of markets. With induced institutional innovation, changed economic circumstances provide incentives for political and social entrepreneurs to organize to bring about institutional change. The result is the promotion of growth and the transformation of the traditional sector. In summary, governments can act either directly or indirectly to foster the development of the institutions necessary for the linking of the various islands of traditional sector economic activity.

However, just as markets may fail to adequately develop, and thus we may speak of market failure, so there may be government failure. That is, government attempts at institutional innovation may benefit the few at the expense of the many. The institutional structure may actually pose a barrier to traditional sector development. This is best illustrated by a reexamination of the Hayami–Ruttan theory of induced technical change. As a brief review, this theory is based on two important assumptions. First, it is assumed that an institutional framework exists through which farmers can convey their needs to public research organizations. Much of our previous discussion involved government's role in creating these necessary institutions. The second assumption implies that farmers as a group have uniform interests and needs. If this is not true, then even if such institutions exist, farmers might have such diverse interests that the form these institutions take and the groups that they serve will take on a great importance. That is, political power instead of economic merit may influence the type of research undertaken and the types of technologies developed.

Within the agricultural sector in a less developed country, there are likely to be numerous groups, each facing different kinds of constraints and different problems. Regional differences in climate, geography, and soil in and of themselves are likely to generate a diversity of interests among farmers concerning technology. Differences in the distribution of certain inputs are also likely to lead to different groups having different interests. Larger, wealthier farmers are likely to have interests much different from those of small farmers and landless workers. One can argue that a dualism is likely to exist within the agricultural sector. Larger farmers are likely to be able to gain better access to certain types of inputs relative to smaller farmers. Specifically, larger farmers are likely to be able to have access to credit on a much cheaper basis than small farmers. Thus, it is likely that they will find it easier to borrow to purchase such commercial inputs as tractors and fertilizers. Alternatively, because larger farmers are more likely to rely on hired labor and the cost of such labor is likely to be higher than the cost of family labor, it is likely that large farmers will find land relatively cheap compared to labor. Alternatively, small farmers are likely to find labor relatively cheap.

Given these differences, it would follow that the types of technology needed by various groups of farmers are likely to differ. Farmers in regions where irrigation is impossible or nonexistent and water supplies are tenuous, at best, may be most interested in drought resistant seed varieties. Alternatively, those in irrigated regions may be interested in seed varieties that are highly responsive to controlled applications of water.

Large scale farmers, because of their cheap access to inputs such as commercial fertilizers, pesticides, and water, may prefer the development of technologies biased toward the use of these inputs. Small scale farmers may find it extremely difficult to use these types of biochemical technologies, because they lack access to the key inputs necessary to make the new technology work. In addition, because the scarcest factor for larger farmers is likely to be labor, they are also unlikely to be interested in biochemical technologies which save land and use labor, unless such techniques can be combined with labor saving mechanical technologies.

The interests of smaller farmers and landless laborers may be quite similar. They would be more interested in technologies that are labor using and land saving. Biochemical technologies may fulfill this need if the key inputs, fertilizer, water, and credit, are made available to them. Lacking these inputs, smaller farmers would be interested in developing husbandry techniques, which are labor intensive but require no significant increases in commercially produced inputs.

In summary, instead of a homogeneous group of farmers, who face similar problems and have similar needs, there are numerous groups with different problems and needs. The question then becomes which needs and wants are going to determine the direction of institutional development and the allocation of research resources. Now, of course, we are entering the realm of political economy, in which the evolution and distribution of political power and social status will be the key elements in determining whose interests are most important.

Alain de Janvry[56] views this process as one of dynamic interaction involving demand and supply. In this process the socioeconomic structure, politico-bureaucratic structure, and innovation producing institutions play central roles. The expected payoff matrix specifies, *ex ante*, the net economic gains and losses that any set of groups within the society expects to result from the implementation of certain specific technical or institutional innovations. The returns from alternative technological innovations will vary by commodity, region (irrigated versus dry land, fertile versus marginal lands), and technological bias. De Janvry also believes that rural inhabitants are not a homogeneous group with common interests. Instead, he sees commercial farmers, the traditional landed elite, subsistence farmers, and landless workers and certain urban groups, such as industrial employers, urban workers, and government workers, as playing important roles. Each of these groups expects to derive certain benefits or to bear certain costs stemming from alternative possible innovations.

The supply–demand interaction is centered on the payoff matrix. Specifically, the demand for technical innovation originates from this matrix. Each group has a latent demand for particular types of innovations, and this demand derives from the expected payoff. The latent demand of all groups is translated into actual demand via the functioning of the politico-bureaucratic system. The most important components of this system are the social system whereby various groups exert direct pressure on bureaucrats to promote the interests of particular groups, the electoral and bureaucratic reward system that converts pressure into political and bureaucratic commitment, and the legislative system that transforms these commitments into laws and budget appropriations. The actual demand for innovations emerges from this filtering process. The relative power of various groups will of course determine whether a group's latent demand will be converted into actual demand. The innovation producing research institutions respond to these actual demands. Within these institutions, the store of physical and human capital will determine the position of the innovation possibility curve. The resulting actual supply of innovation will have an impact on the socio-economic structure and produce a set of actual payoffs for all the various social groups involved.

De Janvry applies this analysis of technological innovation to Argentine agriculture. He argues that the landed elite has determined the actual demand for innovation. Hence, their goals and their needs influence the direction of agricultural research. Because these groups seek to maintain the status quo, they will seek to promote those technologies that they believe will achieve this goal. The status quo, according to de Janvry, can best be promoted by the development and use of mechanical, not biochemical, technology. So there is little actual demand for biochemical technologies, and thus few resources are made available for public research systems. Therefore, mechanical technologies are purchased from private firms, domestic or foreign, and yield increasing biochemical technologies are underdeveloped.

In the de Janvry model the process of induced innovation becomes much more uncertain. Institutional breakdowns may occur that would prevent the development of appropriate technologies. In fact, it is easy to conceive of situations in which technology is developed that is inappropriate from society's perspective, given social opportunity costs. For example, it would be

inappropriate for a labor abundant society to develop labor saving technological innovations if the same research effort is more effective in reducing
the use of the more costly factor.

Much of the theoretical analysis just discussed was stimulated by what was
initially called the *green revolution*. The green revolution began during the
1960s and represented the development of new biochemical technologies
for rice and wheat production. Initially, the new technology was thought to
be the solution to the agricultural problems of less developed nations. It
involved the application of new high yield seeds combined with timely applications of commercial fertilizer, pesticides, and irrigation water. The technology was thought to be scale neutral and thus could be applied to both
large and small farms. Dramatic yield increases occurred in certain regions
of Mexico, India, and the Philippines. Modified varieties of high yielding
seed varieties quickly spread to other regions as well. This would seem to
represent an example of the operation of the induced innovation hypothesis.

However, it was not long before a number of economists began to analyze
the new technology with a more critical eye. It was realized that the technology was very much region specific. That is, seeds developed for one
region could not be readily transferred to others where soil and climate
differ. Thus, research would have to be region specific. Also, although the
technology might be neutral with respect to scale, the institutional structures
in most less developed nations are not. Initially the larger farmers, because
of their better access to credit and other key inputs, were able to adopt the
new technology, smaller farmers were not.[57] Hence, it was possible for the
distribution of income to worsen, and the poorer, smaller farmers might
even be made worse off if the price for their output falls substantially.

Others, such as Ruttan and Binswanger,[58] argue for the unambiguous
benefits of the green revolution for small farmers. They contend that, although larger farmers are generally the first to adopt the technology, small
farmers soon adopt and use the technology introduced by large farmers. In
addition, they argue that this new technology has in fact been labor using
in nature and that this could create additional employment opportunities for
landless laborers. The increased demand for landless laborers might not,
however, benefit small farmers. Furthermore, unevenness in the adoption of
the new technology might leave some parts of the country permanently
poorer. For example, the adoption of new technology tended to occur only
in areas already well endowed with agricultural resources, in particular water
for irrigation. Less well-endowed regions may reap little benefit from the
technology.[59]

The employment creating potential of the technology has also been questioned. Mechanization of farm operations and the use of large tractors has,
in many regions, blunted the employment creating potential of the new

technology. This low employment creation is readily understandable given our previous discussion of decision making by farmers with large and small farms. For larger farms, labor is relatively expensive but for small farms labor is relatively cheap. Thus, large farms will meet their increased labor demand, stemming from the new seed technology, by mechanizing farm operations.

Also, it has been noted that in some regions the application of biochemical technologies has led landlords to resume the direct operation of their own lands, hence to evict their previous tenants. This result is understandable given our previous discussion of tenancy. Wage labor contracts give all of the benefits of entrepreneurial innovation to the landowner. Fixed rent contracts result, in the short run, in all benefits of innovation going to the tenant. With share contracts, the benefits are shared. One would expect that, in periods of rapid technological change, landowners would seek to shift out of fixed rent and share contracts and convert them to wage labor contracts. Of course, this shifting increases the risk burden and the costs of information and the costs of enforcing optimal labor exertion. However, to deal with the latter problem the landlord could, as discussed previously, seek to mechanize.

The biochemical technologies of the 1960s and 1970s illustrate many of the ideas developed in the discussion of the theory of induced innovation. For a number of regions in a variety of less developed nations, the new technology represented the results of the theory of induced innovation. Specifically, those regions already characterized by relatively fertile soil, previous use of commercial fertilizers, and the existence of irrigation systems were faced with the need for a technology that was yield increasing in nature. The farmers in these regions were able to pressure public research institutions to develop new biochemical technologies that significantly raised yields.

Less well-endowed regions faced, of course, different kinds of problems, and the theory of induced innovation breaks down. The lack of reliable sources of water, the unavailability of large quantities of commercial fertilizers, the lack of access to credit, and differences in soil and climate meant that they could not simply borrow technologies developed in other regions. A different type of technology was needed for these poorer regions. However, farmers in these areas generally have less influence over the politico-bureaucratic structure of a nation. As a result, few research resources are allocated to the development of appropriate technologies. These regions are, in effect, left behind.

In summary, the induced technical innovation process may result in the development of inappropriate technologies that do not in general lead to the development of the traditional sector. In this case, the government and its various organizations fail to create an institutional environment conducive to rapid technical change. This occurs because certain groups are able to control the institutional structure in such a manner as to generate technologies that benefit a minority. This is an example of a more general type of institutional innovation that limits rather than promotes development.

In the theory of induced institutional innovation discussed earlier it was argued that changes in exogenous economic circumstances create incentives for political and social entrepreneurs to organize to bring about institutional modifications. The implicit assumption is that these modifications would tend to improve overall productivity. However, it seems likely that for societies with a very unequal distribution of wealth and power, political and social entrepreneurs will perceive opportunities to modify institutional arrangements in a way that benefits a small minority by imposing obstacles to increased productivity for the society in general. In fact Olson[60] has argued that, for a variety of reasons, it is much easier for small groups to organize into an effective unit than for large groups. In addition, the former are more likely to be interested in policies aimed at the redistribution of income whereas the latter tend to be more interested in policies that increase overall productivity. Thus, institutional innovation brought about by small powerful groups is likely to result in slower productivity growth.

Therefore, just as the induced technical innovation theory may break down in the face of a very unequal distribution of power and wealth, so may the theory of induced institutional innovation also break down. In these cases governments will fail in the sense that they will not carry out policies seeking to solve market failure problems that promote overall productivity. In these circumstances, dramatic reforms, perhaps land reform, would be a necessary prerequisite to development of the traditional sector.

CONCLUSION

There are reasons to believe that development strategies that emphasize the displacement of the traditional sector by the modern sector are not likely to succeed. The displacement of the institutional structure of the traditional sector with that of an imported modern sector is likely to result in social disorganization. The costs of this social disorganization are such that the GNP may appear to increase yet the net social product per person may rise slowly if at all or may actually decline. This possibility that dualistic development might be counterproductive is one reason for looking very closely at the traditional sector.

An alternative strategy to concentrating on the modern sector is to rely on transforming the traditional sector and making it dynamic. This strategy will be, to a great extent, an agriculturally based strategy of development. However, increased agricultural productivity can stimulate the development of traditional manufacturing activities. Traditional sector development depends on the possibility that gradual improvement in the traditional sector will transform that sector by leading to institutional changes linking the islands of the traditional sector through markets. This process of growth and induced institutional change may be mutually reinforcing through a positive feedback loop.

Understanding more about the traditional sector is of course important for understanding whether and how this transformation might occur. Much of the theory of the traditional sector is directly related to this possibility of transformation. These theories encompass questions about the inefficiency of traditional sector agriculture and the source of this inefficiency, the implications and evolution of different land tenure institutions, the causes of different types of technological change in agriculture, and the reasons and potential future viability of traditional sector manufacturing.

Finally, one should note that in some areas of the world it may be too late to pursue a traditional sector strategy of development. For example, Latin America has, for the most part, vigorously pursued an import substitution strategy of development that has discriminated against the traditional sector, so as to transfer resources to the modern sector to finance large, capital intensive manufacturing firms. In the process, the bulk of the population has migrated into urban areas where employment opportunities have failed to keep up with the number seeking employment. In this situation, dramatic reforms in trade and industrial policy are going to play a crucial role in the development process. These ideas will be pursued in later chapters.

In analyzing the development of the traditional sector, the prime role for government becomes either to directly or indirectly foster the development of the institutional infrastructure necessary for the transformation of the traditional sector. However, we should be aware that, in societies in which political power and economic wealth are unequally distributed, there exists the likelihood of government failure. In these situations, significant reform may be necessary as a prerequisite for development of the traditional sector.

NOTES

1. See Douglas C. North, *Institutions, Institutional Change and Economic Performance* (Cambridge: Cambridge University Press, 1990).
2. See, for example, Heinz Arndt, "'Market Failure' and Underdevelopment," *World Development* 16 (1988): 219–229.
3. Henry Bruton, "The Search for Development Economics," *World Development* 13 (October–November 1985): 1099–1124.

4. Theodore Schultz, *Transforming Traditional Agriculture* (New Haven, Conn.: Yale University Press, 1964).

5. Bruton, "The Search for Development Economics."

6. Situations in which the institutions of the traditional sector may come to be regarded as illegitimate will be discussed later in the chapter.

7. Bruce F. Jonston and John Mellor, "The Role of Agriculture in Economic Development," *American Economic Review* 51 (1961): 566–593.

8. Robert H. Bates, "Lessons from History or the Perfidy of English Exceptionalism and the Significance of Historical France," *World Politics* 60 (July 1988): 499–516.

9. The first number in each cell represents the return to I and the second number the return to II.

10. Much of this discussion is drawn from David Kreps, "Corporate Culture and Economic Theory," in *Perspectives on Positive Political Economy,* ed. James Alt and Kenneth Shepsle (Cambridge: Cambridge University Press, 1990).

11. Thomas C. Smith, *Native Sources of Japanese Industrialization, 1750–1920* (Berkeley: University of California Press, 1988), p. 138.

12. Ibid, pp. 50–70.

13. Richard Grabowski, "European and East Asian Exceptionalism: Agriculture and Economic Growth," *Journal of International Development* 6 (1994): 443.

14. Ibid.

15. Richard J. Smethurst, *Agricultural Development and Tenancy Disputes in Japan, 1870–1940* (Princeton, N.J.: Princeton University Press, 1986).

16. Ibid.

17. The discussion in the next few paragraphs is based on Yujiro Hayami and Vernon Ruttan, *Agricultural Development: An International Perspective* (Baltimore: Johns Hopkins University Press, 1985).

18. There are many varieties of share tenancy and leasehold arrangements. However, we will not deal with all of these possibilities.

19. Much of this discussion is based upon Steven N. S. Cheung, *The Theory of Share Tenancy* (Chicago: University of Chicago Press, 1969), pp. 42–50.

20. See Pranab Bardhan, *Land, Labor, and Rural Poverty: Essays in Development Economics* (Delhi: Oxford University Press, 1984).

21. Yujiro Hayami and Massao Kikuchi, *Asian Village Economy at the Crossroads: An Economic Approach to Institutional Change* (Baltimore: Johns Hopkins University Press, 1982), pp. 31–32.

22. J. E. Stiglitz, "Incentives and Risk Sharing in Sharecropping," *Review of Economic Studies* 41 (April 1974): 217–255.

23. Hayami and Kikuchi, *Asian Village Economy at the Crossroads,* pp. 32–33.

24. Joseph E. Stiglitz, "The New Development Economics," *World Development* 14 (1986): 257–265.

25. Hayami and Kikuchi, *Asian Village Economy at the Crossroads,* pp. 32–33.

26. Ibid.

27. Ibid., p. 34.

28. Ibid.

29. D. C. North and R. P. Thomas, *The Rise of the Western World* (Cambridge: Cambridge University Press, 1973).
30. David Feeny, "The Demand for and Supply of Institutional Arrangements," in *Rethinking Institutional Analysis and Development: Issues, Alternatives, and Choices,* ed. Vincent Ostrom, David Feeny, and Hartmut Picht (San Francisco: International Center for Economic Growth, 1988), pp. 159–209.
31. Yujiro Hayami and Vernon Ruttan, *Agricultural Development: An International Perspective* (Baltimore: Johns Hopkins University Press, 1985).
32. J. Hicks, *The Theory of Wages* (New York: St. Martin's Press, 1964).
33. There are other definitions of neutrality, such as Harrod neutrality. However, this will not be used in this chapter.
34. H. Habakkuk, *American and British Technology in the Nineteenth Century* (Cambridge: Cambridge University Press, 1962).
35. E. Rothbarth, "Courses of the Superior Efficiency of U.S.A. Industry as Compared with British Industry," *Economic Journal* 56 (1946): 383–390.
36. Nathan Rosenberg, "The Direction of Technological Change: Inducement Mechanisms and Focusing Devices," *Economic Development and Cultural Change* 18 (1969): 1–24.
37. See Yujiro Hayami and Vernon Ruttan, *Agricultural Development: An International Perspective,* 2nd ed. (Baltimore: Johns Hopkins University Press, 1985), p. 92.
38. J. R. Hicks, *The Theory of Wages,* pp. 124–126.
39. Syed Ahmad, "On the Theory of Induced Innovation," *Economic Journal* 76 (June 1966): 344–357.
40. Hayami and Ruttan, *Agricultural Development.*
41. For a summary discussion of these tests, please see Thirtle and Ruttan, *The Role of Demand and Supply in the Generations and Diffusion of Technical Change,* Economic Development Center, University of Minnesota, Bulletin Number 86–5, pp. 50–60.
42. H. P. Binswanger, "A Microeconomic Approach to Induced Innovation," *Economic Journal* 84 (1974): 940–958.
43. See S. Hymer and S. Resnick, "A Model of an Agrarian Economy with Non-Agricultural Activities," *American Economic Review* 59 (September 1969): 493–506.
44. Dennis Anderson, "Small Industry in Developing Countries: A Discussion of Issues," *World Development* 10 (November 1982): 214.
45. E. Staley and R. Morse, *Modern Small-Scale Industry for Developing Countries* (New York: McGraw-Hill, 1965).
46. Anderson, "Small Industry in Developing Countries," p. 921.
47. Yhi-Min Ho and Donald Huddle, "Traditional and Small-Scale Culture Goods in International Trade and Employment," *Journal of Development Studies* 12 (January 1976): 232–251.
48. Kazuo Sato, "The Japanese Economy" (Lecture Notes, Yale University, Spring 1985).
49. The discussion of linkages is based on Gustav Ranis, Frances Stewart, and

Edna Angeles-Reyes, *Linkages in Developing Economies: A Philippine Study* (San Francisco: International Center for Economic Growth, 1990), pp. 8–9.

50. Gustav Ranis and Frances Stewart, "Rural Linkages in the Philippines and Taiwan," in *Macro-Policies for Appropriate Technology in Developing Countries,* ed. Frances Stewart (Boulder, Colo.: Westview Press, 1987), pp. 140–171.

51. Hugh Emrys Evans, "A Virtuous Circle Model of Rural–Urban Development: Evidence from a Kenyan Small Town and Its Hinterland," *Journal of Development Studies* 28 (July 1992): 640–667.

52. Thomas C. Smith, *Native Sources of Japanese Industrialization, 1750–1920* (Berkeley: University of California Press, 1988), pp. 15–49.

53. Jan de Vries, *European Urbanization 1500–1800* (Cambridge, Mass.: Harvard University Press, 1984), p. 245.

54. Franklin Mendels, "Proto-industrialization: The First Phase of the Industrialization Process," *Journal of Economic History* 32 (March 1972): 241–261.

55. Ibid., p. 241.

56. Alain de Janvry, "Social Structure and Biased Technical Change in Argentine Agriculture," in *Induced Innovation: Technology, Institutions and Development*, ed. Hans Binswanger, Vernon Ruttan, *et al.* (Baltimore: Johns Hopkins University Press, 1978), pp. 297–323.

57. Keith Griffen, *The Political Economy of Agrarian Change* (London: Macmillan and Co., 1979).

58. Vernon Ruttan and Hans Binswanger, "Induced Innovation and the Green Revolution," in *Induced Innovation: Technology, Institutions and Development*, ed. Hans Binswanger, Vernon Ruttan, *et al.* (Baltimore: Johns Hopkins University Press, 1978), pp. 358–408.

59. Richard Grabowski, "Induced Innovation, Green Revolution and Income Distribution: Reply," *Economic Development and Cultural Change* 30 (October 1981): 177–181.

60. Mancur Olson, *The Logic of Collective Action: Public Goods and the Theory of Groups* (Cambridge, Mass.: Harvard University Press, 1971).

4

Fertility and Population

Disquieting visions of rising population growth ending any hopes of long-term economic prosperity at times threaten our more sanguine hopes that development is possible. Even within the comforting context of the neo-classical growth models presented in the first chapter, higher rates of population growth unambiguously reduce per capita income. Indeed, few would doubt the need for population growth rates to eventually fall. Any fixed rate of population growth when extrapolated far enough into the future yields population sizes that stretch our ability to imagine. For example, the current world population growth rate of 1.7 percent would increase world population to over 30 billion by the year 2100 and over 150 billion by 2200. A problem with such simple extrapolations, which is shared by most growth models, is that population growth rates are treated as exogenous. Consequently, population does not respond in these models to changing income, education, and occupation. A thorough treatment of the economic determinants of population is needed before we can fruitfully speculate on whether or not endogenizing population growth can brighten these dark visions of perpetual poverty.

Fears of over population are ultimately based on the belief that actions that determine the size or growth rate of the population are socially irrational. Recall from the discussion of limits to rationality in Chapter 2 that social irrationality might exist for rational individuals when individual utility from an action is directly affected by the actions of others. This interaction certainly seems to be a possibility with birth decisions because of the many positive and negative externalities associated with children. Children are necessary for maintaining the human population. Hence, everybody benefits from children. Children also cause congestion from a larger population. Hence, everybody bears some costs of children. In analyzing these interactions and the rationality of population related behavior, economists have typically explored rational behavior of families while sociologists have concentrated on the social norms that lead, in their view, to socially rational behavior. In this chapter, we will discuss these two approaches and the population theories they have generated.

Changes in the size of a population can come through only births, deaths, or migration. In other words,

$$P'(t) = B(t) - D(t) + M(t), \tag{4.1}$$

where $P'(t)$ is the change in population size, $B(t)$ are births, $D(t)$ are deaths, and $M(t)$ is net migration. Population theory concerns the separate determinants of $B(t)$, $D(t)$, and $M(t)$ as well as the complex interaction among population growth and the components of population change (migration, mortality, and fertility). Specific theories concentrate separately on fertility, mortality, or migration; grand theories attempt to explain population growth as the result of interactions among its three components. These grand theories will be considered first. Such theories are the Malthusian theory, transition theory, and neo–Malthusian growth models. Each will be explained in order. Then more specific economic theories, which focus on fertility, will be considered. Finally, a brief treatment of mortality will be introduced. Migration will be left until Chapter 5 when labor markets are considered.

MALTHUS AND MALTHUSIANISM

Perhaps the first person to formally develop a theory of population was T. R. Malthus. Despite the continuing controversy over the appropriate way to interpret Malthus, Malthus is usually formulated in a way that stresses the likelihood that most people are doomed to a tenuous existence, where they are always faced with the threat of starvation. Furthermore, any attempt to alleviate poverty may be less than useful. For example, Leo Rogin stressed this interpretation of the meaning of Malthus's theory: "Essentially, the function of this theory is to justify the imposition of the entire burden of social progress upon the backs of the laboring class, by demonstrating that charity to the poor, whether public or private, tends in the long run to be assimilated into increasing population and the moral degradation of that class."[1]

Many treatments of Malthus begin by posing a Malthusian model where labor is trapped at a low level of income by high fertility where economic growth or income transfer cannot alleviate the poverty faced by workers. Then modifications of the model, which account for rising levels of living, are presented. Like the classical model, these versions assume a subsistence real wage rate exists, s, where the population grows if the real wage rate, w, is greater than *s* and declines for *w* < *s*. The subsistence wage rate is an extension of the classical concept of the natural price of a commodity that is the cost of its production. Ironically, Malthus explicitly rejects the usefulness of the concept of the natural wage rate.

> Mr. Ricardo has defined the natural price of labour to be "that price which is necessary to enable the labourers one with another to subsist, and to perpetuate their race, without either increase or diminution." This I should really be disposed to call a most unnatural price; because in a natural state of things, that is, without great impediments to the progress of wealth and population, such a price could not generally occur for hundreds of years.[2]

The workings of this Malthusian model are illustrated in Figure 4.1. It is typically presented without any consideration of the classical wages fund constraint discussed in Chapter 1. Labor receives its marginal product, and N^* is the size of the labor force where MPL = *s*. For $N < N^*$, the wage rate exceeds subsistence and both the population and the labor force grow. The owners of capital and land constitute a different class and receive rent and profits. Their numbers do not necessarily rise as a result of high income either because second and later sons become workers or because of the prudence of owners. Consequently, workers are driven, through their reproductive powers, to poverty at the subsistence wage rate, whereas owners are not similarly driven to poverty. Note, that charity would temporarily increase *w* but eventually *N* would increase. If all profits were returned to workers, *N* would grow to N_m and everyone would be in poverty. Hence, in this model labor in the long run earns its supply price where the supply price of any commodity is its cost of production.

The model can easily be extended to include a cultural component to the subsistence wage rate. Societies, classes, or individuals have different levels of living that are viewed to be adequate.[3] Males with high aspirations, in Malthus's view, postpone marriage until they can support a family at a level that they desire. Hence, if aspirations rise, then the subsistence level of income will rise, where *subsistence* is defined as the level of income that will just induce the long-term replacement of the labor force. Again, in this sociological version of Malthus, private or public charity will not permanently improve living levels for the poor but will simply induce the poor to have more children. Indeed, in this model, the poor are poor through their own fault because they have low aspirations. Malthus stressed that measures such as the provision of universal education were more likely than charity to improve the conditions of the poor. Education would provide more opportunities and simultaneously raise aspiration levels.

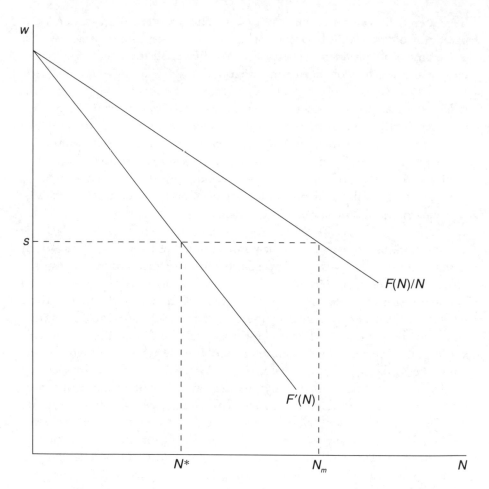

Figure 4.1 The Malthusian model.

Although these models reflect Malthus's view, a few additional points should be stressed.[4] Malthus often did not reason in terms of the natural price of labor, the subsistence wage rate, as did Ricardo. He tended to view wages as the result of a race between a rising number of workers and rising productivity. Because Malthus held that population size could potentially increase more rapidly than production, some forces must act to check population growth. Malthus divided these checks to population growth into two categories: positive or direct checks, which include malnutrition, war, famine, and high infant mortality, and preventative checks, which include late marriage and celibacy. Malthus believed that differences in the relative strengths of these checks determine differences in living levels. Hence, Europe had higher living levels than China because preventative checks were stronger in Europe. Factors acting to strengthen preventative checks in Europe include the practice of apprenticeship and the custom where servants and some other employees live in their employer's household and remain unmarried.

In essence, preventative checks involve the opportunity for people to invest in themselves by postponing family formation or remaining single. The return to this investment is higher income and status, later in life. The apprenticeship system is a good example of a preventative check. An apprentice would go to work for a master craftsman at a very young age and receive board and room. He would slowly learn the trade and eventually become a journeyman. Eventually, he would become a master craftsman and establish his own shop. Only then would he marry. This postponement of marriage to obtain a better life was central to Malthus's preventative checks. It would raise income for two reasons. First, fertility would be reduced because of late marriages. Second, workers would become more productive because of the apprenticeship training.

Malthus contended that industrialization was breaking down preventative checks and that, as a consequence, the fertility rate was rising. Furthermore, because per capita income was thought to ultimately depend upon population size, industrialization would eventually make society worse off unless this deterioration of preventative checks were reversed. Malthus was not entirely pessimistic in that he proposed a way of strengthening preventative checks.

To understand Malthus's proposal, first consider why he thought preventative checks were being weakened by industrialization. One reason was that industrialization was destroying the apprenticeship system. Skilled artisans were being replaced by machine labor. Hence, one avenue whereby a person could postpone marriage to invest in himself was being substantially diminished. Malthus advocated universal education as another way in which people could postpone marriage to invest in themselves. By increasing educational opportunities, a society reduces fertility, because people must delay family formation to take advantage of this opportunity, and increases productivity. This is precisely what Malthus had in mind as a preventative check. A discussion of the extent to which Malthus's empirical contentions were correct and could be explained by his theory will be reserved until the end of the next section.

TRANSITION THEORY

In sharp contrast with the Malthusian view stands the theory of the demographic transition. Malthusian theory predicts that a decline in fertility, caused by an increase in the strength of preventative checks, will lead to greater economic prosperity. Transition theory reverses the direction of causality. Growing economic prosperity is held to cause fertility to fall. Furthermore, population is not viewed as having a tremendous potential to grow unless kept in check. Instead, high fertility needs to be encouraged by society, in the face of high mortality, if the population is to reproduce itself. The solution to possible population pressures is seen to lie in continuing economic development and not in fertility control.

The theory of the demographic transition is usually attributed to Warren S. Thompson and Frank W. Notestein.[5] Transition theory rests on the belief that social norms and mores determine fertility and that social norms and mores eventually adjust to the needs of society. Hence, fertility is socially rational in the long run. Initially, cultural inducements to high fertility were necessary to offset high mortality. Modernization acts first to raise income and reduce mortality. Fertility eventually falls for a variety of reasons, including the gradual response of "religious doctrines, moral codes, laws, education, community, customs, marriage habits, and family organizations" to the new lower level of mortality.[6] Early versions of transition theory do little more than present a taxonomy of the stages of a demographic transition. Later versions stress the ways in which changing institutions affect choices through changing the constraints. Before discussing these new views, the older taxonomy will be presented and discussed.

The demographic transition is typically divided into four stages. In the first stage, mortality is high for numerous reasons, including not only the lack of modern medicine but also the existence of periodic and localized food shortages caused by wars, droughts, and floods. The lack of adequate transportation and political fragmentation leads to local starvation in times of general prosperity. Survival of the tribe or of a kinship group depends upon high numbers of births to offset high mortality. Hence, in all viable societies the prevailing institutions encourage and support high birth rates. In stage two, modernization causes mortality to decline with improvements in transportation, increases in per capita food production, better hygiene, public health projects such as draining swamps, and the introduction (or discovery) of modern medicine. This decline in mortality may be substantial and last for several decades. Births remain high as institutions that encourage high fertility are resistant to change. In stage three, fertility begins to fall. This fall is, partly, a direct response to modernization, as changing economic institutions have a direct affect on fertility and partly an indirect response to low mortality. In the fourth stage, institutions, both economic and social, have been fully modernized. Both mortality and fertility are low.

Like the stage theories discussed in Chapter 1, the terminology in transition theory has become a part of the descriptive language of the discipline. Also, like other stage theories, attention is focused on only a few of the stages. In transition theory, the primary concern is with the third stage and the transition from the second stage. A considerable body of empirical literature owes its justification to testing propositions concerning the transition between these stages. One proposition concerns the existence of a pension motive for having children. Reduced child mortality is thought to eventually lead to reduced fertility as parents realize that they need fewer births to guarantee that a sufficient number survive to care for them when they are no longer productive workers. Other propositions concern the decline of extended families with shared child care, the rise of production outside the household, and rising educational requirements for many jobs. All three factors are thought to increase the costs of raising children. Thus, much of transition theory concerns the direct effects of economic development on fertility. However, a major focus continues to be the indirect effect of development on fertility through the reduction of child mortality. Reduced mortality along with rising income diminish the need for extended families as a form of social insurance.

Direct investigation of the four stage taxonomy has concerned the existence of differences in pretransition fertility, the timing of the mortality–fertility decline, the unevenness of the fertility decline, and the possibility that the decline is reversible. Much of this research has been critical of the taxonomy. For example, premodern societies practiced contraception, differed in fertility rates, and grew at different rates. Furthermore, the countries that developed first may have had low population growth for a long period before economic expansion. This possibility that low fertility caused economic development is a Malthusian proposition and contradicts transition theory. In addition, the empirical evidence seems to be that fertility has initially risen with development, as Malthus contended.[7]

Transition theory has been reformulated to encompass this empirical evidence. In these reformulations, the focus on how society adjusts from a high fertility equilibrium to a low fertility equilibrium is replaced by a concern with how economic development affects fertility. Modernization is thought to eventually lower fertility through changing norms, mores, and institutions. The belief that the population was or will necessarily be in equilibrium (i.e., births equal deaths) is not held to be central to the theory. Hence, recent research has concentrated on how modernization might lower fertility. This has led to theoretical innovation and detailed empirical work on how increased occupational specialization and the resulting rise of exchange has influenced fertility. The reformulated theory is still non–Malthusian in the sense that economic development is thought to lower fertility and not the other way around.

Two reformulations of transition will be considered. The first reformulation to be considered fits in well with the economist's perspective but the second does not. The first reformulation starts with the supposition that the high fertility of families in less developed countries is rational, not only in the sense that it is consistent with maximizing behavior but also in the sense that it is not to be explained in terms of some culturally determined preferences for large families. The key to understanding fertility is to understand the budget constraints of households and how they operate to encourage or discourage large families. A trivial but often studied example concerns differences in the net family resources consumed by a child. In rural families, children are thought to be both producers and consumers whereas in urban families children are largely consumers. Hence, we would expect rural fertility to be higher. Furthermore, a movement toward less family production or rising years of compulsory education would make childbearing more costly and, hence, reduce fertility. A more interesting example of how large families in less developed countries are rewarded begins with the notion of an implicit contract that transfers income or wealth among family members. Children might, for example, be obligated to care for aged parents.

The notion that the understanding of wealth transfers is the key to understanding the demographic transition is associated with John C. Caldwell.[8] For a simple version of Caldwell's theory, consider how fertility is affected as the economy moves from peasant agriculture to a modern economy. For convenience, think of this transformation as occurring in three stages. In the first stage, the unit of production is the household but there are also strong extended family ties where extended family members live in the same area. If land is abundant, larger extended families necessarily enhance the security of family members if there are implicit contracts shifting wealth to family members who are temporarily in need or who are disabled. Larger extended families also increase the power of the family patriarch. Hence, there exist both insurance and power incentives for large families, provided that these large families can be supported. The introduction of a modern sector into this traditional society will eventually change these relationships and consequently change fertility. The availability of land and these incentives for large families will determine extended family size.

In the second stage, some family members are able to earn a living outside peasant agriculture. A move into the modern sector may require two different types of investment. First, the individual or household may have to physically move to a new urban location. This move requires resources for actually moving and for providing for the household during any initial job search in the new location. Second, the potential modern worker may have to obtain some level of education and job skills before he or she can be employed in the modern sector. The resources for this investment may be provided by the extended family. The extended family, or kinship group, benefits from this wealth transfer partly because a diversification of the sources of income enhances the economic security of family members. The migrants into the modern sector may receive increased income for moving but they will also share in the increased security of the kinship group.

During this second stage, the rewards to having large families may increase. Larger families increase the possible diversification of income sources. As long as the extended family system of wealth transfers remains in tact, increased opportunities of moving to the modern sector may actually increase fertility. Furthermore, the fertility of urban households would not be expected to decline.

In the third stage, the implicit contracts underlying the extended family system of wealth transfers may begin to lose strength. Spatial distance from kinship groups and the different lifestyles in urban areas weaken extended family ties. Hence, large families and kinship groups lose their appeal as a means of stabilizing income. Consequently, fertility begins to decline. Note, that Caldwell's wealth transfer theory does not reduce to the simple suggestion that children are a source of current security, of investment funds, of political power, and so forth.

Having considered Caldwell's reformulation of transition theory, we will briefly consider another reformulation. This reformulation has alternately been called the *revisionist approach* or the *Princeton School approach*. This view is not compatible with the economic approach because it rejects rationality. This rejection is based on an interpretation of data gathered by the Princeton project. This project concentrated on the timing of the fertility decline in Europe, which began in the later part of the 19th century. They found that marital fertility seemed to decline simultaneously across Europe. They interpret this simultaneity to mean that socioeconomic and demographic variables have little if any impact on the timing of the demographic transition. At best, variables like infant mortality, income, occupation, and education, for a much earlier time, made the decline possible because they may have eventually changed the culture. However, cultural variables determined when the transition was to occur and how birth control innovations were to be diffused throughout the population.[9]

These interpretations of the historical evidence reflect the long-standing view of the Princeton School that socioeconomic variables have little or no impact on fertility in either developed or less developed countries. In studies of U.S. fertility, married couples were asked questions about how many children they expected to have during their lifetimes. They typically responded in ranges such as "two to four." Their mean response was found not to be correlated with socioeconomic variables. The responses did, however, differ by religion. The conclusion drawn by the Princeton School was that fertility is largely determined by culture and that socioeconomic variables influence fertility mainly by their long-range impact on culture or, less important, by influencing the spacing of births but not the number of births.[10]

Considerable empirical attention has been paid to the views of the Princeton School. We will discuss only the examination of the European fertility decline, because it is directly relevant to evaluating both Malthus and transition theory. Considerable doubt has been cast on the Princeton School conclusions. For example, Dov Friedlander, Jona Schellekeus, and Eliahu Ben-Moshe found that, contrary to the Princeton School view, socioeconomic variables played the dominant role in the decline of fertility in England and Wales.[11] C. R. Winegarden and Mark Wheeler found that income played an important explanatory role for Europe, again, contrary to the Princeton School view.[12]

Winegarden and Wheeler contend that rising income would increase fertility for low levels of income but reduce fertility for high levels of income. Their reasoning is based on the household production model of fertility that will be discussed in the section on economic theories. Basically, parents derive satisfaction from both the number of children and from the expenditures they make for each child. At low levels of income, they choose to have more children as income rises and make little change in expenditures per child. Eventually, as income rises past some critical level, rising expenditures dominate parent's choices, and they have fewer children in order to spend more on each child. Winegarden and Wheeler find that for Germany, Norway, Sweden, and the United Kingdom, fertility did rise and then fall as income rose. This quadratic income–fertility relationship is consistent with Caldwell's view of transition theory but not with the Princeton School view.

Winegarden and Wheeler note that this quadratic relationship explains the slight rise and then decline in fertility observed in the years considered by the Princeton project. Another study, the Cambridge project, looked at the 18th and early 19th century. This project found that a fertility rise occurred a long time before the period considered by Winegarden and Wheeler.[13] The total fertility rate (see the Appendix to this chapter for a definition) rose sharply beginning in the middle of the 18th century. This rise was partly or largely the result of a decline of almost three years in the age at which women marry.

In conclusion, the new historical evidence suggests that neither standard transition theory nor the revisionist Princeton School theory help much in understanding European fertility. Malthus's view, however, is consistent with the evidence. Fertility did rise with industrialization as Malthus contended. This rise was the result of a declining age at marriage. These changes could be interpreted as being the result of a weakening of preventative checks.

ENDOGENOUS POPULATION GROWTH MODELS (NEO-MALTHUSIAN)

The neoclassical growth model developed in Chapter 1 will now be extended to include endogenous population growth. Recall that these models were Malthusian in the sense that a decline in the rate of population increase leads to an increase in per capita income both in the short-run and long-run steady states. Making the population growth rate endogenous may either reinforce the Malthusian nature of these models or lend support to transition theory, which emphasizes that rising income causes population growth rates to fall. There are two linkages between population growth and the other variables in the model. First, income may affect population growth either through its impact on mortality or by changing fertility. Second, the rate of growth of population might influence the savings function. Both possibilities will be considered.

Early models of endogenous population growth emphasized a demographic trap. The rate of population growth might at first rise with income and then decline for higher levels of income. This possibility is illustrated in Figure 4.2 for the neoclassical growth model developed in Chapter 1. For $k < k_1^*$, the economy will grow (k will rise). However, k_1^* is a steady state because $\dot{k} < 0$ (i.e., capital intensity falls) for $k_1^* < k < k_2^*$. In terms proposed by Richard Nelson, k_1^* is a low income demographic trap.[14] If the economy can grow past k_2^*, then the economy could move to an era of unrestrained economic growth.

In the demographic trap models, the demographic transition cannot occur because of a rapidly expanding population. Either a "big push" is required to move the economy out of poverty or a stringent population control policy is needed to lower fertility. If combined with the savings trap model of Chapter 1, the prospects become gloomier. More savings and investment are required for the economy to grow when the population growth rises just to maintain the current level of capital per worker. Furthermore, high fertility may cause low savings because children consume more than they produce.

The notion that high fertility is detrimental to economic development is widely held by policy makers. Family planning programs are now seen as an important component of the development efforts of a nation. Such an emphasis has not always been the case. Ten years ago, family planning programs were sold on the notion that they helped parents to better achieve their own family size goals. The notion that the government should take an active role in trying to reduce desired fertility was seen as being both unlikely to succeed and undesirable. Attitudes have changed, but many question the need for active programs to reduce fertility. For example, Julian Simon, Allen C. Kelley, and Jeffrey G. Williamson, and others doubt that high fertility

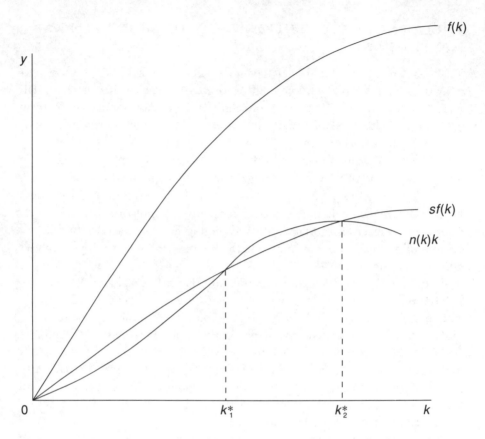

Figure 4.2 The demographic trap.

is particularly detrimental to development.[15] However, the current mainstream view, particularly within the context of neoclassical growth models, is that rapid population growth hinders development.[16]

This detrimental effect of high population growth on development can also be found in the dualistic, neoclassical growth model developed by Dale Jorgenson.[17] Land and labor are the inputs in the agricultural sector whereas capital and labor are used in the industrial sector. Let R be the resources or land used, L be agricultural labor, and N be manufacturing labor. Let agricultural output be

$$Y = e^{\alpha t}R^{\beta}L^{1-\beta} \tag{4.2}$$

and manufacturing output be

$$X = e^{\lambda t}K^{b}N^{1-b}. \tag{4.3}$$

These functions, of course, assume constant returns to scale. The superscripts α and λ are the rates of technical progress in the two sectors.

Consider first the agricultural sector. Let the quantity of land, R, be fixed and fully utilized, $R = \bar{R}$. Output is then

$$Y = Ae^{\alpha t}L^{1-\beta}, \tag{4.4}$$

where $A = \bar{R}^{\beta}$. Per worker output is then

$$y = Y/L = Ae^{\alpha t}L^{-\beta}. \tag{4.5}$$

The rate of growth of output per agricultural worker is then

$$\hat{y} = \alpha - \beta\hat{L}. \tag{4.6}$$

Assuming that $\hat{L}$ is also the rate of growth of the population, the rate of growth of per capita output is equal to the rate of technical innovation minus the rate of population growth times land's share of output, β.

The population growth rate is assumed to be

$$\hat{L} = \min(\gamma y - \sigma, \varepsilon), \tag{4.7}$$

where σ is the mortality rate, ε is the maximum possible rate of population growth, and γy is the birth rate as a proportion of per capita income. Hence, it is assumed that the population growth rate rises with income up to some biological maximum.

For

$$\gamma y - \sigma < \varepsilon, \tag{4.8}$$

the growth rate of agricultural output per person (equation (4.6)) becomes

$$\hat{y} = \alpha + \beta\sigma - \beta\gamma y \tag{4.9}$$

or

$$\dot{y} = (\alpha + \beta\sigma)y - \beta\gamma y^2. \tag{4.10}$$

Setting $\dot{y} = 0$ in equation (4.10) yields the quadratic

$$(\alpha + \beta\sigma)y - \beta\gamma y^2 = 0, \tag{4.11}$$

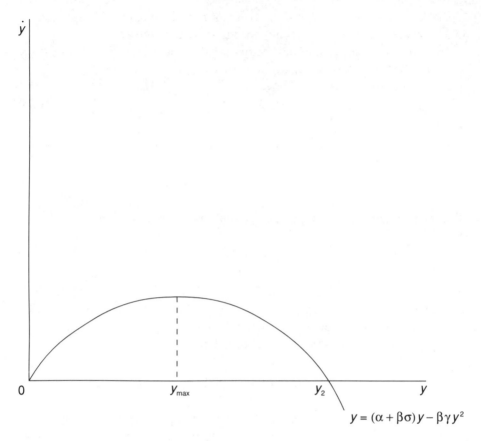

Figure 4.3   Growth in agriculture.

which has two solutions. Obviously $y = 0$ is a solution. With no income there is no population. The second solution is

$$y = (\alpha + \beta\sigma)/\beta\gamma. \tag{4.12}$$

Further note that $\dot{y}$ is at its maximum when

$$\partial\dot{y}/\partial y = \alpha + \beta\sigma - 2\beta\gamma y = 0 \tag{4.13}$$

or

$$y_{max} = (\alpha + \beta\sigma)/2\beta\gamma. \tag{4.14}$$

For $0 < y < y_{max}$, $\partial\dot{y}/\partial y > 0$ and for $y > y_{max}$, $\partial\dot{y}/\partial y < 0$. The solutions are illustrated by Figure 4.3.

In interpreting Figure 4.3 it is important to note that the path $\dot{y} = (\alpha + \beta\sigma)y - \beta\gamma y^2$ is the actual path for output in the agricultural sector when equation (4.8) is satisfied. In terms of y, equation (4.8) becomes

$$y < (\varepsilon + \sigma)/\gamma. \tag{4.15}$$

If $y_2 < (\varepsilon + \sigma)/\gamma$ then the economy will reach y_2 and y_2 is stable. However, if $y_2 > (\varepsilon + \sigma)/\gamma$, no solution exists and the economy can continue to grow indefinitely. A solution at y_2 can be interpreted as a low income steady state, which will exist if

$$\alpha/\beta < \varepsilon. \tag{4.16}$$

Because $(1 - \beta)$ is the elasticity of output with respect to labor, a steady state becomes more likely the lower is this elasticity and the lower is the rate of technical progress. Finally, the rate of growth when $\alpha/\beta > \varepsilon$ becomes

$$\hat{y} = \alpha - \beta\varepsilon. \tag{4.17}$$

Before introducing manufacturing into the model, consider the possibility that the food supply will not support a nonagricultural population. If $\alpha/\beta < \varepsilon$, the economy will be stuck at a low level income trap. For an agricultural economy to, by itself, move out of this low level output trap, α would have to rise, β fall, or ε fall. If the country emerges from the low level trap, an agricultural surplus will begin to emerge. Jorgenson defines the agricultural surplus as

$$S = y - (\varepsilon + \sigma)/\gamma. \tag{4.18}$$

In other words, the difference between actual per capita income and the level of per capita income at which population growth reaches its maximum is assumed by Jorgenson to be made available to industrial workers. This surplus allows the establishment and expansion of the industrial sector. In the industrial sector, the wage rate for labor is equal to the marginal product of labor; that is, profits are maximized. The wage rate in the agricultural sector is assumed to be determined in some traditional manner and total agricultural income, both wage and property, is assumed to be consumed. Thus, investment in the industrial sector is financed solely from the income of the owners of capital in this sector. Finally, labor will flow from the agricultural sector to the industrial sector as long as the wage in the latter sector exceeds the agricultural income that could be earned in the former.

The process of growth in the industrial sector can now be outlined. Once the agricultural surplus appears, it is somehow transferred to the industrial sector along with labor. The profits that occur in the emerging sector are assumed to be reinvested and the industrial sector further expands. This expansion draws additional labor and surplus from agriculture. Note that workers in the modern sector do not save. A wage differential is assumed to exist between the two sectors. This wage differential attracts labor to the modern industrial sector causing the labor force in manufacturing to grow more rapidly than in agriculture. Consequently, the economy would become increasingly urban.

There have been numerous other endogenous population growth models, but the neoclassical model and the dualistic model presented here capture the flavor of these models. In both models, the economy can be trapped at a low level of income. If the economy can be moved beyond this trap, the growth process can become self-sustaining. The implicit fertility theory underlying these models is, however, quite naive. It focuses only on the relationship between income and fertility (or mortality). In the next section, attention will be centered on the relationship between income and fertility. Various theories of fertility will be discussed in terms of how they explain the impact of changing income on fertility.

ECONOMIC THEORIES

Early economic theories assumed, ceteris paribus, a positive relationship between income and fertility coupled with a negative relationship between income and mortality. In terms of choice theory, children are assumed to be normal goods. A rise in income would then increase population growth rates both by increasing fertility and reducing mortality. In empirical work, however, this positive relationship between births and income is difficult to find. For example, families in prosperous countries tend to have fewer children than those in low income countries. In terms of choice theory children appear to be inferior goods. Of course, as Malthus contended, the very factors that lead to high income may be the cause of low fertility. Higher educational levels, enhanced social mobility, and increased access to contraception will have independent negative effects on fertility and will likely be positively related to income. Hence, economic development might increase fertility, because higher income allows parents to support more children, or reduce fertility, as increased economic opportunities raise educational levels, enhance social mobility, and so forth.

Much of economic theory has been centered around explaining why, ceteris paribus, fertility seems to fall as income rises. The negative relationship requires explanation because it is difficult to think of children as an inferior good. Inferior goods are usually thought of as low quality, inexpensive substitutes for some higher quality good. An example might be that potatoes are a substitute for meat as a protein source. As income rises, the demand for potatoes falls. If children are analogous to potatoes, what is the "meat" that people prefer?

Three basic explanations of the negative income–fertility relationship have been proposed by economists. The first explanation is that the costs of raising children are mechanically linked to parents' income and consumption. Parents do not in this explanation feed their children inferior diets so that parents can eat well. Quoting Duesenberry, "Children may eat a different menu from their parents, but if so, it is because they *like* peanut-butter sandwiches."[18] The rising cost per child may offset rising family income and result in fewer children. The second explanation, consistent with Malthus, is that children and income are chosen jointly. Families, choosing to have many children, are also choosing lower income. For example, the wife may be sacrificing market income to raise children. Third, parents may decide to spend more resources per child as income rises, making children appear to be more expensive. Parents derive satisfaction from consuming child services, which consists of average resources devoted to each child times the number of children. As income rises, parents may consume more child services by substituting the quality of children (resources per child) for the quantity of children. This third possibility adds a new dimension to Malthus's argument that a person can achieve higher income and lower fertility by investing in education and training. Here families can achieve higher future income for their children by having fewer children and investing more resources in each child.

Rising Costs per Child

The first explanation of the negative income–fertility relationships, that expenditures per child are mechanically linked to income, is the basis for one of the most influential theories of fertility (at least in terms of the criticism it generated). This theory, developed by Harvey Leibenstein, presents childbearing choice in terms of the utility and disutility associated with what is called the *marginal child*.[19] The theory is oriented toward explaining the "next child decision," which is whether or not a family wishes an additional birth. Parents are seen as weighing the disutility of the nth child, D_n, against the utility of that child, U_n. Both the utility and disutility of an additional child are viewed as being functions of the parents' income, y, with

$$\frac{\partial D_n}{\partial y} > 0 \text{ and } \frac{\partial U_n}{\partial y} < 0, \tag{4.19}$$

and of the number of children. It is assumed that D_n rises and U_n falls as n increases.

Leibenstein supported these conjectures with a discussion of the sources of utility and disutility. Children provide utility directly to the parent as a consumer good and indirectly as a producer of income and as old age security. Leibenstein conjectured that the utility the child provides as a consumer good is largely independent of the parents' income. However, the utility of the marginal child, coming from the other two roles of the child (as a producer and as a source of old age security), is assumed to decline with income. Numerous arguments are advanced. For example, children are used less as producers as income rises, and higher income opens up alternative sources of old age security. Consequently, it is assumed that $\partial U_n/\partial y < 0$. The sources of disutility associated with the marginal child are the direct costs, such as food and clothing, of raising a child and the indirect costs associated with income and other opportunities foregone by the parents in order to raise the child. Although Leibenstein is less certain as to how these sources of disutility vary with income, he considers the case where $\partial D_n/\partial y > 0$. We will return to a discussion of the basic premises of the model after we discuss its implications.

Consider the example illustrated in Figure 4.4. Here, the parents desire at least n children if income is less than y_1 because for $y < y_1$, $U_n > D_n$. However, for $y > y_1$, $D_n > U_n$ and the parents desire fewer than n children. For $y < y_2$, note that $U_{n-1} > D_{n-1}$ and the parents desire at least $n - 1$ children (they desire exactly $n - 1$ children for $y_1 < y \leq y_2$). Hence, at least in this example, income and fertility are negatively related.

The categorization of variables as sources of costs versus benefits is arbitrary in Leibenstein's theory. Parents are assumed to receive utility from the income received by children working and disutility from goods and services devoted to raising the children. No explanation is given as to why the opposite does not hold. For instance, parents might receive satisfaction from nurturing children and actually enjoy giving a gift to a child. Leibenstein's parents view the pleasures of having children as independent of the resources devoted to each child. Hence, the rational parent would want to reduce expenditures on children to the subsistence level unless they are constrained from doing so. These constraints arise from class norms. Parents are not free to reduce expenditures per child below some given level because of social pressures and penalties. Hence, the limitation of choice by social norms is not merely an added constraint in Leibenstein's theory but its raison d'être. The reason why these socially determined costs rise with income is because socioeconomic status is presumed to largely determine expenditures per child. Because the socioeconomic status of a group or class is positively associated with income, the costs of nurturing children will rise with income.

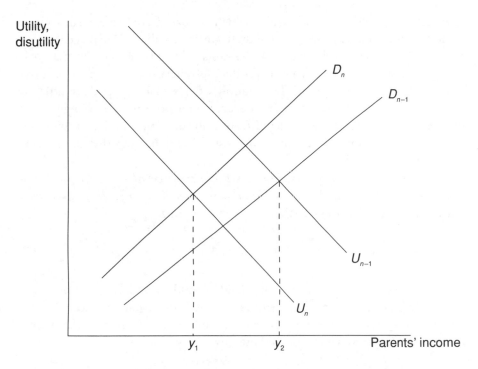

Figure 4.4   The marginal child.

While Leibenstein subsequently modified his views,[20] his theory still stresses the importance of social group or class in determining expenditures per child. An implication of this view, which Leibenstein uses as support, is that within a social group fertility might rise with income. The disutility of children would fall with income if the marginal utility of goods and services foregone to raise a child declines; that is, if there is diminishing marginal utility of income. Hence, fertility might be negatively associated with income in the aggregate and positively associated with income within each socioeconomic group.

This later view of Leibenstein's is consistent with the classical view of fertility posited by Ricardo and Marx and extended by Sydney Coontz.[21] In Coontz's model, the supply price of labor, that is, the cost of rearing a child, is determined by occupation. Physicians cost more to rear than Ph.D. economists and hence are paid more. Physicians also tend to raise more physicians than do other occupational groups and consequently have a higher cost of raising their children. Coontz, however, contends that wealthy physicians have more children than less wealthy physicians. In Coontz's view, child-bearing is positively related to income once we control for the supply price of labor; that is, the costs of raising children to enter a given occupation.

A difficulty with Coontz's view, which is shared by Leibenstein's view, is that it does not explain why children are raised for a given occupation. Hence, there is no explanation for the costs of child rearing. No reason is given for assuming that physicians produce physicians or any fixed occupational structure of offspring. The notion of a social group does little to alleviate this difficulty unless it can be explained how people change social groups. Unless parents are restricted to one social group, they may pick the group with the norms concerning the costs of childbearing that the parents find most congenial.

Another application of Leibenstein's theory concerns the existence of a "pension motive" for having children. Jeffrey S. Hammer presents a two period consumption model where parents maximize

$$u = u(c_1, c_2). \tag{4.20}$$

where c_1 and c_2 are the parents' first and second period consumption, respectively.[22] The parents earn income in the first period but none in the second. They receive income either from children raised in the first period or from first period savings. Consequently,

$$c_1 = y - c(N; x) - s$$

and   (4.21)

$$c_2 = R(N; z) + s(1 + r),$$

where y is income, N is the number of surviving children, x and z are vectors of exogenous variables, s is savings, $c(N; x)$ is the cost per surviving child, $R(N; z)$ is the pension received from surviving children, and r is the rate of interest. Consequently, children are viewed as assets that compete with savings as a source of pensions. Any factor that increases the return to children relative to savings will cause parents to desire more children. For example, a fall in infant mortality might reduce the costs of raising surviving children and consequently increase the pension demand for children. This result is just the opposite of the prediction of transition theory. Because a decline in infant mortality could increase fertility, Hammer suggests that financial deepening by raising the return on savings, might be an important force working to reduce fertility as an economy develops.

Another application where it is convenient to assume fixed cost per child is in dealing with son preference.[23] The basic idea behind son preference is that there are different costs and rewards to sons than to daughters. Parents maximize

$$u = u(S, D, X)$$

subject to   (4.22)

$$y = c_s S + c_d D + X,$$

where S is the number of sons, D is the number of daughters, X is other goods (or commodities), c_s is the price of sons, and c_d is the price of daughters. u^* is optimum utility. Son preference exists if each $u^*(S + 1, D, X) > u^*(S, D + 1, X)$ for all S, D, given X. There is mixed evidence supporting the hypothesis of son preference for many societies.

Children and Income

The second explanation of the negative income–fertility relationship is that parents jointly choose income and the number of children. This explanation is forcefully presented by Richard Easterlin, who introduced the concept of "potential income."[24] Actual, observed income is a function of the number of children in a family. In other words, $Y = Y(N)$, where Y is actual income and N is the number of children, with $\partial Y/\partial N < 0$. Potential income is the income the parents could earn if they had no children: that is, $Y_p = Y(0)$ is potential income. Easterlin contends that empirical studies which look at fertility as a function of actual income are biased toward showing a low or negative income–fertility relationship because fertility is a function of potential income and not actual income. For example, suppose the family budget constraint is given by

$$Y = A + w_h(T - L_h) + w_w(T - L_w)$$ (4.23)

where A is nonwage income or wealth, T is the time in the period, w_h and w_w are the market wage rates for husband and wife, respectively, and L_h and L_w are the nonworking hours of husband and wife, respectively. As the number of children increases, the family may have to increase nonworking hours, $L = L_h + L_w$, in order to care for children. Income, Y, will consequently fall.

The reader will, of course, recognize the budget constraint in equation (4.23) as coming from the second chapter. We can modify the household leisure choice discussion of the second chapter to incorporate fertility decisions. Let the household maximize

$$u = u(X, NC, L_{Xh}, L_{Xw}, L_{Ch}, L_{Cw}, N).$$ (4.24)

Subject to

$$Y = A + w_h(T - L_h) + w_w(T - L_w) = P_X X' + P_C NC',$$

with

$$L_h = L_{Xh} + L_{Ch} \qquad (4.25)$$

and

$$L_w = L_{Xw} + L_{Cw},$$

where X is a vector of goods consumed by the parents, NC is a vector of goods consumed by the children (N is the number of children and C is the goods vector consumed per child), L_{Xh} and L_{Xw} are the leisure times not devoted to child rearing by the husband or wife, L_{Ch} and L_{Cw} are the leisure times devoted to the children, P_X and P_C are price vectors, and the remaining variables are defined as in equation (4.23).

To apply the discussion to fertility, it is useful to assume that the utility function can be written as

$$u = u[s(X), q(C)N, L_X, L_C, N] \qquad (4.26)$$

where $s(X)$ and $q(C)N$ are aggregate goods. Furthermore, the husband's and wife's leisure are assumed to be perfect substitutes. The budget constraint can then be written as

$$Y = A + w_h(T - L_h) + w_w(T - L_w) = P_s s + (P_q q)N \qquad (4.27)$$

where P_s and P_q are the prices of the aggregate goods $s(X)$ and $q(C)$. The assumption that L_h and L_w are perfect substitutes implies that the wage earner with the higher income will work full-time. Hence, if $w_h > w_w$, the husband's income would be treated as exogenous. The demand for children could then be expressed as a function of the wife's wage rate, the husband's income (i.e., $A + w_h(T - L_h)$), the prices of child related goods, and other prices.

This model has the advantage over Leibenstein's model that expenditures per child is included as a decision variable. It is still possible to introduce socioeconomic considerations. For example, the utility function can be written in Stone-Geary form, where

$$u = u[s(X - \overline{X}), q(C - \overline{C}), L_X - \overline{L}_X, L_C - \overline{L}_C, N], \qquad (4.28)$$

with $\overline{X}, \overline{C}, \overline{L}_X, \overline{L}_C$ being interpreted as subsistence levels that may be sociologically or physically determined. Rising income may reduce fertility for two different reasons. First, $\overline{X}$ or $\overline{C}$ might rise with income as parents move into higher status groups. The rise in $\overline{C}$ could be interpreted as an increased cost per child. Second, for a given $\overline{C}$, parents might choose to spend more per child as income rises. In this case expenditures per child would be a normal good. The demand for children could then fall with income because parents choose to spend more per child as income rises. Hence, the resolution of the seeming paradox, that children appear to be inferior goods, does not require the assumption that expenditures per child are exogenous and that they tend to rise with income.

Note that social norms are introduced into the model as affecting tastes; that is, the utility function. There are, of course, other ways in which norms might influence fertility. For instance, in Caldwell's model, social norms create an implicit contract between members of a kinship group that influence fertility through the budget constraint. Economists are often skeptical about explanations of behavior that hinge on differences in tastes. Nonetheless, this model is best known for a taste formation conjecture made by Easterlin. Again the emphasis is on income. The income of young adults relative to the income of their parents 10 to 15 years earlier is seen as a crucial variable because of the hypothesis that $s(X)$ and $q(C)$ are systematically influenced by this relative income.[25]

The relative income hypothesis or, as it is also called, the Easterlin hypothesis, has been used to explain fertility swings in developed countries. It does, however, suggest some research questions for less developed nations. The hypothesis starts with the assumption that tastes, including persons' visions of the good life, are largely formed during their teenage years when they were in the parents' households. The levels of living toward which people aspire were largely formulated in these years. In terms of equation (4.28), it was during these years that $\overline{X}$ and $\overline{C}$ were determined. Higher levels of relative income imply that young couples can more easily achieve $\overline{X}$ and $\overline{C}$ for any given number of children. Consequently, parents with high relative income are able to have more children and still achieve the standard of living to which they aspire. Such parents are thought to start their families earlier and have larger families. An implication of this hypothesis is that countries which first experience rapid growth will see fertility rates rise because relative income rises. Eventually, however, fertility will fall, partly because relative income falls and partly because of the long-run negative impact of economic development on fertility.

Quality of Children

The third explanation of the negative income–fertility relationship is based on the idea that, by changing expenditures per child, parents are in effect choosing different qualities of children. When income rises parents might increase the quality of their children, the number, or quantity, of children or both. This explanation can perhaps be best understood as a natural extension of Malthus's view of education as a preventative check. In Malthus, fertility would be reduced by increasing the ability of people to invest in themselves by postponing children to obtain an education. With effective contraception parents have an additional avenue of investment. They can have fewer children in order to invest in their children's education.

The quantity–quality choice is usually associated with Gary S. Becker. Becker introduced the consideration of the quality of children within a human capital framework.[26] Although the subsequent literature has not extended some of Becker's original insights, a brief consideration of Becker's original article will help us to compare Becker with Leibenstein. Furthermore, the seminal article has insights of particular interest to development economics. Once Becker's human capital model is discussed, we will turn our attention to the "new economic demography," which emphasizes the quality–quantity tradeoff.

In his 1960 article, Becker viewed the decision of whether to have another child as being analogous to investing in a consumer durable. A key element in that investment decision is the cost of the consumer durable. The cost of a child was defined to be the present value of expenditures on the child plus the imputed present value of the parents' time minus the present value of the child's monetary and nonmonetary contributions to the parents' income. In other words, the cost of a child is

$$C = \sum_{a=0}^{n}(E(a) + PS(a) - Y(a) - CS(a))/(1 + r)^a, \qquad (4.29)$$

where a is the age of the child, $E(a)$ are expenditures on the child, $PS(a)$ is the imputed value of parents' services to the child, $Y(a)$ is the income of the child, $CS(a)$ is the imputed value of the child's services to the parents, r is the discount rate, and n is the time horizon. The time horizon, Becker argued, is the age at which the child leaves the household because net remittances are negligible.

Thus far, Becker's notion of costs is similar to Leibenstein's in that C might be thought of as being determined by social institutions. Becker, however, considers why parents might choose different levels of C. The reason is obvious given the consumer durable analogy. Higher priced consumer durables are often of higher quality. For example, the cost might be higher for a Mercedes Benz than for a Volkswagen. A person who buys a Mercedes Benz does so because it is of higher quality. Similarly, a parent might devote more time and goods to raising a child because they wish in a sense to increase the quality of the child.

Before evaluating the analogy, consider its implications. First, the purchases of consumer durables are likely to be procyclical because such purchases can be postponed in hard times. Second, the sign of the long-run trend in the income–fertility relationships is indeterminate. As permanent income rises, parents would be expected to increase the quality per child just as they would be expected to purchase more expensive cars. Fertility, that is, the quantity of children, might rise or decline with permanent income. Just as the number of cars a person owns might rise with income or fall as the person decides that one expensive but reliable car is better than two cheap cars. Becker thought that the relationship would be positive if we controlled for the effectiveness of contraception, which he thought would be positively associated with income. Becker suggested that differences in the effectiveness of contraception might explain much of the negative income–fertility relationship found in cross-sectional studies. Similarly, the negative income–fertility trend found in long-run time series might be partly explained by a growing effectiveness of contraception. Indeed, Becker believed that fertility falls with rising income partly because with economic development a greater proportion of conscious family planning occurs.

The assumption that the effectiveness of birth control varied directly with income was made by Becker because he wished to avoid assuming that tastes vary systematically with income. Quoting Becker:

> It is tempting to conclude from this evidence either that tastes vary systematically with income, perhaps being related to relative income [in the sense of Duesenberry], or that the number of children is an inferior good. Ultimately, systematic variations in tastes may have to be recognized; but for the present it seems possible to explain the available data within the framework outlined in section I, without assuming that the number of children is an inferior good . . . tastes are not the only variable that may have varied systematically with income, for there is a good deal of general evidence that contraceptive knowledge has been positively related to income.[27]

The abandonment of the assumption about the effectiveness of contraception led to a neglect of Becker's original human capital model. The concept of the quality of children was kept but placed within a model of household production as developed in Chapter 2. Because some of the insights gained from the household production model can be incorporated into the human capital model, we will compare the two models after briefly presenting the new economic demography.

In the new economic demography, parents are seen as maximizing the utility from consuming household produced commodities. Three aggregate commodities considered are the quality of the ith child Q_i, the number of children N, and other commodities S. An additional restriction, which would be interesting to relax when considering gender or birth order, is to set $Q_i = Q$ for all $i = 1, 2, \ldots, N$. The household maximizes

$$u = u(S, Q, N). \tag{4.30}$$

Subject to

$$Q = f(t_C/N, X_C/N),$$

$$S = g(t_s, X_s), \tag{4.31}$$

and the income constraint

$$y = H + wL = PX'.$$

Q represents the quality per child, t_C and X_C are time and goods used to produce child quality, t_s and X_s are time and goods used to produce other commodities, H is the (exogenous) husband's income, w is the wife's wage rate, L is the wife's working hours, and X and P are vectors of goods purchased on the market and their prices, respectively. The same assumptions are made here as were made in Chapter 2 (i.e., the husband's time is unproductive at home and f and g are linearly homogenous with no joint production). L is given by $L = T - t$, where T is total time, H is the sum of nonlabor wealth and the husband's wage income.

Note that the sex of children is not considered nor are the costs of giving birth to a child. In a more detailed treatment of the new economic demography, we would want to introduce these (and more) considerations. For illustrative purposes, let child services be defined as C, where

$$C = NQ = f(t_C, X_C). \tag{4.32}$$

Equation (4.32) comes from equation (4.31), the assumption that f is linearly homogenous and the implicit assumption that N is costless to produce. The budget set can be written as

$$\tau(NQ, S, H, T) = 0. \tag{4.33}$$

The household selects the optimum quantities of t_C, t_s, X_C, X_s, N, Q, S, and L, denoted as t_c^*, t_s^*, X_c^*, X_s^*, N^*, Q^*, S^*, and L^*. Recall from Chapter

2 that the optimum is described in terms of the implicit prices of the commodities. Hence, the household maximizes

$$u(S, N, Q).$$

Subject to   (4.34)

$$I = \pi_C NQ + \pi_s S,$$

where $I = H + wT$ is full income, π_C is the shadow price of child services and π_s is the shadow price of the other, nonchild commodity. The constraint is linear under the assumptions made, if the wife earns some income by producing goods or by selling her labor.[28] The budget demand for the three commodities can be expressed as

$$N^* = N(I, \pi_C, \pi_s),$$

$$Q^* = Q(I, \pi_C, \pi_s), \text{ and} \qquad (4.35)$$

$$S^* = S(I, \pi_C, \pi_s).$$

The fertility decisions of a household can now be easily described in terms of indifference curves. Consider the effect of an increase in the husband's income. Full income would clearly rise. Because income has increased and the time available to the household, T, has remained the same, it seems reasonable to suppose, as we did in Chapter 2, that the shadow price of the most time intensive commodity would rise relative to the other commodity. If we assume that child services are relatively time intensive, π_s/π_C would fall. The resulting new equilibrium is illustrated in Figure 4.5. Note that $I' > I$ but that $\pi_s'/\pi_C' < \pi_s/\pi_C$. The household in this case consumes more of both C and S at (C_2, S_2) than at (C_1, S_1). This might be thought of as the usual case. In addition, the household will substitute market goods for time in the production of both C and S.

Now consider the question of the sign of $\partial N^*/\partial H$ for the situation where both C and S are "normal" in the sense that the household consumes more of each commodity when the husband's income rises. The household can substitute Q for N in the production of C. The rectangular hyperbola $Q = C/N$ gives the combinations of N and Q that can be used to produce any given C as illustrated in Figure 4.6. C_1 and C_2 are two quantities of child services that the household might elect to consume. The indifference curves for the quantity–quality choice will in general depend upon the levels of S and C that are selected. Let u_1 be the optimal curve from the family of curves associated with the choice (C_1, S_1) and u_2 be the optimal curve from the (C_2, S_2) family of indifference curves. Note that the elasticity of substitution along

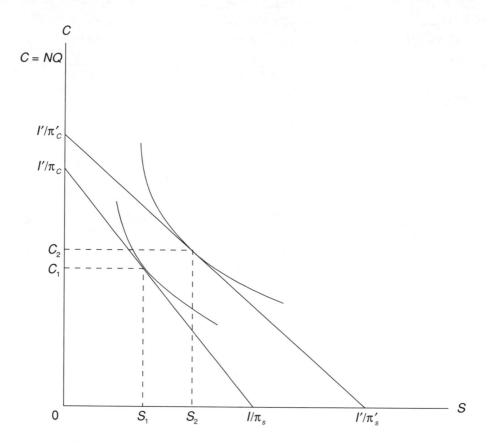

Figure 4.5 Effect of rising income on the demand for child services.

the indifference curves must be less than for the quality–quantity constraint. Otherwise, there would be no solution. In the example, the household markedly increases the quality per child while slightly reducing N (the discreteness of N is ignored). Hence, even though the demand for child services has risen with a rise in income and C is then a normal "commodity," N has fallen.

It is, of course, still possible to introduce the notion that there is some socially determined level of child quality. Proponents of using household production models to analyze fertility have not been sympathetic to such an approach. The idea that changes in social norms, tastes, or values largely determine changes in fertility is not rejected. It is merely argued that an economic analysis of fertility ought to largely rest on arguments about constraints and not preferences. Consequently, they do not introduce arguments like $\overline{C}$ and $\overline{S}$ into the utility function as in the more eclectic model in the

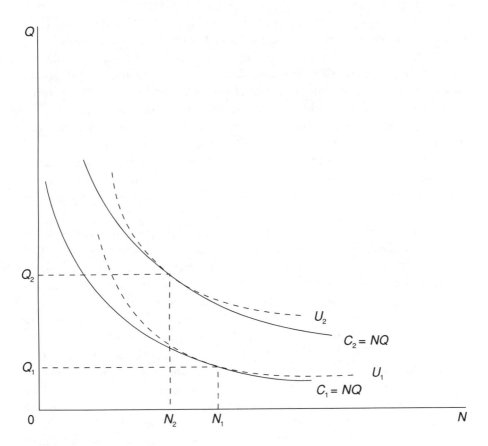

Figure 4.6 The number and quality of children.

last section. Proponents of household production models, of course, also argue that they allow the time required to raise children to be directly incorporated into the explanation of fertility. This incorporation of time as an input into the quality of children is the major advantage of the household production model over the earlier consumer durable approach.

It should be emphasized that both the household production model and the more socioeconomic choice model associated with Easterlin assume a great deal of information on the part of decision makers when these approaches are applied to fertility. Households choose the optimal number of children based on lifetime budget constraints including lifetime levels of income, prices, production technology, and so forth. Because none of these variables, if definable, is actually observed, it is not possible to move directly to empirical measurement and tests. Nevertheless, these models are useful in explaining empirical relationships in actual data. Still the models should be interpreted as being suggestive rather than systematic.

One shortcoming of lifetime decision models is that they do not directly explain dynamic relationships. The consumer durable approach does better in this respect. The expected pecuniary costs and benefits of a child are explicitly discounted. Consequently, differences in the timing of these net costs as well as changes in the expected time path of income can be introduced into models of fertility. For example, the demand for consumer durables is thought to be sensitive to swings in income. Consequently, children might be postponed during recessions, accounting for the positive relationship between income and fertility over the business cycle that is often found. Total lifetime fertility, however, may be little influenced by episodic business conditions. The consumer durable analogy is therefore suggestive of how these dynamic questions can be formulated.

A notable feature of the dynamics of fertility decisions is that children are born sequentially. To have the $(n + 1)$th birth, parents must have first had n births. The consumer durable analogy is amenable to viewing birth decisions as occurring one at a time. Parents do not need to know the optimum lifetime number of children to decide whether or not they wish to have another child. They need to know only if and when they want at least one more birth. This next child decision depends upon both current and expected prices, and wages, along with the anticipated pleasures of raising one more child. Parents may have some anticipated family size, but many events can intervene to change their plans. Formulating fertility theory solely in terms of these lifetime plans may be unnecessarily restrictive. The consumer durable analogy is capable of avoiding these restrictions within the context of an economic theory. Fertility is still viewed as a choice variable. These economic approaches are in contrast to the socioeconomic approaches, to be discussed in the next section, that do not view fertility as a choice variable.

PROXIMATE DETERMINANTS APPROACHES

There is a long tradition of viewing fertility as being largely the unintended consequence of numerous decisions throughout parents' lifetimes. Deliberate and effective family planning is thought to be largely absent in many current societies and in societies throughout history. Conscious and effective birth control is thought to be fairly recent in demographic history. Episodic events such as wars and unemployment, along with customs concerning the age at marriage, how long the child is nursed, the frequency of coition, and so forth, are held to largely determine the deviation of fertility from some natural fertility level. Attention is focused on explaining fertility in terms of the mechanisms by which fertility is determined. These mechanisms are called the *proximate determinants of fertility.*[29]

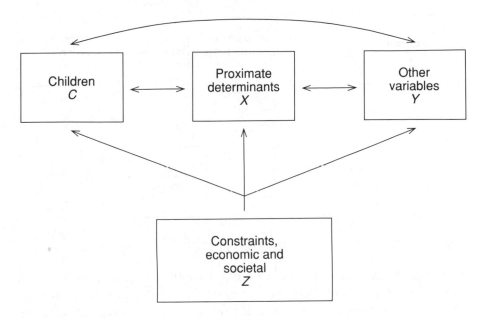

Figure 4.7 Choice theoretical approach.

The idea behind the proximate determinants approach is illustrated in Figures 4.7 and 4.8. Choice variables are placed in three categories: child related variables, C; proximate determinant variables, X; and other nonchild related choice variables, Y. In standard demand theory, prices, wage rates, and other exogenous (to the family) variables determine the demand for C, X, and Y. The constraints may include social constraints such as the acceptable numbers of children, expenditures per child, and so forth. The arrows show causal linkages. The directional arrows show mutually dependent choice variables.

Note that in Figure 4.7 the demand for children (C), for proximate determinants (X), and for all other variables (Y) is simultaneously chosen. In other words, the family chooses

$$C = C(Z),$$

$$X_i = X_i(Z), \text{ and} \tag{4.36}$$

$$Y_j = Y_j(Z), \text{ for all } i, j,$$

where Z represents a vector of exogenous constraint variable. For example, parents simultaneously decide how many movies to attend, how many times to have sexual intercourse, and the number of children they desire. All variables are jointly chosen, so it does not make sense to speak of increased

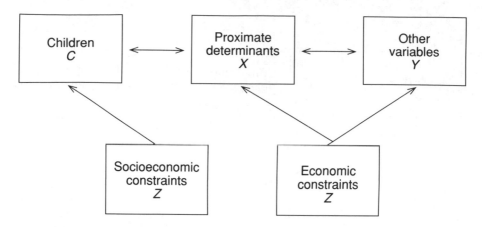

Figure 4.8   Proximate determinants approach.

movie attendance causing a reduction in fertility. Of course, an increased availability of movies or theaters could cause the anecdotal decline in fertility through the reduction in the costs of attending movies compared with the costs of children.

In the proximate determinants approach, the causal assumptions under-lying Figure 4.8 are changed. Although the precise specification of causality can vary within this approach, Figure 4.8 can serve as an illustration. Fertility is assumed not to be the result of conscious choice. Parents still choose proximate determinants and other variables subject to economic constraints. These choices imply some level of fertility, but this level of fertility is not itself an object of choice. Consequently, attitudes about family size do not affect the behavior of the family. Hence, it is meaningful to talk of a change in a proximate determinant causing a change in fertility and not as being merely a mechanism by which parents control fertility. These proximate determinants involve sensitive behavior in many cultures, so they may be particularly subject to cultural constraints. Advocates of a proximate deter-minants approach contend that as a society modernizes both the proximate determinants and the number of children progressively become more subject to individual choice.

It is worth noting that the proximate determinants approach as illustrated in Figure 4.8 appears to be a special case of the choice theoretical approach illustrated in Figure 4.7. Indeed, with suitable data, a structural model of Figure 4.7 could be estimated so that the assumed relationship underlying both figures could be tested. In the absence of such data, a choice of methods must be made. Those preferring Figure 4.7 would estimate fertility directly as a function of constraint variables. The underlying assumption is that it is not necessary to know the combination of methods parents use to achieve some probable family size in order to analyze their choice. Those preferring the proximate determinants approach place more emphasis on proximate determinants such as the frequency and timing of coition, the length of lactation, the age at marriage, and the practice and effectiveness of contraception. Because it is assumed that these practices are chosen without completely considering their impact on fertility, it is held that they are partially exogenous with respect to fertility. Consequently, these practices could be viewed as causes of fertility as will be further explained in the next section.

MORTALITY

Fears that a new plague may radically alter prospects of living a normal life span have recently surfaced in parts of the world that for generations have been immune from such fears. Like a primordial nightmare, the emergence of AIDS brings the prospect that here is a natural devastation our science may not be able to control. A catastrophic swing in mortality once again threatens to be more important than fertility in determining the immediate course of population growth. Like previous plagues, this embryonic plague threatens to transform our society. Yet we are reminded that the poor in much of the world have always faced the prospects of a short life. Mortality has likewise played a powerful role in shaping the institutions of societies facing poverty. This role is important in theories of social change, like the theory of the demographic transition described earlier. Our attention will be focused both on the causes of mortality itself and on the interrelationship between mortality and fertility.

In discussing the causes of mortality we are immediately confronted with a thorny methodological issue that was raised in the proximate determinants approach to fertility. To what extent is high mortality a rational response to people's economic situation? For example, people who smoke die sooner on the average than nonsmokers. Does smoking cause, for example, lung cancer? There is a sense in which the answer to this question, despite the professed reservations of tobacco companies and some smokers, is obviously yes. Medically, smoking causes cancer. Yet, this obvious answer is question begging. It does not address the ultimate cause of smoking. If smokers are rational, they simultaneously choose both smoking and a higher probability of dying each year. In other words, both smoking and cancer are endogenous choice variables to be explained by preferences and constraints. If we wish to view health choices as being rational, then the economic causes of mortality are to be viewed in terms of the reaction of families to changes in the constraints to household choices.

Turning to a question of vital concern to less developed countries, how are we to formulate questions concerning infant mortality? If we view infant mortality as a choice variable then we are left with the difficulty of explaining why governments should wish to change those choices. To focus on this difficulty, note that we have just supposed families to be choosing their optimal infant mortality rate given their budget constraint. Therefore, for a given income distribution, the level of infant mortality in society should be optimal in the absence of market imperfections such as externalities. Standard welfare economics (to be discussed in Chapter 6) would suggest that we should no more try to directly control the demand for infant mortality than the demand for any other commodity. However, to limit our concern with high infant mortality to addressing market imperfections seems, to put it mildly, unsatisfying. Nevertheless, viewing mortality as a choice variable has led to some useful theoretical insights and interesting empirical results. The implications of rationality assumptions in mortality will be briefly discussed. First, infant mortality and its relationship to fertility will be discussed within the context of choice theory. Then the notion of health economics and the household production of health will be applied to the discussion of mortality. Finally, some implications of nonrational choice for the study of mortality will be mentioned.

Typically, economic models of fertility and infant mortality concentrate on fertility as a function of infant mortality where infant mortality is assumed to be exogenous.[30] The number of surviving children is assumed to be an argument in the family utility function. Higher infant mortality rates reduce the demand for surviving children by raising the average costs per surviving child. Fertility (the demand for births) is viewed as an increasing function of both the optimal number of surviving children and the child mortality rate. These models justify estimating fertility as a function of infant or child mortality within the framework of a single equation model.

However, simultaneity between fertility and child mortality is implied by choice theory. Households in choosing to have fewer children, with more resources devoted to each child, are simultaneously choosing lower child mortality. Within this context, an exogenous change in childhood mortality through say the elimination of a childhood disease would likely cause both a reduction in births and a further reduction in mortality as parents find it relatively less expensive to invest in the quality versus the quantity of children. In the single equation model, a reduction in infant mortality increases the demand for surviving children because the costs per child are reduced. There is also an increase in resources devoted to each child because the cost of child quality is also reduced. In a simultaneous equation model, there is feedback from increased child quality to a further reduction in infant mortality. In both single equation and simultaneous equation models, the derived demand for births is reduced.

Although it is usually assumed that a fall in infant mortality reduces the demand for births, there are two competing hypotheses about the size of this effect. They are called the *child replacement hypothesis* and the *child survival hypothesis*. In the child replacement hypothesis, parents are viewed as reacting to the death of their own infant by increasing their number of births. Parents are not viewed as reacting to infant mortality rates in general. Because births are costly, the death of a child increases the costs of having any given number of surviving children, reducing the demand for surviving children. Hence, the child replacement hypothesis implies an incomplete replacement of infant deaths. Therefore, if N is the desired number of children, B is the desired number of births, and m is the probability of an infant or child death, the child replacement hypothesis implies that $\dfrac{\partial B/\partial m}{N} < 1$. Perfect replacement implies

$$B = N(1 + m)$$

or   (4.37)

$$\partial B/\partial m = N.$$

The child survival hypothesis implies a greater than proportionate response to a change in the child mortality rate. In this conjecture, parents are viewed as basing B on their estimate of the probability a child will survive. Hence, if parents wish N children they will on the average have

$$B = N/(1 - m) \qquad (4.38)$$

births. By taking the derivative of equation (4.38), we have

$$\partial B/\partial m = N/(1 - m)^2 > N \qquad (4.39)$$

implying a greater than proportional response to child mortality. There is mixed evidence in support of whether the child survival or replacement hypothesis holds.[31]

Returning to mortality, the notion that health in general and infant mortality are choice variables is emphasized in health economics. Michael Grossman, Mark R. Rosenzweig, and T. Paul Schultz among others treat health as being essentially a home produced commodity.[32] For example, Rosenzweig and Schultz consider health as produced by some initial health endowment plus resources devoted towards improving health. Households maximize a function like

$$U = U(H,\ X,\ Y) \qquad\qquad\qquad (4.40)$$

where H is health, Y are commodities affecting health (negatively or positively) from which the household directly derives satisfaction, and X are
commodities that do not affect health. For example, Y might include
cigarette smoking. The household production of health can be written as

$$H = H(Y,\ I,\ E), \qquad\qquad\qquad (4.41)$$

where I are commodities that influence utility only indirectly through their
impact on health, and E is the health endowment of the family. The family
maximizes utility subject to the health production function and a budget
constraint. A change in prices, income, or the health production function is
seen to influence the demand for H, X, and Y. Like any other commodity,
health is ultimately a function of prices and income.

As income rises, families will be able to consume more health and other
commodities that affect health. Health policy would then consist of the
provision of public health services and, because of externalities of inocula-
tion, mandatory vaccination. The provision of clean drinking water, health
clinics, and health information can dramatically reduce mortality. Advocacy
of these health measures are all consistent with the assumption that health
choices are rational.

There are two basic objections to the rationality assumption when it
comes to the health care decisions of families. First, the welfare of some
family members may receive little or no weight during times of economic
difficulty. In particular, younger female children in large families may receive little attention. It has been postulated that such children have higher
death rates during times of economic stress than male children. Second, as
in the proximate determinants approach, households may not maximize over
the whole range of alternatives. In this approach, households are viewed as
exercising choice over a subset of outcomes but exercising little control over
the remaining outcomes. Consider the tradeoff between higher life expectancy with the more immediate pleasures of smoking. The linkages may be
only dimly understood by the smoker. If smoking and health are not jointly
chosen, it becomes possible to view smoking as causing cancer. Similarly,
early decisions concerning diet, exercise, water supply, and vaccinations have
a considerable impact on health and mortality. If these decisions are not
entirely rational, then health can be said to be caused by these variables. It
seems reasonable to suppose some degree of irrationality in decisions affecting mortality. Consequently, studies of mortality determinants can be given
a choice theoretical basis.

CONCLUSION

Population questions have long been a concern in development economics. Simple projections obviously suggest that population cannot grow at current rapid rates without eventually eliminating any progress that has been made. If, as many contend, fertility falls as income rises, then economic growth could achieve a high income, low fertility equilibrium. This view is incorporated into neoclassical growth models with endogenous population growth as formulated by Nelson and others. This view is consistent with demographic transition theory. Furthermore, it is a central feature of the fertility theories of Leibenstein, Becker, and Easterlin.

There are, of course, many other reasons why fertility might fall with economic development. Development may increase the rewards to delaying family formation in order to obtain human capital. Diversified occupational opportunities may eventually reduce fertility by weakening extended family ties, which are thought to enhance fertility. The availability of income security through government insurance may also reduce the pension motive for children. Finally, an increased diversity of lifestyles made possible by development may lead to time and goods being allocated away from children and child related activities. The list is lengthy and would come under what Malthus called the *strengthening of preventative checks*. If these other factors are important sources of fertility decline, then the existence of a negative relationship between income and fertility is not as important because fertility could still fall as the economy develops.

Explanations of why fertility is related to a variable in a given way have been more controversial than the variables themselves. For example, economists have pointed out that family income may not be the best notion of income to correlate with fertility because, to some extent, families that decide to earn more income are simultaneously choosing to have fewer children. Potential or full income is a more appropriate concept. This view has had fairly quick acceptance among sociologists. However, the reason why fertility is thought to fall as full income rises is more controversial. Becker and others treat tastes as constant and explain the relationship in terms of changed optimal household production. Easterlin, Leibenstein, and others treat tastes as partly endogenous and explain the relationship largely in terms of changed tastes.

The question of rationality has received more attention for fertility and mortality related behavior than it has for almost all other economic choices. Those questioning rationality often focus on intermediate variables such as contraception use, age at marriage, and so forth. Those more comfortable with rationality focus on births. These different research programs are, of

course, related. Both help to provide a richer knowledge of population economics and both are relevant to economic development.

APPENDIX: DEMOGRAPHIC MEASURES

There are a confusing array of demographic measures. The student of population needs to be aware of a few measures and terms to read the empirical
literature. These measures result partly from the fact that demographic
decisions require a time horizon of a life span. For example, there are many
years during which parents can bear children. A change in an exogenous
variable may alter the timing of the next birth, the total desired number of
births, or both. Furthermore, parents are more likely to have children at
some ages than others. Thus, the age distribution of parents matters. In
this appendix, some demographic measures will be defined and discussed.

Aggregate Measures

The age structure of human populations affects average behavior in pre-
dictable ways. The very young and the aged are more vulnerable to death.
Persons between the ages of 6 and 18 are more likely to be attending school.
Women between the ages of 18 and 30 are the most likely to be having
children. The examples of behavior where age is important are numerous.
This dependence of behavior on age both presents difficulties and provides
advantages for the analysis of such behavior. The difficulties come from the
need to normalize for differences in age structure. The advantages come
from the added predictive power of being able to calculate the age structure
for the near future. Many demographic measures are designed to correct for
the influence of age structure on births, deaths, marriages, and so forth. In
this section, these measures will be developed and explained.[33]

The simplest measures are the crude birth rate $b(t)$ and the crude death
rate $d(t)$. The crude birth rate is given by

$$b(t) = B(t)/\overline{P}(t) \tag{4.42}$$

and the crude death rate by

$$d(t) = D(t)/\overline{P}(t) \tag{4.43}$$

where $B(t)$ and $D(t)$ are births and deaths occurring in period t and $\overline{P}(t)$ is
the mean population size for period t. For example, if birth and death rates
are uniform throughout the period, $\overline{P}(t)$ is the midperiod population. The
difference between the crude birth rate and the crude death rate is the
instantaneous rate of natural population increase $r(t)$. In other words

$$r(t) = b(t) - d(t). \tag{4.44}$$

For example, the 1983 reported crude birth and death rates for Indonesia are 0.034 and 0.013 for a 0.021 rate of natural increase. The same rates for Tunisia are 0.033, 0.009, and 0.024, respectively.

Although we may ultimately wish to predict equation (4.44), the crude birth and death rates are not good measures of fertility or mortality. For example, the crude death rate for both Tunisia and the United States is 0.009 even though life expectancy in the United States is 75 years versus 62 years in Tunisia. Obviously, a greater proportion of the population is in low mortality years in Tunisia than in the United States. Life expectancy and infant mortality are better mortality measures because they do not depend on the age structure. The natural way of introducing these rates is to consider a cohort (i.e., a group) of persons all born at the same time and to follow this birth cohort through time. A *cohort* is defined as a group of persons experiencing the same event during the same period of time. Let ℓ_x be the proportion of persons surviving to age x. Let q_n be the proportion of persons dying when they are aged n years. Then

$$q_n = 1 - \ell_{n+1}/\ell_n = \frac{\ell_n - \ell_{n+1}}{\ell_n}. \tag{4.45}$$

For example, if 950 persons of an initial 1,000 born, survive to age one; $q_0 = 1 - \dfrac{.95}{1.0} = .05$, if 935 persons live to age two, $q_1 = 1 - \dfrac{.935}{.95} = .016$, and so forth. Cohort infant mortality, the proportion of person dying within the first year is $q_0 = 1 - \ell_1/\ell_0$. In discrete form, life expectancy at birth can be written as

$$e_0 = 0.5 + \sum_{n=1}^{\infty} \ell_n \tag{4.46}$$

The reason for adding 0.5 to the summation in equation (4.46) comes from the assumption that people die uniformly throughout the year and consequently that persons dying in year n live an average of one half of that year.

It is important to note that neither infant mortality nor life expectancy depends upon the age structure of the population. A practical difficulty must be overcome if these rates are to be useful. Data on cohorts generally are not available. Indeed, if we are concerned with the life expectancy of birth cohorts through time, data on the future mortality of current cohorts (cohorts with currently living members) is in principle not available. Consequently, life tables are constructed using period (usually of length one year) data. The easiest period life table to calculate is to simply substitute the proportion of persons age n who die in a given year for (ℓ_n/ℓ_{n+1}) in equation (4.45). Because $\ell_0 \equiv 1$, ℓ_{n+1} can be recursively calculated for $n = 0, 1, 2,$ . . . . Hence, e_0 in equation (4.46) can be calculated using these period rates. This calculation is exact for a stationary population where the number of person of each age does not change. Otherwise, a correction must be made for changing births or age structure. For example, if deaths occur uniformly throughout year t, then

$$q_n = \delta_n(1 - \ell_{n+1}/\ell_n) \tag{4.47}$$

where $\delta_n = .5(1 + P_n/P_n^0)$ and where P_n^0 is the population aged n at the beginning of year t and P_n is the populated aged n at the beginning of the next year. If the population is stationary, $\delta = 1$ and no correction is needed. For a growing population, simply using annual rates underestimates mortality.

The measure of fertility that is analogous to life expectancy is the cohort (total) fertility rate. The cohort fertility rate (CFR) gives the average number of children who would be born to a cohort of women if those women experienced no mortality. Corrections for mortality can be made using ℓ_n from a life table. To find CFR we need to first know the number of births occurring to women of each age in the cohort. Let $f(n)$ represent the probability a woman (of a given cohort) will give birth at age n. Then the total average number of births for that cohort is given by

$$\text{CFR} = \sum_{n=14}^{49} f(n). \tag{4.48}$$

The reason for only summing age-specific birth rates for ages 14 through 49 is that few if any births occur to women of other ages (i.e., $f(n) = 0$ for these excluded ages). Hence, if CFR = 3.5, women of that cohort would have had an average of 3.5 births had they lived through age 49.

Not only is the cohort fertility rate independent of the age structure of the population, but it is easy to formulate as the decision variable within the context of fertility theory where the period of analysis is the lifetime of the family. As was the case with mortality, the cohort fertility rate can not be computed for women currently in their childbearing years. Consequently, the proportion of women aged n who give birth to a child in a given year can be substituted for $f(n)$ in equation (4.48). The summation is called the (period) *total fertility rate* (TFR). The same correction can be applied to the total fertility rate as was done with life expectancy in equation (4.47). Hence, for each year

$$\text{TFR} = \sum_{n=14}^{49} \delta_n f(n). \tag{4.49}$$

The 1983 total fertility rate was 4.3 for Indonesia and 4.9 for Tunisia even though, as we noted, Indonesia has a slightly higher crude birth rate. This discrepancy exists because a larger proportion of Indonesia's population is in the chief childbearing years.

Individual Measures

Thus far, the vital rates that have been discussed are measures of the fertility or the mortality of a population. These aggregate measures cannot measure the fertility or mortality of individual persons or households, because they are continuous whereas individual vital events are discrete. A person dies once. A woman has N children, where N is a nonnegative integer. In dealing with individual vital events, different measures are required. These measures will be divided into four types. The first type of measure, a proximity measure, is derived from looking at the proximate cause of an event. For example, the use of contraception might be used as a measure of fertility. The second type of measure, a timing measure, begins with the spacing of vital events. The third type of measure, a frequency measure, concerns the number of times that event has occurred. Finally, the fourth type of measure, a likelihood measure, is found by looking at the perceived likelihood an event will occur. For example, the number of children that women claim they want in responding to a survey might be used as a measure of fertility. Proximity and likelihood measures might more properly be considered as determinants of fertility and not a substitute for more direct fertility measures. Consequently, only timing and frequency measures will be considered.

Timing Measures

Timing models involve the analysis of the time it takes for an individual, a household, or some other entity of analysis to change states from its current state. Life tables are a timing model. They are constructed from the time it takes numerous individuals to die (i.e., their age at death). Fertility models can be similarly constructed. The probability of another birth can be estimated as a function of time using data on the spacing of births. These timing models were originally developed for mortality and have alternatively been called *failure time models, survival models,* or *hazard models.* These models are generating increasing interest in demographic research.[34]

To make the analysis less abstract, consider the timing of a specific vital event such as another birth. Suppose a group of women all had a child at time $t = 0$ and that we wish to describe the distribution through time of subsequent births. For the moment, neglect the possibility of mortality. Three functions useful in describing the distribution of subsequent births through time are the survivor function, the probability density function, and the hazard function. The survival function gives the proportion of the women who have not yet had an additional birth by time t. In other words,

$$F(t) = P(T \geq t), \ 0 < t < \infty \qquad (4.50)$$

is the cumulative probability of having the next birth spaced at least T periods after the last birth. The probability density function is given by

$$f(t) = \lim_{\Delta t \to 0^+} \frac{P(t \leq T < t + \Delta t)}{\Delta t} = -\frac{dF(t)}{dt}. \qquad (4.51)$$

Finally, the hazard function gives the instantaneous rate of subsequent births at time t and is given by

$$\lambda(t) = \lim_{\Delta t \to 0^+} \frac{P(t \leq T < t + \Delta t | T \geq t)}{\Delta t} = \frac{f(t)}{F(t)}. \qquad (4.52)$$

Typically, assumptions are made about the hazard function, which is then estimated given the data. For example, if λ is constant through time, the survival function is exponential and is written as

$$F(t) = e^{-\lambda t}. \qquad (4.53)$$

The density function is then

$$f(t) = \lambda e^{-\lambda t}. \qquad (4.54)$$

The exponential distribution can be easily extended to include a vector of exogenous variables that change λ in a proportional way. For example, let

$$\lambda(t; \ X) = \lambda C(\beta X), \qquad (4.55)$$

where $\beta X = \beta_0 + \beta_1 X_1 + \beta_2 X_2 + \ldots + \beta_n X_n$. Typically $C(\beta X) = e^{\beta X}$. Hence,

$$\lambda(t;\ X) = \lambda e^{\beta X}. \tag{4.56}$$

Thus λ and β are estimated as functions of observed values of survival time and X. The attraction of exponential models is that the log survival time $y = \log T$ can be written as a linear function. To see this, substitute equation (4.56) into (4.53) to find the survival function

$$F(t) = \exp(-te^{\beta X}). \tag{4.57}$$

The probability density function of the log of the survivor function can be written in linear form and estimated as

$$Y = -\log\lambda - ZP + w \tag{4.58}$$

where w is an error term with the probability density function

$$\exp(w - e_w), \quad -\infty < w < \infty. \tag{4.59}$$

These exponential hazard models along with their generalization, the proportional hazard model, written as

$$\lambda(t;\ X) = \lambda_0(t)e^{\beta X}, \tag{4.60}$$

where $\lambda_0(t)$ is an arbitrary baseline hazard function and can be estimated using standard statistical packages.

Proponents of failure time models for analyzing vital events point out that these models can handle truncated data when the truncations are random. A limitation of these models is that they provide a joint estimation of the timing of an event and the probability that event will occur (before the person exits the state for some other reason). For example, decisions about the timing of births and the total number of births may be based on different considerations and respond to different variables. Spacing decisions might be based largely on socially acceptable notions of which spacing is best for the psychological development of the children, whereas decisions on whether or not to have another child might respond more to the economic situation of the family. Combining separate decisions into a single model might give false impressions of the childbearing process.

A simple alternative to the hazard model approach for measuring fertility is to concentrate on the probability of another birth.[35] Let y be the probability that a woman will have at least one more birth within a specified period of time, say, within five years. Then y can be estimated as a function of a vector of exogenous variables X. A useful probability model for such an estimation is to let

$$y = 1/(1 + e^{\alpha X}), \tag{4.61}$$

where α is a vector of constants. Note that equation (4.61) has the desirable property that $0 \le y \le 1$. Equation (4.61) is called a *logit probability model,* and the function is called a *logistics function.* Note that linear probability models are inappropriate because y is unbounded. Although a negative probability might be interpreted as parents wishing they could undo a birth, there is no natural interpretation of $p > 1$. The probability of another child can also be estimated separately for each birth order. Let $y(N)$ be the probability that a woman with n births will have at least one more birth. Hence, $y(N)$ can be estimated by looking at the birth histories of women who have had at least N births and observing the proportion of these women who have had at least one subsequent birth. After having estimated the probability of another birth, the timing of that birth can be estimated separately.

The Frequency of an Event

The concept of fertility that is of ultimate interest in studying individual fertility is the quantity of children. The quantity of children is the number of children ever born to women who have completed childbearing. For example, if the probability of another birth, y, is constant over birth order, then the expected quantity of children is $E(N) = y/(1 - y)$, and the probability that the woman will have exactly N children is given by $P(N)$ $= (1 - y)y^N$. If y varies by birth order, $E(N) + \sum_{n=1}^{N} nP(n)$ and $P(N) = (1 - y_N)y_{N-1}y_{N-2} \ldots y_1$. $E(N)$ and $P(N)$ could be calculated from estimates of birth probabilities. Typically, however, the number of children ever born (CEB) is directly used as the fertility measure.

CEB has the advantage that it is readily available from surveys, censuses, and vital statistics data. It is also an easy variable to use. An obvious difficulty is that CEB is obviously correlated with age. Alternative estimation procedures that can be illuminating are to estimate CEB for a few age groups or to include the woman's age (preferably the log of the age) as one of the right-hand variables.

NOTES

1. Leo Rogin, *The Meaning and Validity of Economic Theory* (New York: Harper and Brothers, 1956), p. 162.

2. Thomas R. Malthus, *Principles of Political Economy*, in *Works and Correspondences by David Ricardo*, 10 vols., Vol. 1, ed. Piero Sraffa (Cambridge: Cambridge University Press, 1955), pp. 227–228.

3. See D. E. C. Eversley, *Social Theories of Fertility and the Malthusian Debate* (Oxford: Clarendon Press, 1959).

4. See William Petersen, *Malthus* (Cambridge, Mass.: Harvard University Press, 1979). See also, of course, Thomas R. Malthus, *An Essay on the Principle of Population*, 5th ed. (London: Ward, Lock and Co., 1980).

5. Warren S. Thompson, "Population," *American Journal of Sociology* (May, 1929): 959–975. Frank W. Notestein, "Population – the Long View," in *Food for the World,* ed. Theodore W. Schultz, pp. 36–57 (Chicago: University of Chicago Press, 1949).

6. Notestein, ibid., pp. 39–40.

7. Tim Dyson and Mike Murphy, "The Onset of Fertility Transition," *Population and Development Review* (September 1985): 399–440.

8. John C. Caldwell, *Theory of Fertility Decline* (New York: Academic Press, 1982). Caldwell's view of wealth transfers also plays a role in migration theory.

9. See Ansley J. Coale and Susan Colts Watkins, *The Decline of Fertility in Europe* (Princeton, N.J.: Princeton University Press, 1986); John Knodel and Etievie van de Walle, "Lessons From the Past: Policy Implications of Historical Fertility Studies," *Population and Development Review* 2 (June 1979): 217–245; and Ron J. Lesthaeghe, *The Decline of Belgian Fertility, 1800–1970* (Princeton, N.J.: Princeton University Press, 1977).

10. See Ronald Freedman, Pascak K. Whelpton, and Arthur A. Campbell, *Family Planning Sterility and Population Growth* (New York: McGraw-Hill, 1959); and Whelpton, Campbell, and John E. Patterson, *Fertility and Family Planning in the United States* (Princeton, N.J.: Princeton University Press, 1966).

11. Dov Friedlander, Jona Schellekens, and Eliahu Ben-Moshe, "The Transition from High to Low Marital Fertility: Cultural or Socioeconomic Determinants?" *Economic Development and Cultural Change* 39 (January 1991): 331–352.

12. C. R. Winegarden and Mark Wheeler, "The Role of Economic Growth in the Fertility Transition in Western Europe: Econometric Evidence," *Economica* 59 (November 1992): 383–501.

13. See R. D. Lee and R. S. Schofield, "British Population in the Eighteenth Century," in *The Economic History of Britain Since 1700:* Vol. 1. *1700–1860,* ed. Roderick Floud and Donald McCloskey (Cambridge: Cambridge University Press, 1981). For similar evidence on European population see Massimo Livi-Bacci, *A Concise History of World Population* (Oxford: Basil Blackwell, 1992), p. 59.

14. Richard R. Nelson, "A Theory of the Low-Level Equilibrium Trap in Underdeveloped Countries," *American Economic Review* (December 1956): 894–902; and Stephen Enke, "The Economic Consequences of Rapid Population Growth," *Economic Journal* (December 1971): 800–811.

15. See Julian L. Simon, *The Economics of Population Growth* (Princeton, N.J.: Princeton University Press, 1977); and Allen C. Kelly and Jeffrey G. Williamson,

Lessons from Japanese Development: An Analytical Economic History (Chicago: University of Chicago Press, 1974).

16. See Geoffrey McNicholl, "Consequences of Rapid Population Growth: An Overview and Assessment," *Population and Development Review* (June 1984): 177–240.

17. See Dale W. Jorgenson, "The Development of a Dual Economy," *Economic Journal* (June 1961): 309–334; and "Surplus Agricultural Labor and the Development of a Dual Economy," *Oxford Economic Papers* (November 1967): 288–312.

18. James Duesenberry, comment on "An Economic Analysis of Fertility" by Gary S. Becker, in *Demographic and Economic Change in Developed Countries* (Princeton, N.J.: Princeton University Press, 1960).

19. Harvey Leibenstein, *Economic Backwardness and Economic Growth* (New York: Wiley, 1957).

20. Leibenstein, "An Interpretation of the Economic Theory of Fertility: Promising Path or Blind Alley?" *Journal of Economic Literature* (June 1974): 457–479.

21. Sydney Coontz, *Population Theories and the Economic Interpretation* (London: Routledge and Kegan Paul Ltd., 1957).

22. Jeffrey S. Hammer, "Children and Savings in Less Developed Countries," *Journal of Development Economics* (October 1986): 107–118.

23. See Yoram Ben-Porath and Finis Welch, "Do Sex Preferences Really Matter?" *Quarterly Journal of Economics* 9 (1976): 285–307; and Hassan Y. Aly and M. P. Shields, "Son Preference and Contraception in Egypt," *Economic Development and Cultural Change* 39 (January 1991): 353–370.

24. Richard A. Easterlin, "Towards a Socioeconomic Theory of Fertility: A Survey of Recent Research on Economic Factors in American Fertility," in *Fertility and Family Planning: A World View*, ed. S. J. Behrman, Leslie Corsa, Jr. and Ronald Freeman, pp. 126–156 (Ann Arbor: University of Michigan Press, 1969).

25. Richard A. Easterlin, *Population, Labor Force and Long Swings in Economic Growth: The American Experience*, General Series 86 (New York: National Bureau of Economic Research, 1968).

26. Gary S. Becker, "An Economic Analysis of Fertility," in *Demographic and Economic Change in Developed Countries* (Princeton, N.J.: Princeton University Press, 1960), pp. 209–231.

27. Ibid., p. 218.

28. See Robert J. Willis, "A New Approach to the Economic Theory of Fertility Behavior," *Journal of Political Economy* (March–April Supplement 1973): S14–S64; and Robert A. Pollak and Michael L. Wachter, "The Relevance of the Household Production Function and Its Implications for the Allocation of Time," *Journal of Political Economy* (April 1975): 255–277. For a general text, see T. Paul Schultz, *Economics of Population* (Reading, Mass.: Addison Wesley, 1981). See also W. Keith Bryant, *The Economic Organization of the Household* (Cambridge: Cambridge University Press, 1990). If the wife specializes in household production, the constraint is nonlinear.

29. See Richard A. Easterlin, Robert A. Pollak, and Michael L. Wachter, "Toward a More General Economic Model of Fertility Determination: Endogenous Preferences and Natural Fertility," in *Population and Economic Change in Developing Countries*, ed. Richard A. Easterlin, Universities National Bureau Conference Report 30 (Chicago: University of Chicago Press, 1980).

30. For reviews of the literature on infant mortality and fertility, see Samuel H. Preston, "Health Programs and Population Growth," *Population and Development Review* (December 1975): 139–200; Susan C. M. Scrimshaw, "Infant Mortality and Behavior in the Regulation of Family Size," *Population and Development Review* (September 1978): 383–405; and T. Paul Schultz, *Economics of Population*, Chapter 5. For a study of whether there is a causal relationship between infant mortality and fertility, see Abdur R. Chowdhury, "The Infant Mortality–Fertility Debate: Some International Evidence," *Southern Economic Journal* 54 (January 1988): 666–674.

31. See M. P. Shields and Ronald L. Tracy, "Four Themes in Fertility Research," *Southern Economic Journal* (July 1986): 201–216.

32. Michael Grossman, "On the Concept of Health Capital and the Demand for Health," *Journal of Political Economy* (March–April 1972): 223–255; and Mark R. Rosenzweig and T. Paul Schultz, "Estimating a Household Production Function: Heterogeneity, the Demand for Health Inputs and Their Effects on Birth Weights," *Journal of Political Economy* (October 1983): 723–746.

33. Donald J. Bogue, *Principles of Demography* (New York: Wiley, 1969); Mortimer Spiegelman, *Introduction of Demography*, rev. ed. (Cambridge, Mass.: Harvard University Press, 1968).

34. See James J. Heckman and Robert J. Willis, "Estimation of a Stochastic Model of Reproduction: An Econometric Approach," in *Household Production and Consumption*, ed. Nestor E. Terleckyj, Conference on Research in Income and Wealth (New York: National Bureau of Economic Research, 1975), pp. 103–121; John L. Newman and Charles E. McCulloch, "A Hazard Rate Approach to the Timing of Births," *Econometrica* (July 1984): 939–961; and John D. Kalbfleisch and Ross L. Prentice, *The Statistical Analysis of Failure Time Data* (New York: Wiley, 1980).

35. See N. K. Namboodiri, "Which Couples at Given Parities Expect to Have Additional Births? An Exercise in Discriminant Analysis," *Demography* (1974): 45–56; and Michael P. Shields and Steve W. Tsui, "The Probability of Another Child in Costa Rica," *Economic Development and Cultural Change* (July 1983): 787–808.

5

Labor

There are many potential differences between labor markets in developed and less developed countries. For example, social welfare programs, which provide unemployment insurance, pensions, workers compensation, job placement services, and many other benefits are largely lacking in less developed countries. The lack of these programs leads to important behavioral differences in labor markets. One of these differences concerns the possibility that demand deficiencies will result in measured unemployment. Unemployment might be disguised by workers taking temporary jobs in subsistence agriculture or in a subsistence service sector, which contribute little to the output of society. Such employment is often called *disguised unemployment*. Disguised unemployment in this sense may also exist in market, industrial economies like the United States, but it is thought to be more pervasive in less developed countries. Much of the literature on labor markets in less developed countries has been dominated by this insight. It is particularly important in dualistic models of development.

Rapid urbanization is another feature of less developed countries, whereas developed countries are already largely urbanized. The pace of this urbanization seems to be quicker in current less developed countries than was the case in the past for today's developed countries (DCs). The cause and implications of this urbanization, as workers shift from agriculture and other rural occupations to urban occupations, is another matter of considerable interest for labor economics in less developed countries (LDCs).

A related feature of LDC labor markets is the substantial difference in wage rates between sectors of the economy. Workers in the modern sector of the economy, such as government employees, employees of large multinational firms, and union workers in general, earn substantially more than rural workers or urban workers in the traditional sector. An understanding of possible reasons for these differences is important both for coming to terms with the notion of disguised unemployment and for formulating an

169

appropriate wage policy for less developed countries. Of particular concern are questions regarding the sources of these wage differences. Are they the result of high wage policies by the government or powerful labor unions that favor some workers over others, or are they the result of competitive market forces? Each possibility suggests a different set of desirable policy actions.

Another feature of labor markets in less developed countries is the contrast in production methods. Some sectors use highly capitalized industries, which have modern production methods, in contrast with other sectors using more traditional production techniques. The extent to which this should and does occur underlies a debate concerning the appropriate technology for less developed countries.

A final feature of less developed countries is relatively low levels of education in comparison with developed countries. If we think of education as human capital, the relative scarcity of human capital should imply high rates of return to the individual for investment in human capital. These high rates of return do not seem to exist. For this and other reasons there is emerging interest in education and development.

This chapter is organized around these five concerns of labor economics in less developed countries. In order, the form that unemployment takes, migration theory, the efficiency wage hypothesis, technology choice, and the role of human capital will be discussed.

UNEMPLOYMENT

Unemployment is, of course, one dimension of the poverty problem. A nation whose economy is not generating jobs at a fast enough rate to absorb a growing population is a nation where poverty is likely to be increasing. It has long been recognized that unemployment is not the only response to a sluggish growth in the number of jobs. Those without gainful employment may turn to theft, beggary, or marginal pursuits, such as selling matches, flowers, or candy on street corners, in a desperate attempt to generate enough income to survive.

Most poor people in less developed nations cannot afford to be unemployed in the sense that they are idle, for even a short period of time. They must find some means of helping to support themselves and their families. Whether their efforts should be defined as employment, unemployment, or disguised unemployment is the subject of this section.

Workers in less developed nations often find employment in the informal sector. In this sector, the production unit is generally very small and often consists of family run enterprises. The production techniques used are generally

scale neutral and labor intensive in nature. In addition, the level of technology utilized is limited. Therefore, the jobs in this sector are typically low
productivity jobs that generate low incomes. It is tempting to view these
low productivity activities as being disguised unemployment. That is, the
individual appears to be employed but is in reality generating very little
increase in output. The marginal product of the individual's labor is quite
low; in fact, it may be well below the real wage actually being received. This
view of disguised unemployment was discussed by Arthur Lewis[1] in some
detail when he referred to the traditional sector.

However, the notion of disguised unemployment is fraught with difficulties. As Amartya Sen points out, the notions of disguised unemployment and, indeed, of employment itself are complex.[2] To illustrate this
complexity, Sen considers a beggar. Is the beggar to be classified as employed
or unemployed? Suppose by *employed* we mean that a person is producing
a good or service for income. The beggar receives income for his or her
effort. The beggar may also be thought of as providing a service by raising
the social consciousness of those observing the beggar. If we, as it seems
reasonable, deem the beggar to be unemployed, by what criteria are we to
judge an artist to be employed? Was not Shakespeare producing the same
service, raising our social consciousness, as the beggar? There is no unim-
peachable way of classifying persons as employed or unemployed. Consequently, there is considerable disagreement as to the definition and, hence,
the extent of disguised unemployment.[3]

Furthermore, the notion of disguised unemployment should be different
for LDCs than for the DCs, for which the term was invented. To see this
difference, consider a developed country with a homogeneous labor force
and a real wage rate of w, where w does not need to clear the market.
Consider a worker who would like to work L^* hours at wage rate w. The
worker, however, is self-employed with MPL $< w$ and earnings $y = L \cdot$ MPL.
This example illustrates disguised unemployment because MPL $< w$. The
person would accept employment at the market wage rate if employment
were available.

For the family worker in a less developed nation, the situation is different.
Let N be the number of family workers and suppose they all work the same
number of hours. Further suppose they all receive the same share of the
income of the family enterprise. In addition to receiving an equal share of
rent from the family enterprise, each worker receives MPL(L/N), where L
is total family labor. Rent from the enterprise will largely consist of land
rent, but rent from reputation or location might also be included. The total
earnings of a family worker are then

$$y = (R/N) + \text{MPL}(L/N), \tag{5.1}$$

where R is rent. Notice that we are assuming that only family members receive a share of the rent. Hence, if a person were to leave the family enterprise and take other employment, his or her total income would be $wL*$. Now it is possible to have $(R + MPL \cdot L)/N > wL*$ even though MPL $< w$. There is no disguised unemployment because the person would not voluntarily accept the job outside the family enterprise. Disguised unemployment exists if $(R + MPL \cdot L*)/N < wL*$. Family members would then accept employment at the market wage rate if employment were available.

Of course, the difference in meaning of disguised unemployment for developed and less developed nations would disappear if each family worker could retain access to a share of rent, even if that worker is involved in employment outside the family firm. In that case, if MPL $< w$, the person would indeed accept outside employment at the market wage, if it were available, and still retain a rental share. This sort of situation would prevail where the objective is to maximize family income.

One additional point should be made concerning disguised unemployment. The family firms, which generate such job opportunities, are often not linked very closely to input and output markets. More specifically, using the language of Chapter 3, they often appear to be economic islands where within each island economic efficiency prevails, but across islands there are substantial differences in technology. Much of the low productivity of this informal sector would seem to result from its lack of linkage via markets. This lack of linkage is, to a great extent, often the result of active government discrimination against firms in this sector. That is, most governments in developing nations have utilized policies that subsidize large scale, capital intensive production in the modern sector. This subsidization has usually involved credit subsidies as well as direct and indirect market protection (via tariffs, quotas, etc.). Such policies, of course, actively discriminate against firms in the informal sector and isolate them from access to the inputs necessary for modernization and productivity improvement. Thus much of the low productivity and disguised unemployment attributed to this sector may be the result of government policies that actively discriminate against it in favor of the modern sector. Therefore, it is possible that informal sector firms may play an important role in generating a more labor intensive process of overall economic development.

MIGRATION

Explaining rural to urban labor migration and evaluating its consequences are important for understanding economic development. Urbanization certainly seems to be a consequence of economic growth. Those countries that have higher per capita income also have larger proportions of their population residing in urban areas. For the most part, this urbanization has been viewed as desirable. For example, in dualistic theories of growth and development, migration is seen as a key to economic growth. Development is seen as a process where labor is transferred from a low productivity, rural sector to a high productivity, urban sector thereby increasing output as a whole. This view is strikingly illustrated in the dualistic growth models discussed in Chapter 1.

The views of migration that are most consistent with dualistic models view the potential migrant either as a supplier of labor or as an investor in human capital. These two views and the research that they have generated will be outlined in this section. A third approach, which views the migrant as a consumer of regional amenities such as public goods, will also be sketched. Finally, a new approach, which views the potential migrant as a producer of home produced commodities, will be outlined. These four views will be classified as the labor-flow view, the human capital view, the urban amenities view, and the household production view, respectively.[4]

The Labor-Flow View

In labor-flow models, migration is viewed as being labor's response to regional labor market disequilibrium. To illustrate this adjustment process consider a simple production function with two inputs, labor and capital. Furthermore, assume each input is paid its marginal product. Let MPL and MPK be the marginal products of labor and capital in a region where labor is relatively abundant, and let MPL′ and MPK′ be the marginal products for labor scarce regions. Assuming normal inputs, where the marginal product of a factor is positively related to the quantity of the other factor employed, MPL < MPL′ and MPK > MPK′. If only real returns are important, equilibrium exists when factors of production receive the same real return in each region (i.e., when MPL = MPL′ and MPK = MPK′). This equilibrium will be achieved because factors, both capital and labor, will flow to the region where they have the greatest return. As labor flows to the high wage region, MPL′ will fall (and MPK′ rise) due to the increased supply of workers in the high wage region. Similarly, MPL will rise (and MPK fall) with the reduction of workers in the low wage region. Capital should, of course, flow in the opposite direction as labor reinforcing these changes in factor prices. This adjustment will continue until real regional wage differentials are entirely explained by regional wage rigidities and the resulting unemployment or by moving costs.

In dualistic development theories, the labor-flow model, in its simplest form, can be stated as

$$M = \beta(w - s), \; \beta > 0, \tag{5.2}$$

where M represents net rural to urban migration, w is the real urban wage rate, s is the real rural wage rate, typically assumed to be at subsistence, and β is a scalar that represents barriers to migration, imperfect information, moving costs, and artificial barriers that restrict the speed of adjustment. Note that, if w falls as the size of the urban labor force rises (i.e., if labor and capital are substitutes and if the labor force grows more rapidly than the capital stock), then migration will fall through time as the urban–rural real wage differential narrows. Indeed, the eventual narrowing of real wage differentials is a major prediction of the model. The apparent failure of real wages to narrow has generated much empirical research and several innovations.[5]

It is important to properly define the real wage rates in the model. In general, it is thought that the costs of living are higher in urban areas than in rural areas. Hence, nominal wage rates are expected to be higher in cities. In terms of equation (5.2), $M = 0$ when $w = s$. Because w and s are real wage rates, the nominal wage rate in equilibrium (i.e., when $w = s$) is higher in the urban area. These wage rates should, of course, be made occupation or skill specific to obtain the relevant comparison.

One influential view of why real regional wage rates may not narrow was stated by Gunnar Myrdal.[6] Regional differences in skill or education may be self-perpetuating because higher skilled and better educated individuals are the most likely to migrate out of depressed regions. If this education is paid for largely by those living in the depressed region, the exodus of the most skilled persons will further impoverish the region resulting in higher out-migration in the future. Myrdal presented this drain of skilled persons as an example of a vicious cycle.

Another explanation for the failure of urban–rural real wage differentials to narrow concentrates on employment differentials that can occur when labor markets fail to function perfectly. Union or government restrictions on hiring, restrictive land tenure laws, discrimination, and high wage policies of governments, private employers, or unions may be a cause of such failure. In early dualistic models it was assumed that there is no unemployment in the urban sector and no observed unemployment in the rural sector. Rural workers simply shared jobs and could be transferred to the urban sector without cost. Later models introduce urban unemployment. Potential migrants must look not only at the wage rate they would earn if employed but must also look at the probability they will be employed. In the Harris–Todaro model, the probability a potential migrant will be unemployed is assumed to be the proportion of the urban labor force that is currently unemployed.[7] This assumption allows equation (5.2) to be rewritten as

$$M = \beta(\delta w - s), \tag{5.3}$$

where $\delta = 1 - u$ and u is the urban unemployment rate. Hence, δ is the employment rate and δw is real expected urban wage income. There is assumed to be no rural unemployment.

The simple Harris–Todaro formulation in equation (5.3) has many implications for trade theory and public economics as well as for labor economics in developing countries. The model will reappear in the chapter on public economics. For the moment, consider the implications of equation (5.3) for regional wage differentials. If $\delta w - s > 0$, labor will flow into the urban area lowering δw. Note that it is not necessary that wage rates be flexible for δw to fall. The equilibrating mechanism might be a rise in unemployment. δw will continue to fall until $\delta w = s$. Hence, migration may not necessarily cause regional wage differentials to narrow.

Another notable feature of the model is that job creation may increase both the number of unemployed workers and the rate of unemployment. Suppose the labor market is initially in equilibrium in the sense that $\delta w = s$ with w and s fixed. The creation of urban jobs will initially increase δ resulting in more rural to urban migration in response to the increased probability of employment. Equilibrium is restored when $1/\delta$ rural workers move to the urban area for each job created. The unemployment rate in the urban market returns to its former level with a larger urban labor force and with more urban workers unemployed. However, the unemployment rate in the economy as a whole rises because the urban sector increases in relative importance in the economy.

The Harris–Todaro model suggests two ways of lowering unemployment rates. Urban jobs could be made less attractive or rural jobs could be made more attractive. For example, a fall in the urban wage rate would make urban jobs less attractive. A fall in w would reduce δw and workers would leave the urban area. Consequently, δ would rise (unemployment would fall) offsetting the fall in w. Similarly, a rise in traditional, rural income, s, would lead to an increase in δ as urban workers move to the rural area. If a decline in w is thought to be undesirable, policy could be directed at improving the traditional, rural economy as the best way of reducing urban unemployment. This implication of the Harris–Todaro model is supportive of the notion that development policy has unwisely neglected traditional sector, rural development.

The Harris–Todaro migration model, like the labor-flow model from which it is derived, views migration in a narrow context, where net migration occurs as a response to opportunities to earn higher income. The model is an aggregate model, where aggregate migration responds to regional variables. It does not directly address the question of why some persons move and others stay. The next model to be discussed does address the question of who moves. Migration is viewed as an investment decision. Investment involves returns over time. The reason for incorporating time into the migration decision is that the costs and benefits of a move occur at different times. Hence, there is no easy way of incorporating costs into equations (5.2) or (5.3). These costs might properly be thought of as including a period of job search in the urban area. Recent migrants may be much more likely to be unemployed than established residents. Hence, unemployment, and the resulting temporary loss in income, might be better viewed as an investment required to earn higher future income. The migrant might, then, be properly viewed as an investor in human capital and not simply as a supplier of labor.

The Human Capital View

In the human capital view of migration, migration is viewed as an investment decision like any other investment decision. Costs are incurred in anticipation of future gains. Central to the investment decision is the identification of the costs and returns from migration. Larry Sjaastad provides an influential methodology for identifying these costs and returns.[8] One question of concern to Sjaastad was how to account for regional amenities in the migration investment decision. Should enhanced regional amenities enter in the migration investment decision and counted as a gain from migration? Consider, for example, the Harris–Todaro equation. If urban lifestyles are attractive per se, then should equation (5.3) be rewritten as $M = \beta(\delta w - s + a)$, where a represents the psychic net return from urban amenities? High urban unemployment would then partly be the result of the attractiveness of urban living.

Sjaastad suggested a simple answer to the question of how to count urban amenities. These amenities are already reflected in the differences in rent on land. In other words, land in desirable locations costs more than in undesirable locations. Because differences in land costs are perhaps the major cause of differences in the costs of living, potential migrants are faced with paying for these regional amenities in the form of higher living costs. In the aggregate, the value of regional amenities may be largely canceled by increased living costs. Hence, aggregate migration can be explained by regional amenities only if the availability of regional amenities has not yet been reflected in land costs. Furthermore, differences in living costs might play little role in migration because they are offset by the value of regional amenities. Consequently, the analysis of investment in migration can concentrate on differences in expected income.

In the human capital view, persons or families look at the net present value of a move. Net present value, in a simple dualistic model, is given by

$$V = \sum_{t=1}^{n} (y_t - s)/(1 + r)^t - C, \qquad (5.4)$$

where t is time, $y_t = \delta_t w$ is urban income, r is the rate of time discount, and C is the cost of moving. For now note that in equation (5.4) the costs of moving are assumed to occur before the move. The wage rates are assumed to be constant. However, expected income is different for each year because the probability of unemployment is assumed to depend upon time. The concentration on unemployment probabilities is from Todaro.[9] Note that if δ_t is constant and if $C = 0$, then the model collapses to the labor-flow model in equation (5.3). For any time $\tau > 0$, if $\delta_t = 0$ for $t < \tau$ and $\delta_t = 1$ for $t \geq \tau$, then unemployment merely increases the cost of a move. The expected duration of the initial job search (i.e., τ) and not the average regional unemployment rate becomes the crucial unemployment variable.

The explicit treatment of migration as an investment decision provides a further explanation of why regional wage differentials may not narrow. The costs of a move must be covered by the discounted differences in income. The human capital model moves away from the aggregate labor-flow model to an emphasis on individual decisions. Persons or families with a positive net present value from migration move. Those with a negative net present value stay.

Empirical studies concentrate on determining which characteristics of individuals or families make them prone to migrate. These characteristics are introduced to the studies in terms of how they are thought to influence the costs or benefits of a move. Age, education, marital status, occupation, sex, employment status, income, and the number of children are all characteristics that have been included in studies of migration, because they are thought to systematically influence the costs or benefits of a move. Regional characteristics such as average employment rates and average income and the distribution of that income have been included in human capital models as affecting the expected costs or benefits of a move.

In terms of policy, one of the more important variables is education, which is thought to lead to more migration. Migrants are risk takers, as are any other investors, and education may both reduce risk and enhance the ability of a person to bear risk. Education will reduce risk to the extent that it represents general human capital enabling the person to adjust to a wider variety of occupations and lifestyles. Education makes it easier to bear risk because it represents higher life time wealth, enabling the person to bear a temporary loss in income.

Nonmonetary, psychic, costs and benefits may also be included in the model. Caution should be exercised, however, when dealing with these psychic costs. For example, some persons may be reluctant to leave friends, relatives, and the comfortable lifestyle of their birthplace. This reluctance is a *psychic cost*. Other persons may be eager to escape the restrictive lifestyle of their birthplace. This eagerness is called a *psychic benefit*. The persistence of regional wage differentials might be explained in terms of psychic costs, whereas the higher mobility of some subgroups of people may be explained in terms of psychic benefits. However, unless relative magnitudes of the costs and benefits can be independently assigned, the explanation is not testable.

The Regional Amenities View

The regional amenities view concentrates on migration as a decision to purchase regional amenities unavailable at the original location. These amenities include public goods such as education, roads, water supply, and sewage. They also include physical aspects of the region such as climate and private goods that are not available at other locations. The consumer pays for the availability of these amenities through taxes, to pay for public goods, and land rent. As consumers move to a region to purchase amenities, land rent rises and will continue to rise until households are in equilibrium. Hence, migration is seen as equilibrating both the labor market (as in the labor-flow view) and the land market, with the emphasis on the land market.

Regional wage differentials are still viewed as a key determinant in explaining migration. Wage differentials determine the quantity of market goods and services that a person can purchase. The greater the difference in real income, the greater is the quantity of market goods that can be purchased and the greater is the level of utility, ceteris paribus. Externalities in consumption, however, may create regional differences in the variety and kinds of market goods available. For example, the variety of movies shown in an area depends on the market size. In addition, locations differ in terms of the availability of nonmarket public goods and nonproduced regional amenities.

Much of the recent literature on migration in developed countries has focused on the migrant as a consumer of nonmarket regional amenities. One hypothesis that has received some attention is that, as a society becomes more prosperous, regional amenities will replace pecuniary motives in the migration process.[10] Regional amenities are assumed to be luxury goods, which are not purchased at low income. Expenditures on these goods rises as a proportion of income once income rises above some critical level. Because less developed countries are by definition low income countries, this hypothesis implies that regional amenities will not play an important role in the migration of people in less developed countries.

There is reason to believe that regional amenities do, however, play an important role in less developed countries. Urban areas offer a lifestyle that is often not available in rural areas. As a country develops and incomes rise, families can be expected to shift their consumption patterns. Recall in Chapter 4 that, as income rises, families generally choose to have fewer children and to increase expenditures per child. This was interpreted in terms of choosing a higher quality of children and lower quantity. Some of these expenditures on children involve health and educational amenities, which are more readily available in urban areas. Hence, as education and income rise, families will tend to migrate to areas that have lower costs of raising higher quality children.[11]

The Household Production Approach

Recall the distinction drawn in Chapter 4 between the fertility theories associated with Easterlin and Becker. These theories are respectively referred to as the *Pennsylvania School* and the *Chicago School*. In Pennsylvania School models, differences in tastes play a major role in explaining differences in fertility. In Chicago School models, the same behavior is explained in terms of differences in the production technology of the household. A similar difference exists in migration theory. In the regional amenities view, tastes play an important role. Tastes are thought to vary with the life cycle and with education. Educated persons are thought to have a taste for areas with better schooling, cultural surroundings, and more diversity in available lifestyles. In the Chicago view, emphasis would be placed on household production.[12]

The household production view of migration can be most sharply contrasted with the other three views by considering a nuclear family where the wife devotes all of her time to household production. Such a wife plays no basic role in the labor-flow, human capital, and regional amenities approaches other than that she adds to the costs of a move. For a wife working for wages, the income lost from quitting at the old location represents a cost of the move. Unless she works, her contribution to moving costs comes largely through influencing psychic costs. For example, no economic role is attached to differences in the level of education of wives unless their education is translated into actual earned income or into differences in the tastes of their family. In contrast, in the household production approach, the education of the wife specializing in home production can be given a concrete interpretation. Education enhances the ability of the wife to produce commodities. The value of the wife's household production at the old location is a cost of a move. The value of her home production at the new location is a benefit of a move.

Employment and the level of market earnings of the wife are usually thought to be negatively associated with moves of the family to a new labor market.[13] The reason for this negative relationship is that these earnings are assumed to be difficult to transfer. In many instances household production may also be difficult to transfer. For less developed countries, where wives seldom work for wages, household production is important in the migration decision. To a considerable extent, food is prepared, clothing is made and repaired, and both children and the elderly are cared for in the home. In addition, a large proportion of the goods consumed by the family is produced in the family's own garden or earned in the informal, traditional sector where renumerations are seldom reported. These activities may be costly to transfer. Upon moving, the household may need to plant a new garden, find new markets for goods produced by the household and sold on the market, and establish new relations for the care of dependent members of the family.

Consider the choice between living in an urban area with readily available urban amenities or in a rural area that allows for close contact with relatives and friends. In the urban area, the shadow prices of educational activities and recreational activities might be low, but the shadow price of contacts with friends or relatives could be high. If the family lives in the rural area, the family could produce commodities associated with urban amenities by occasionally making trips to the urban center for educational, recreational, and health services. However, the costs of these trips to the city would increase the costs of producing urban amenity commodities while living in the rural location. Living in an urban area might greatly reduce the costs of urban related commodities. However, commuting, phone calls, and letters would be required to produce contacts with friends and relatives thereby increasing the costs of such contacts. Hence, location will affect both the shadow prices of home produced commodities and the full income of the family.

Similar to the case with the regional amenities model, households will move to the region with the best combination of market income, market prices, and region specific factors, such as public goods, that affect household production. With development and increases in education and income, the bundle of commodities that households wish to produce and consume will change. In particular, as incomes rise it will become more important for families to use time more efficiently as they substitute goods for time in household production. To the extent that urban areas are relatively time saving, families will move to cities as income rises with development.[14]

EFFICIENCY WAGE MODELS

Efficiency wage models postulate a very simple deviation from perfect competition and explore the implications of this deviation. The productivity of workers is assumed to depend upon their wage rate. This hypothesis fits in nicely with the Harris–Todaro migration model because it explains why urban wage rates might be set above the market clearing level even when competition exists. In standard competitive models, the employer can choose how much of each factor to employ at a given vector of factor prices. Prices above the market level clearly would not be paid because they reduce profits. In efficiency wage models, the employer not only chooses the number of workers to hire but also has a meaningful choice concerning wage rates. The increased productivity resulting from higher wages may more than offset the additional costs.

Belaboring an obvious point about perfect competition will help explain how efficiency wage models work.[15] In competition there is no reason to pay a worker more than the market clearing wage rate because the employer wishes to minimize the cost per unit of labor. The market clearing wage rate is the minimum wage rate that the employer can charge. There is no reason to pay a worker ten dollars an hour if that worker or an equivalent worker (in terms of productivity per hour) can be hired for five dollars an hour. The wage rate, w, is simply the cost per unit of labor that the employer wishes to minimize.

Turning now to efficiency wages, consider a simple neoclassical production function of the form $Q = [\sigma(w)N, X]$ where N is labor, X is a vector of other inputs and $\sigma(w)$ augments the productivity of labor and is a positive function of the real wage rate. Hence, $L = \sigma N$. To illustrate the role of $\sigma(w)$, note that σN and not N is the labor input in the production function. The value of σN can be increased by increasing either N or σ. The cost per unit of efficiency labor (i.e., of σN) is not w but $w/\sigma(w)$. As in the standard competitive model, the firm will hire inputs at the minimum cost. The wage rate that minimizes $w/\sigma(w)$ is called the *efficiency wage rate*.

The efficiency wage rate is shown in Figure 5.1. The firm wishes to set w/σ as low as possible or, alternatively, to set σ/w as high as possible. Each value of σ/w is a different ray from the origin. The efficiency wage is found by rotating σ/w to its highest value as long as it satisfies the constraint that $\sigma = \sigma(w)$. Here, σ/w is maximized subject to $\sigma = \sigma(w)$ at the point of tangency between σ/w and $\sigma(w)$.

Having defined the efficiency wage, three reasons why productivity might depend upon the wage rate will be considered before addressing the implications of the model. Two of these reasons require little explanation. First,

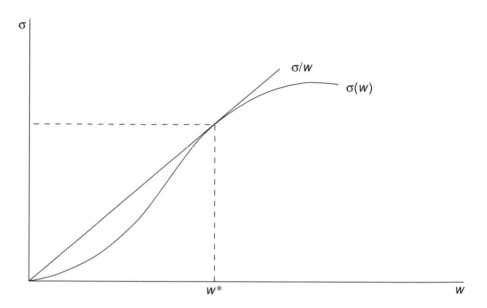

Figure 5.1 The efficiency wage rate.

higher wages might increase a person's physical ability to work. Higher wages, at very low income levels, will increase the ability of workers to purchase adequate food and medical services, increasing their physical productivity. Second, higher wages may be necessary to attract more productive workers. The third reason that higher wages might increase the effort of workers requires more explanation.

Employers must monitor a worker's activities if the employers are to know how well the worker is performing. A worker who is not performing satisfactorily might be disciplined in a number of ways. Ultimately, the worker can be fired. To monitor workers, the employer must incur expenses. For many jobs, the costs of constant monitoring might be extremely high. Hence, the employer might check on the worker's activities only occasionally. A worker who is not performing satisfactorily can be fired. The threat of being fired might not be enough to induce much effort if a worker can quickly obtain another job at the same wage rate. Hence, by paying wages above some prevailing wage rate, employers can assure that workers will have something to lose if they are fired. Paying higher wages will then increase the effort of workers and, hence, their productivity.

The simplest version of the efficiency wage model makes the simplifying assumption that the industry in question is small with respect to the rest of the economy. Hence, changes in employment or in the wage rate in the industry will not affect wage rates in the rest of the economy. Furthermore,

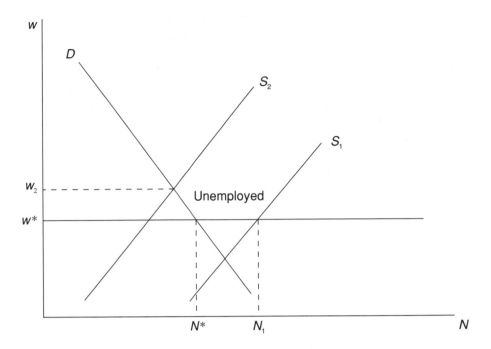

Figure 5.2   Unemployment and the efficiency wage.

suppose that each firm in the industry is identical, assuring that each firm has
the same efficiency wage rate.

It is important to note that a profit maximizing firm will not pay less than
the efficiency wage rate w^* because w^* is the wage rate that each firm would
choose, if it were free to do so. However, the equilibrium wage rate in the
industry could be above w^*. Let us turn our attention to Figure 5.2. S_1 and
S_2 are two different supply curves of labor in the industry and D is demand.
Note that D is not defined below w^* because no firm will pay a lower wage.
For S_2, demand intersects supply above w^* and w_2 is the market clearing
wage rate. All the standard neoclassical propositions for competitive firms
(under the usual assumptions) hold as long as demand intersects supply above
w^*. For example, an increase in the supply of labor if demand and supply
still intersect above w^*, will cause a fall in the wage rate.

We get quite different results if supply and demand do not intersect
above w^* as is the case for S_1. Firms can hire all the labor they want at the
efficiency wage rate and will hire N^* units of labor. Because the quantity
of labor supplied at w^* is N_1, the labor market cannot clear, and some form of
unemployment develops. Note that this unemployment is not the result of
unions or a legal floor on the wage rate. Employers are paying the profit maximizing wage rate and will not reduce that wage rate further. Furthermore,

the many standard propositions of neoclassical economics for competitive firms do not hold. For example, a rise in the supply of labor simply causes more unemployment and does not result in a decline in the wage rate. The reader can verify this claim by simply shifting S_1 to the right.

Nothing in the efficiency wage model requires that the economy be dualistic.[16] However, the model is often applied to dual economies within the context of a Harris–Todaro model. The existence of a fairly elastic supply of labor below the efficiency wage rate means that the market clearing wage rate would be below the efficiency wage. Hence, the efficiency wage model would be relevant.

The efficiency wage hypothesis may shed some light as to how dualism evolves and why it persists. Specifically, it would seem that the relationship between productivity and wages, $\sigma(w)$, is likely to be related to the complexity and size of the firm, the attitude of workers in general, and the stake that workers have in the success of the firm. In industries in which the optimal scale of operations is quite large, firms will find it very difficult to monitor the effort of workers due to the increased layers of bureaucracy needed to manage such a firm. As a result, wage rates among such large modern sector firms are likely to be well above wage rates for firms in the traditional sector, which tend to be much smaller. In addition, the difficulty of monitoring workers in larger firms is also likely to lead to the substitution of capital for labor.

The attitude of workers may also be extremely important. In smaller, traditional sector firms the workers may very well take pride in their work, whereas in larger firms this pride may be less likely. The latter is because in larger firms the degree of specialization may have reached such lengths that it is difficult for the worker to have a sense of pride. Therefore, the wage rate paid by larger firms would be higher than that for smaller firms to promote diligent work in the former.

Finally, in family enterprises, which characterize the traditional sector, it is likely that workers feel they have an important stake in the firm. This is because most of the workers in these types of enterprises are family members. As a result, wages will be lower and these firms are likely to use less capital per worker. Alternatively with larger firms, workers feel less commitment to the firm and therefore must be paid higher wages to reduce shirking. It follows that these firms will try to substitute capital for labor whenever possible.

In summary, the efficiency wage hypothesis sheds considerable light on the existence of dualism. Specifically, firms in the traditional sector are not necessarily technologically backward relative to firms in the modern sector. The differences in wage rates and in capital intensity are due to differences in worker behavior related to the size of the firm. Larger firms must pay higher wages to reduce shirking, whereas smaller firms can rely upon their small size and the dedication of their workers. In addition, larger firms will seek to substitute capital for their troublesome labor. Of course, this does not rule out the possibility that firms in the traditional sector are technologically backward, but there appears to be no a priori reason why that need be the case.

APPROPRIATE TECHNIQUE AND APPROPRIATE TECHNOLOGY

Compared with developed countries, less developed countries are labor abundant and capital scarce. Hence, labor costs should be relatively low and capital costs high. Because labor is abundant and is often believed to be underutilized, production ought to be geared toward using labor. There are three basic ways of using more labor, which are often classified under the heading of choosing the appropriate technology. The first choice concerns the appropriate technique. The appropriate technique refers to which capital–labor ratio should be chosen for a given production function. The second choice concerns the appropriate technology. The appropriate technology refers to which production function should be used when two or more production functions are available. The third choice refers to the appropriate product mix and concerns which goods should be produced. The appropriate technique and the appropriate technology will be discussed in the remainder of this chapter. The appropriate product mix is largely a question of comparative advantage, which will be discussed in Chapter 7 on trade.

The Appropriate Technique

The question of the appropriate technique concerns which capital–labor ratio should be chosen from among a number of options available for a given production function. Consider the production function $Q = F(K, L)$ illustrated in Figure 5.3. The isoquants (Q_0, Q_1, and Q_2) are drawn to illustrate that in some sense it is possible to choose any capital–labor combination along each isoquant. Although there may be a limited number of known production techniques from which to choose, this possibility, which will be mentioned shortly, does not appreciably change the discussion of the appropriate technique.

The production technique can be identified with the capital–labor ratio. Consider three such capital–labor ratios $(K/L)_0$, $(K/L)_1$, and $(K/L)_2$, which are shown as rays from the origin. Suppose that the capital and labor available for use in production are K_0 and L_0. If all the capital and labor were used, output would be Q_0 and the capital–labor ratio would be $(K/L)_0$. In

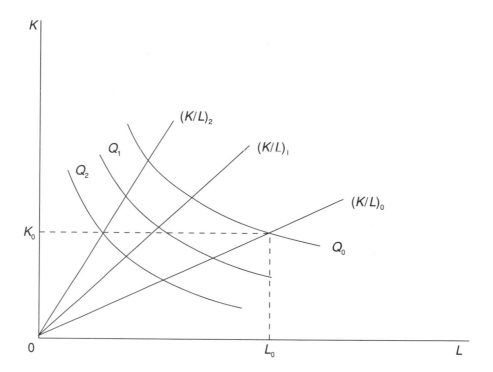

Figure 5.3   Choice of a capital–labor ratio.

other words, if $(K/L)_0$ were chosen, labor and capital could be fully employed and output would be at its maximum level of Q_0. $(K/L)_0$ is the
appropriate technique because it maximizes production, given the production function and given factor endowments of K_0 and L_0. If the technique
$(K/L)_2$ were chosen, there would be unemployed labor and output would
only be $Q_2 < Q_0$.

Consider the following question: Why would profit maximizing firms
choose capital–labor ratio $(K/L)_2$ if $(K/L)_0$ is available? In discussing the
numerous answers to this question, recall that a profit maximizing firm will
produce at the point where the isoquant is tangent to the firm's expenditure
constraint (i.e., where the marginal rate of technical substitution equals the
slope of the expenditure constraint). The slope of the expenditure constraint
is w/r, where w is the real wage rate and r is the cost of capital services. As
we move along an isoquant substituting capital for labor, the slope of that
isoquant rises. Hence, as w/r rises, the profit maximizing capital–labor ratio
will also rise. Thus, high capital–labor ratios are associated with high costs
of labor relative to capital.

Returning to Figure 5.3, the capital–labor ratio $(K/L)_2$ would be chosen
over $(K/L)_0$ for a sufficiently higher (actual or expected) w/r. Recall that the

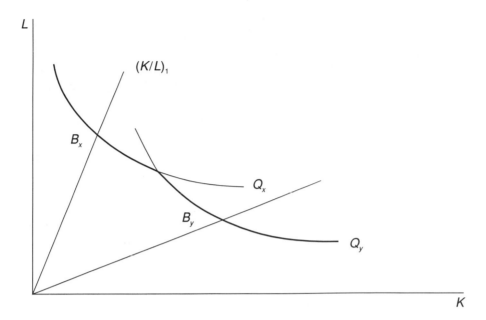

Figure 5.4 The choice of appropriate technique.

result of choosing $(K/L)_2$ is lower real output and unused labor. This output loss results from a factor–price distortion, where either r is too low or w is too high. For example, r might be too low because interest rates are kept artificially low while credit is rationed. Firms with access to inexpensive credit would thereby find an incentive to use too much capital and too little labor. Or, w might be too high because of government high wage policies, strong labor unions, or the desire of foreign corporations to purchase peaceful labor relations. Note that the high wage rate cannot be due to firms paying an efficiency wage rate above the market clearing rate because the isoquants in Figure 5.3 are independent of the wage rate. Consequently, the unemployment, due to a high wage rate, leads to lower output because the higher wage rate does not increase the productivity of labor.

A notable feature of the discussion, thus far, of the appropriate technique is that it is static. Furthermore, it has been implicitly assumed that both capital and labor are homogeneous and can be costlessly shifted from production using one technique to production with any other technique. In considering the appropriate technology, the assumption that capital can be costlessly shifted between production technologies is dropped. It is still possible, however, to frame the question of the appropriate technology in the static framework used for analyzing the appropriate technique.

Consider Figure 5.4, where two different isoquants are shown, Q_x and Q_y, from two different production functions, $x(K, L)$ and $y(K, L)$. Suppose we have carefully selected the isoquants to be of the same output level so that $Q_x = Q_y = Q$. If we use technique $(K/L)_1$, the production function $x(K, L)$ is the appropriate technology. Output Q could be produced at point B_x using less capital and more labor than at B_y. Similarly, for technique $(K/L)_2$, $y(K, L)$ is the appropriate technology because Q could be produced more cheaply at B_y. Note that ex ante we can choose the technology to suite the appropriate technique. Hence, ex ante, the two technologies can be combined by finding the envelope of the isoquants, for the same level of output, as is shown by the dark portions of Q_y and Q_x. Then, ex ante, the question of the appropriate technique and the appropriate technology become the same. However, ex post, once the capital has been constructed, capital may not be easily shifted between technologies and the choice of technology must be analyzed differently. Capital might be capable of shifting only from one technology to another as it depreciates and is slowly replaced with a different type of capital. It is to this dynamic problem that we will now turn.

The Appropriate Technology

In the choice of the appropriate technology, capital is not treated as homogeneous but as consisting of a collection of machines, tools, and buildings. Once a machine has been constructed, it cannot readily be transformed into another type of machine. The choice of technology to a great extent involves the choice of which machine to use in producing a given good. A different technology can be adopted only slowly as old machines wear out or are sold and new machines are constructed or purchased. The choice of the appropriate technology is framed in this inherently dynamic framework.

Depreciation or maintenance costs of capital play an important role in analyzing the appropriate technology. The only role that these costs play in the static framework is in determining the cost of capital services and hence in determining the rate of profits on each production technique or each type of technology. The adoption of a more profitable (net of depreciation) technology can dramatically change the real costs of depreciation of old machines, machines using the old technology. The net result can be a sudden spurt of growth or a decline in real, full capacity output for the economy as a whole.

The problem of choosing the appropriate technology is illustrated in Figure 5.5. The economy is initially growing at a rate of g_0, which depends upon the savings rate, the capital–output ratio, and the depreciation rate. At time t a new technology is introduced with a different capital–output ratio. This technology can be introduced only by purchasing or constructing new machines. The old machines will eventually be replaced by new machines as the old machines depreciate. The economy will eventually reach some

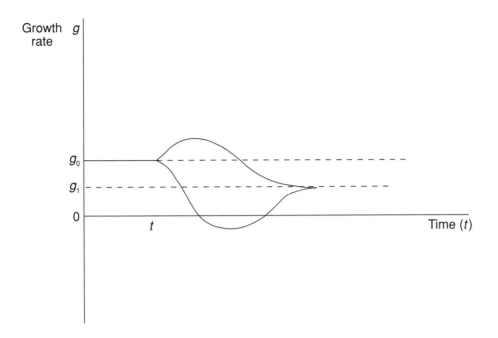

Figure 5.5   Growth and technology.

new rate of growth, g_1, which depends upon the new capital–output ratio and the new savings rate. The latter may differ from the old one because savings rates may depend on both the profit and growth rate and upon the new depreciation rate. In Figure 5.5, g_1 is less than g_0 but g_1 could just as well exceed g_0.

In Figure 5.5, two paths of output growth are shown. On one path, the economic growth rate rises. This increase, however, is only temporary. As the old machines are replaced, the growth rate declines until the economy eventually grows at a slower rate than would have grown if the new technology were not introduced. Hence, the adoption of the new technology might appear to be good for the economy because short-term economic growth has been increased even though these short-term gains will be more than offset by long-term losses. On the other path output actually falls and the economy, even though it eventually grows, never reaches the old, g_0, growth rate. Looking at Figure 5.5 might help explain why a country that appears to have adopted the wrong technology might initially experience rapid growth. This growth, however, comes at the cost of lower future growth.

Before showing how growth paths such as those illustrated in Figure 5.5 might occur, it will help to place the problem in a historical setting. There was considerable fear in the early 19th century that machines would make

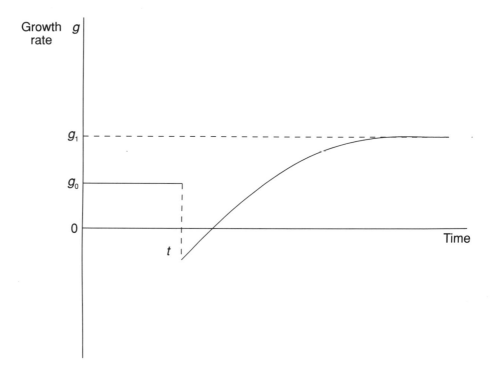

Figure 5.6 The Ricardian case.

workers unnecessary and would thereby replace workers by depriving them of the opportunity to earn a living. These concerns are perhaps best represented by movements such as the Luddites, who sabotaged machines because they felt that the machine was the source of deprivation. Classical economists such as Ricardo argued that mechanization was good both for workers and for society as a whole. Ricardo then shocked his followers by changing his mind. Ricardo showed that the introduction of new machines, although more profitable than the old machines, could reduce both real output and employment. However, he argued that these effects were only temporary and that output would necessarily recover and be higher than it would have been with the old machines.

Ricardo's case is illustrated in Figure 5.6 by the lower growth path. Note that a discontinuous jump in the growth path occurs at time t. This jump is due to the assumption that, once the more profitable machines become available, no old machines are purchased. Old machines are still used, but they are eventually replaced through depreciation. Output falls and continues to fall for some time as the growth rate becomes negative. In this example, $g_1 > g_0$ so the introduction of new machines eventually increases output.

For Ricardo's model, real output for the economy as a whole will decline, upon the introduction of a new, more profitable type of machine, if

$$g_0 < \delta(\Delta\alpha)/\alpha \tag{5.5}$$

where δ is the physical depreciation rate of the old machines and $\Delta\alpha$ is the increase in the capital–output ratio associated with the new machines. Obviously, if equation (5.5) holds, output can decline only if the capital–output ratio rises, $\Delta\alpha > 0$. The proof of inequality (5.5) is fairly simple but involves some tedious algebra.[17] It will not be repeated here. If inequality (5.5) is reversed, output will initially rise above both g_0 and g_1. A slightly more complicated expression will hold when savings also depend on wage income.

To see how output might fall, we need to first look at the relationship between capital and production. Remember that we are dealing with a fixed-coefficient (Leontief) production function. A Leontief production function takes the form

$$X = \min\{K/\alpha,\ L/\beta\} \tag{5.6}$$

where K is capital, L is labor, and the coefficients β and α are constants. Assuming a labor surplus economy (as did Ricardo), L does not constrain output. Assuming profit maximization, $K/\alpha = L/\beta$. Output is then

$$X = K/\alpha \tag{5.7}$$

and the demand for labor is

$$L = (\beta/\alpha)K. \tag{5.8}$$

Note that α/β is the capital–labor ratio and that α is the capital–output ratio.

Equation (5.6) implicitly assumes that there is only one type of capital in existence. Let M represent the number of these machines and p represent their cost in terms of real output. Here, p is assumed to be constant. In Ricardo, p is constant because capital is produced using only labor as an input at a constant real wage rate. Alternatively, p might simply be assumed to be purchased at a constant price for a small open economy. Capital is measured in terms of its real cost. Hence, $K = pM$. Equations (5.7) and (5.8) can be rewritten as

$$X = aM, \text{ where } a = p/\alpha, \tag{5.7'}$$

and

$$L = bM, \text{ where } b = p\beta/\alpha. \tag{5.8'}$$

From looking at equations (5.7') and (5.8'), it is clear that the capital–output ratio, α, can be written as $\alpha = p/a$ and that the capital–labor ratio, α/β, is p/b.

The choice of an appropriate technology involves the question of whether an economy should slowly replace an old technology as the machines depreciate and start constructing new machines described by different technical coefficients. Let p', a', and b' be coefficients for the new technology with $a' \geq a$, $p' > p$, $b' < b$, and $p'/a' > p/a$. Note that, although the capital–output ratio rises ($p'/a' > p/a$), the labor required to produce a unit of output ($\beta = b/a$) falls, implying that the new technology can be more profitable. Because these machines are more profitable, profit maximizing firms will cease buying old machines, allowing them to depreciate with time.

We now return to why the adoption of the more profitable technology might cause real output to decline. The real depreciation costs of old machines will rise once the new machines are introduced. The real costs of depreciation is the cost of maintaining output at its current level. When only the old machines are in use, depreciation is δM. If these machines are not replaced, output would fall by $a(\delta M)$. The real cost of depreciation is δMp, which is the amount that is sufficient to purchase the δM old machines required to produce $a\delta M$ units of output. However, new machines cost more. Hence, δMp is enough to purchase only $\delta Mp/p'$ new machines, which would produce $a'\delta Mp/p'$ units of output. However, $a'\delta Mp/p' < a\delta M$. To verify this inequality, note that it can be simplified as $p'/a' > p/a$, or that the capital–output ratio has risen. Hence, the savings required to offset depreciation would rise with the introduction of the new technology. If inequality (5.5) holds, output will decline. Hence, in a dynamic model, profit maximization may lead to a seemingly superior technology being introduced that will not only hurt workers but result in an actual decline in real output. This result was, of course, the essence of Ricardo's claim on machinery.

Ricardo held that $g_1 > g_0$ because savings are assumed to be profits in excess of capitalist consumption. It is natural to suppose savings to be positively related to the rate of profits. Let r be the marginal propensity to save out of income when the old machines are exclusively in use. Let r' be the propensity to save when the new machines are introduced. If savings are positively related to the profit rate, then $r' > r$. From the Harrod–Domar model in Chapter 1, $g_0 = [(r - \delta)/(p/a)]$ and $g_1 = [(r' - \delta')/(p'/a')]$. The rise in savings, $r' - r$, will have to be sufficiently large to offset the rise in the capital–output rate, $p'/a' - p/a$, if g_1 is to be larger than g_0. For example, $g_1 > g_0$ for $\delta = \delta'$, if $r'/r > (p'/a')/(p/a)$. Obviously, this condition might not hold, and output growth could be lower in the long run. A particularly troublesome implication for LDCs is that the adoption of a too capital-intensive technology will seem desirable when it is introduced but will slow the long-run growth of the economy. This possibility was illustrated in the upper growth path shown in Figure 5.5.

EDUCATION

Education influences many aspects of the labor market. The availability of skilled labor and not just the number of workers may be the most important factor behind the type of production methods chosen and the type of goods that are produced. Education may also influence the adaptability of workers and their ability to adjust to new production methods. Another aspect of education is that it may influence a worker's efficiency. Workers with more education may be more productive. In terms of the notion of the efficiency wage, σ may be a function of w because a higher wage rate will attract more productive workers where workers are more productive because they are better educated. Through its impact on the labor market, education may be an important determinant of development. The postwar German economic miracle is a possible example of the importance of education. In this section, education, productivity, and development will be discussed. We will con-centrate on incorporating education into a theory of development and on whether the government should subsidize education.

Differences in individual earnings by educational levels may be a result of underlying effects of education on productivity. If more education increases workers' marginal product, a higher wage rate will be the result of this higher productivity. For illustration, let $\sigma(s)$ be the relative productiveness or efficiency of a worker, where s represents years of completed schooling. In hiring a worker, the employer is concerned not with the number of workers hired, N, but with the number of workers weighted by their pro-ductivity, $L = \sigma(s)N$, where L is an efficiency unit of labor. In perfect competition, the employer will hire efficiency units of labor up to the point where their marginal product equals their real wage rate. More formally, let $Q = f(K, L)$ be real output and w the fixed real wage rate per efficiency unit of labor. In other words,

$$w = \partial Q/\partial L. \tag{5.9}$$

To see how much a worker of a given efficiency, σ, will earn, note that the marginal product of N is

$$\partial Q/\partial N = (\partial Q/\partial L)\sigma.$$

Hence, the marginal product of L is

$$\partial Q/\partial L = (\partial Q/\partial N)/\sigma. \qquad (5.10)$$

Combining (5.9) and (5.10) yields

$$w = (\partial Q/\partial N)/\sigma \text{ or } w\sigma = \partial Q/\partial N. \qquad (5.11)$$

Equation (5.11) provides an explanation of differences in real wage rates. Here, $w\sigma$ is the real wage rate for a worker of productivity σ. Hence, workers who are more productive are paid accordingly, receiving the marginal product of their efforts. Education, which increases σ, is rewarded through higher wages. Individual workers with more education produce and earn more, and societies with higher average levels of education also produce and earn more.

It is widely recognized that not all of the differences in wage rates by educational attainment can be attributed to the production enhancing effects of education. In the labor economics of developed countries, the terms *credentialism* and *segmented labor markets* are often used to describe reasons, other than its impact on productivity, why a person's education and wage rate are positively correlated. The basic idea behind these views is that for various reasons labor markets fail to clear and job rationing occurs. Job rationing means that noneconomic criteria are used to select persons to hire from a pool of applicants. Those applicants with higher degrees may be employed even though their additional years of schooling do not help them to better fulfill the requirements of the job. Education and wage rates would be positively correlated even though education does not enhance productivity.

The efficiency wage hypothesis provides an interesting example where a positive correlation between education and productivity does not imply that education increases productivity. Recall that in the efficiency wage hypothesis, wage rates will in part be determined by the costs of monitoring workers' effort and performance. Consider two types of jobs, high responsibility jobs and low responsibility jobs. The performance of workers in high responsibility jobs is costly to monitor. Hence, such workers are paid more to encourage effort. For a homogeneous labor force, the workers chosen to fill these high responsibility positions will have to be selected using some noneconomic criteria. Male workers or workers of the same race, caste, or religion of the owners might be given preference over other workers. Furthermore, these chosen workers would be more productive and receive higher wages than other workers even though the labor force is homogeneous. If education is one such noneconomic criterion, then education will appear to increase worker productivity even though it is merely a screening device for preferred jobs.

For the most part, however, education is thought to increase earnings, not because education is a screening device, but because it makes workers more productive. Thus, not only will the relative education of a worker increase his or her earnings, but higher average levels of education in an economy will increase average productivity and, hence, earnings. Partly for this reason, the provision of more education has been the goal of many countries seeking economic development. Investment in human capital is seen as being as important or more important in explaining relative levels of per capita income than investment in physical capital.

The impact of education on productivity is crucial in the neoclassical tradition. Recall from the discussion of the new growth theory that, without externalities in some type of investment, growth rates and factor returns will converge. One type of investment that could generate these externalities is investment in human capital, education. To see the role of education in explaining differences in factor returns consider the Cobb–Douglas production function

$$Q = BK^{\alpha}L^{1-\alpha} \tag{5.12}$$

where $L = \sigma(s)N$ is the number of efficiency units of labor, K is total capital, Q is the total output, and B and α describe the technology. B may depend on many factors including education. There may be production externalities for both education and capital. Workers with more education may, through example, increase the productivity of workers with less education. This externality has been assigned an important role in explaining real wage rates, real rates of return to capital, and in justifying public support for education.

The importance of externalities of education can be seen by looking at the marginal product of schooling. Let r be the rate of return to physical capital. If investment in human capital is similar to investment in physical capital, investment will proceed up to the point where the rates of return are equalized. The marginal product of schooling for an individual (MPSI) is

$$\text{MPSI} = [(1 - \alpha)BK^{\alpha}L^{-\alpha}]\sigma'(s)N. \tag{5.13}$$

Multiplying by L/L and substituting equation (5.12) yields

$$\text{MPSI} = (1 - \alpha)Q\sigma'/\sigma. \tag{5.14}$$

The marginal product for society, however, is

$$\partial Q/\partial s = B(\partial B/\partial s)K^\alpha L^{1-\alpha} + \text{MPSI}, \qquad (5.15)$$

or, for $B = A[\sigma(s)]^\gamma$, $\gamma > 0$,

$$\partial Q/\partial s = [\gamma A + (1 - \alpha)]Q\sigma'/\sigma, \qquad (5.15')$$

where A is equal to a constant. Because $\gamma > 0$, $\partial Q/\partial s > \text{MPSI}$, and there will be too little investment in education. Hence, education should be subsidized.

Recall from the labor-flow model of migration that migration or capital mobility will equalize wage rates and profit rates between sectors, regions, or nations if resources are mobile. There will, of course, be some immobility of resources between sectors but the two rates of return should be related. A high rate of return to capital should correspond to a high rate of return to education. This simple observation causes considerable difficulty for the neoclassical model. LDCs have less capital per worker and a less educated labor force than do industrialized countries. Consequently, the rates of return to capital and education should therefore be much higher in LDCs. These high rates of return should both generate high domestic savings rates and attract foreign investment. That these rates of return are not substantially higher in LDCs has been explained as being due to positive externalities of education by Lucas.[18]

An example will help clarify the role of externalities in explaining profit rates. First, substituting for L and B in equation (5.12) and simplifying yields

$$Q = A\sigma^\gamma K^\alpha L^{1-\alpha} = A\sigma^\gamma K^\alpha (N\sigma)^{1-\alpha} = A\sigma^{1+\gamma-\alpha}K^\alpha N^{1-\alpha}. \qquad (5.16)$$

Output per worker is then

$$q = Q/N = A\sigma^{1+\gamma-\alpha}k^\alpha, \qquad (5.17)$$

where $k = K/N$. The rate of return on capital can be found by differentiating (5.17) with respect to k. This yields

$$r = \alpha q/k. \qquad (5.18)$$

Let $\alpha = 0.4$, $A = 20$, and $\gamma = 0.4$. The coefficients are meant to be only illustrative but values for α and γ are similar to those suggested by Lucas. Note that $1 - \alpha + \gamma = 1$ in this example so that equations (5.17) becomes

$$q = 200\sigma k^{0.4}. \qquad (5.17')$$

Equation (5.18) is

$$r = 0.4q/k. \qquad (5.18')$$

First consider the return to capital in an industrialized country with an educated labor force where $k = 100,000$ and $\sigma = 10$. Substituting into (5.17') yields per worker output, $q = 20,000$ and a real rate of return to capital of $r = 0.08$ or 8 percent. Now consider a poorer, less developed country with $q = 500$. In other words, per worker income is about 40 times higher in the rich country than in the poor country. Per capita income would also be about 40 times higher in the rich country, depending upon the proportion of each population that is in the labor force.

This income difference might be the result of differences in technology, capital per worker, or education. We will see that, without externalities to education, any explanation might imply unrealistically large profit rate differentials or unrealistically small wage rate differentials. In concentrating on education, we will assume that there are no differences in technology. In the model considered, no externalities are associated with capital. To focus on education externalities, we will first assume that the labor force is homogeneous, so that all the differences in per capita output are explained by capital. Then we will focus on education. Finally, we will consider the importance of education externalities versus private returns to education.

To focus on capital, suppose labor in the two countries is homogeneous so that $\sigma = 10$ in the LDC. From equation (5.17'), the capital per worker required to produce $q = 500$ is

$$k^{0.4} = (500/200)$$

or

$$k = (2.5)^{2.5} = 9.88.$$

From equation (5.18'), the rate of profits is

$$r = 0.4(500)/9.88 = 20.24.$$

Now a profit rate of 20.24 (2,024%) would clearly be noticed and would quickly attract both foreign capital and domestic savings. Consequently, differences in capital per worker cannot explain the differences in income that exist. Any explanation has to include differences in education.

Differences in education coupled with differences in capital per worker can provide a reasonable difference in profit rates. We will first specify a profit rate for the LDC that seems reasonable. Then we will solve (5.18′) for k given r. Then we will find the value of σ in (5.17′) for the LDC. Suppose for the LDC that $r = .16$, twice the value for the DC. Capital per worker is given by equation (5.18′) as

$$0.16 = .4(500/k)$$

or

$$k = .4(500/.16) = 1,250.$$

Substituting into equation (5.17′) yields

$$500 = 20\sigma(1,250)^{.4}$$

or

$$\sigma = 1.44.$$

In other words, labor is $10/1.44 = 6.94$ times more productive in the industrialized country than in the LDC. The higher per capita income of the industrialized country has three sources. These sources are higher capital per worker, more efficient workers, and the more productive economy caused by education externalities. The production function in the industrialized country has a technology coefficient of $B = 20(10)^{.4} = 50.2$ versus $B = 20(1.44)^{.4} = 23.1$ for the LDC.

The positive production externalities of education play an important role in the neoclassical model. Otherwise, the competitive wage rates of skilled workers implied by the model would be unrealistically high. For an average worker, the real wage rate is $y = w\sigma = \partial Q/\partial N = (1 - \alpha)q$. In the industrialized country, the average worker earns $(0.6)20,000 = 12,000$. This implies $w = 1,200$. In the LDC, the average worker earns 300 implying $w = 208.33$. Hence, a worker with the same skill level, σ, will earn $1,200/208.33 = 5.76$ times as much in the industrialized country than in the LDC due to having more capital to work with coupled with the external effects of having more productive coworkers. If all the effects of education are internalized, the skilled worker would earn much more in the LDC.

To get some feeling for the importance of these externalities, assume all the affects of education are internalized (consider the preceding example with the difference that $\gamma = 0$). Differences in output not explained by differences in capital per worker would be the result of differences in σ, which must be larger than in the previous example. For the industrialized country,

$$20,000 = 20\sigma^{.6}(100,000)^{.4}$$

or

$$\sigma = 46.42.$$

For the LDC,

$$500 = 20\sigma^{.6}(1,250)^{.4}$$

or

$$\sigma = 1.84.$$

Here, $w = 258.5$ in the industrialized country and $w = 163.04$ in the LDC. Hence, a worker of the same skill level would earn only 1.59 times as much in the richer country, or conversely, would earn 63 percent less in the LDC. This implied wage rate in the LDC is much too high.

To see that this wage rate is too high, suppose each unit of output and, hence, of capital is worth $2.50. Then average wage income in the industrialized country is $30,000 per worker and average total income per worker is $2.5(20,000) = $50,000. If the labor force is 40 percent of the total population, average per capita income is $42,000, which is about the U.S. average. The model implied that, for example, an Indian worker with the average level of education of a U.S. worker (slightly more than a high school diploma) would earn 63 percent of the $30,000 that a U.S. worker earns. The Indian worker would then receive $18,900. Surely the model cannot be correct. An explanation of income differences cannot be based on differences in the efficiency of individuals any more than it can be based on differences in capital per worker. Hence, those emphasizing human capital and development, such as T. W. Schultz, have looked at external and other effects of education.

Education, in T. W. Schultz's view, can act both to create disequilibrium in a society and to enhance adjustment to disequilibrium.[19] Education creates disequilibrium by creating economies of scale. Economies of scale mean that output can be increased more rapidly than inputs by some reorganization of production. Returns to scale will eventually be competed away as entrepreneurs, by shifting resources into the increasing returns industry, expand production until the increasing returns are eliminated. Education also enhances the speed of adjustment in Schultz's view and has a doubly beneficial effect on growth.

In terms of the fragmented economies of less developed countries, education will tend to improve labor productivity within an island of economic activity. Expanded production will increase the degree of specialization and induce trade with other economic islands. Here, again, education plays a role in increasing the speed of this extension of trade. As some sectors expand more rapidly than others, education will again play a role as education enhances the adjustment to this uneven expansion. Hence, education may play a much wider role in economic development than merely enhancing the skills of workers. As we have seen from our numerical exercise, this role does not need to be enormously extensive to explain why inputs in less developed countries receive so little. In the example, with $\gamma = 0.4$, the implications seemed fairly reasonable. Hence, these externalities in education do and will continue to play an important role in neoclassical views of development. Education has not received similar attention in other views.

CONCLUSION

This chapter dealt with five issues with respect to labor in less developed countries. First, it was argued that in such countries open unemployment may be significant, but an even more important problem is the existence of low productivity, low income jobs. This problem is generally labeled *disguised unemployment*. In this context workers cannot afford to be unemployed, thus they seek employment in the traditional sector. This latter sector is often discriminated against through a variety of government policies.

The disguised unemployment problem is exacerbated by the rapid extent to which labor has migrated from rural to urban areas. The reasons for this migration were explored by examining the four major theories developed to explain the migration process. These theories differ rather dramatically in their emphasis. However, they all revolve around examining those factors that attract people to urban areas or increase the probability that an individual will choose to migrate. It was found that the amenities available to individuals in urban areas as well as higher wages may lead people to migrate. However, it is obvious that in all of these theories government policies can significantly influence the relative benefits and costs of moving. In addition, an urban bias does seem to have characterized government policy making. Much of this bias has resulted in subsidizing the modern sector at the expense of the rural sector, thus promoting a very rapid urbanization process.

The unemployment and underemployment resulting from such urbanization is intensified by other factors pertaining to labor markets in less developed countries. Specifically, if the efficiency wage hypothesis is correct, then unemployment would rise as the supply of labor increases, even if labor markets in the modern sector are perfectly competitive, as illustrated in Figure 5.2. In addition, the low productivity of jobs in the informal sector may, to some extent, be the result of low wages (not the cost), with the latter being caused by discrimination against this sector in public policy.

Penultimately, wage and capital rental rate distortions may have caused inappropriate techniques of production to be utilized in the modern sector. Therefore the growth that does occur there results in very slow growth in employment opportunities. From a dynamic perspective, high capital to output ratios associated with modern technologies may have reduced output in some cases. A more insidious possibility is that the growth rate of output will initially rise, only to fall to a lower rate in the long run. Policy makers who survive based on the short run may be delighted to see the adoption of such a technology and even encourage its adoption.

Finally, education plays an important role in the development process. The returns to education must be partly external if we are to make sense out of what we know about differences in per capita income, profit rates, and wage rates. Because there is reason to believe that substantial external benefits to education exist, education should be encouraged and subsidized. These subsidies should be directed toward the type of education most likely to yield external benefits. It is not clear whether these external benefits are more pervasive for primary, secondary, or higher education. Some hard evidence on where these externalities are to be found seems important for developing a rational education policy.

NOTES

1. Arthur Lewis, "Economic Development with Unlimited Supplies of Labour," *The Manchester School* (May 1954): 139–191.
2. Amartya Sen, *Employment, Technology and Development* (Oxford: Clarendon Press, 1975).
3. A necessary condition for any notion of disguised unemployment for homogeneous labor would seem to be that the person would accept a job at a higher wage rate if it were available.
4. For a survey of these views see G. M. Shields and M. P. Shields, "The Emergence of Migration Theory and a Suggested New Direction," *Journal of Economic Surveys* 3 (1989): 277–304.
5. See Gian S. Sahota, "An Economic Analysis of Internal Migration in Brazil," *Journal of Political Economy* 76 (March–April 1968): 218–245; and Richard J. Cebula, *The Determinants of Human Migration* (Lexington, Mass.: D. C. Heath and Company, 1979).
6. Gunnar Myrdal, *Rich Land and Poor* (New York: Harper and Row, 1957).
7. John R. Harris and Michael P. Todaro, "Migration, Unemployment and Development: A Two-Sector Analysis," *American Economic Review* 60 (March 1970): 126–142.
8. Larry A. Sjaastad, "The Costs and Returns of Human Migration," *Journal of Political Economy*, Supplement 70 (October 1962): 80–93.
9. Todaro, "A Model of Labor Migration and Urban Unemployment in Less Developed Countries," *American Economic Review* (March 1969): 138–148.

10. See R. P. Shaw, *Migration Theory and Fact: A Review and Bibliography of Current Literature* (Philadelphia: Regional Science Research Institute); P. E. Graves and P. D. Linneman, "Household Migration: Theoretical and Empirical Results," *Journal of Urban Economics* 6 (1979): 383–404; and Michael J. Greenwood and Gary L. Hunt, "Jobs versus Amenities in the Analysis of Metropolitan Migration," *Journal of Urban Economics* 25 (1989): 1–16.

11. See T. P. Schultz, "Heterogeneous Preferences and Migration Self-Selection, Regional Prices and Programs, and the Behavior of Migrants in Colombia," in *Research in Population Economics*, ed. T. P. Schultz, vol. 6, pp. 163–181 (Greenwich, Conn.: JAI Press).

12. See G. M. Shields and M. P. Shields, "Family Migration and Nonmarket Activities in Costa Rica," *Economic Development and Cultural Change* (October 1989): 73–88.

13. See Jacob Mincer, "Family Migration Decisions," *Journal of Political Economy* (October 1978): 749–773.

14. See M. P. Shields, "Time, Hedonic Migration and Household Production," *Journal of Regional Science* (February 1995): 117–134.

15. For a discussion of efficiency wage models and some of their applications, see Joseph E. Stiglitz, "Alternative Theories of Wage Determination and Unemployment: The Efficiency Wage Model," in *The Theory and Experience of Economic Development: Essays in Honor of Sir W. Arthur Lewis*, ed. M. Gersovita, C. F. Diaz-Alejandro, G. Ranis, and M. R. Rosenzweig, pp. 78–106 (Boston: G. Allen and Unwin Press, 1982).

16. Kaushik Basu, *The Less Developed Economy: A Critique of Contemporary Theory* (Oxford: Basil Blackwell, 1984); Hadi S. Esfahani and Djavad Salehi-Isfahani, "Effort Observability and Worker Productivity: Towards an Explanation of Economic Dualism," *Economic Journal* 99 (September 1989): 818–836.

17. M. P. Shields, "The Machinery Question: Can Technological Improvements Reduce Real Output?" *Economica* (May 1989): 215–224.

18. See Robert E. Lucas, Jr., "Why Doesn't Capital Flow from Rich to Poor Countries?" *American Economic Review* (May 1990): 92–96.

19. T. W. Shultz, "On Investing in Specialized Human Capital to Attain Increasing Returns," in *The State of Development Economics*, ed. G. Ranis and T. P. Schultz, pp. 339–352 (Oxford: Basil Blackwell, 1988).

6

Public Economics

Under conditions of perfect competition, private and social profitability are identical. That is, investments that are privately profitable are also profitable from society's point of view. However, in the real world and, in particular, in developing nations, the conditions for perfect competition are not met. This can be due to externalities, the existence of public goods, and other sorts of market imperfections. Under these conditions private and social profitability are no longer synonymous, implying that one cannot assume that private allocation of resources will be socially optimal. This creates the possibility that the state can utilize policy to improve upon the allocation of resources.

For the state to achieve a socially optimal allocation of resources, it must have a mechanism for evaluating various alternative allocations. Projects found to be socially optimal will then have to be financed so that the state must also be concerned with how to raise revenue without distorting the allocation of resources in an inefficient manner. Therefore, two main topics of this chapter will concern mechanisms for determining appropriate projects for government spending and taxation policies. However, it must be pointed out that, throughout the analysis, the state will be assumed to be benevolent in nature. That is, the state is interested in promoting the welfare of its citizens. Although this is a highly debatable assumption, which will be addressed in detail in Chapter 8, a benevolent state is assumed because public economics concerns how a benevolent state should behave.

The chapter unfolds as follows. First, the notions of consumer surplus and welfare economics will be introduced. Next, shadow prices and their role in evaluating appropriate government decisions are discussed, along with examples of particular concern to developing countries. Finally, revenues and how these revenues are and should be raised will be considered.

WELFARE ECONOMICS AND CONSUMER SURPLUS

Welfare economics is concerned with the conditions whereby we can conclude that one state of the world is preferable to another state. Should the
government of Egypt, for example, eliminate ceilings on the price of wheat?
There are many social, political, and economic dimensions to answering this
question. It begins by postulating rational human beings with well-defined
utility functions. *Social welfare* is defined as a function of the utility of each
individual. Let w be social welfare and u_i be the utility of the ith person. Then
social welfare is

$$w = w(u_1, u_2, \ldots, u_n),$$

where there are n persons in the society. The welfare function is usually
assumed to be Paretian, which means that welfare improves if one person
is made better off while nobody else is made worse off.[1]

Already some serious questions could be raised concerning the welfare
function. First, neither w or u_i is observable. It seems odd to formulate an
analysis of how one unobservable variable depends on another. Second, the
function is defined for n persons and their preferences. What happens if one
person dies, or moves, or is born? We then need a new welfare function.
Consequently, we will face more difficulties when comparing two states of
the world that cause different numbers of persons to exist. These questions
are interesting, but they will be shunted aside so that we can concentrate on
central elements of welfare theory.

We have already set out a condition whereby one state of the world, state
A, is preferable to another, state B. State A is preferred to state B if at least
one person is better off in A, $u_j^A > u_j^B$ for some person j, and nobody is worse
off, $u_i^A \geq u_i^B$ for all persons i, where u_i^A, u_i^B represent the utility of the ith person
in states A and B, respectively. There are a surprisingly large number of
examples where this condition holds.

Many of the problems in development economics involve choices between
states of the world where income and, hence, utility is redistributed. Some
people are made better off while others are made worse off. A common
practice is to identify net gains in utility with consumer and producer surplus.
Returning to the example of price ceilings on wheat, consider Figure 6.1.
In this example, the price ceiling is $\overline{P}$, which is below the world price P_W.
At $\overline{P}$, $\overline{Q}_S$ is produced domestically and $\overline{Q}_D$ is demanded. Suppose the
government purchases $\overline{Q}_D - \overline{Q}_S$ wheat at the world price P_w and then sells
the wheat to consumers at $\overline{P}$ so that no shortage exists. The effect of this
market intervention on social welfare can be illustrated in Table 6.1.

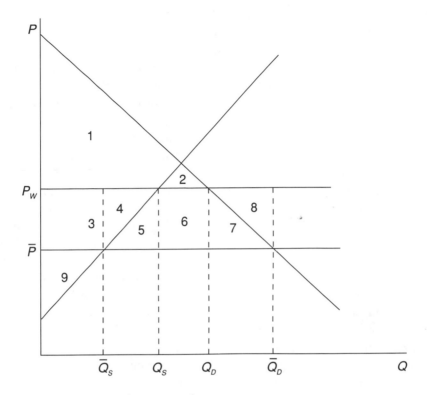

Figure 6.1 Price ceilings on wheat.

Table 6.1 The effect of market intervention.

	Without Intervention	With Intervention
Consumer Surplus	1 + 2	1+ 2 + 3 + 4 + 5 + 6 + 7
Producer Surplus	3 + 4 + 9	9
Government Costs		− (4 + 5 + 6 + 7 + 8)
Net Gain	1 + 2 + 3 + 4 + 9	1 + 2 + 3 + 9 − 8

Without the intervention, the domestic price would be P_w, the world price. Q_S would be supplied domestically and Q_D demanded with imports of $Q_D - Q_S$. Consumer surplus, the area between the demand curve and the price, P_W, is area (1 + 2). Producer surplus, the area between the supply curve and price, is area (3 + 4 + 9). The net gain, or the net contribution to welfare, in this market is area (1 + 2 + 3 + 4 + 9). Note that producer surplus going to foreigners is excluded from the analysis.

With the intervention, consumer surplus rises to area (1 + 2 + 3 + 4 + 5 + 6 + 7) while producer surplus falls to area 9. Consumers do not gain the entire increase in consumer surplus because they must largely pay the government costs of the program. The government loses area (4 + 5 + 6 + 7 + 8) in importing $\overline{Q}_D - \overline{Q}_S$ units of wheat at price P_W and reselling it at price $\overline{P}$. Thus net consumer surplus becomes area (1 + 2 + 3 − 8). The net loss of the program is area (4 + 8). This assumes that there are no administrative costs of the program. The actual costs to the government would be higher if these costs are included.

This example can illustrate three basic possibilities. First, if area 3 is smaller than area 8, consumers are better off without intervention if they have to pay government costs. Because producers are better off without intervention, both consumers and producers gain by moving to the market solution with price P_W. Hence, if we ignore the redistribution among consumers, social welfare would unambiguously be higher at the market solution. Second, if area 3 is greater than area 8, consumers lose (area 3 − 8) and producers gain (area 3 + 4) by moving to the market solution. However, area 3 + 4 > 3 − 8, and as a result, producers could compensate consumers for their loss, making everybody better off. If a practical compensation scheme is found and carried out social welfare is again unambiguously higher at the market solution. Third, like the second possibility, area 3 − 8 is positive and compensation is either not paid or is impractical. Can anything be said in this third case? There is a temptation to say that, because the winners (producers) could compensate the losers (consumers) through lump sum transfers, potential welfare is higher.[2] We should then move to the more efficient market solution and worry about the distribution of income later. This view has been pervasive in areas like trade policy but has not been accepted in appraising government investment and the construction of infrastructure. This partial acceptance in practice comes despite the widespread understanding that this third possibility and the compensation principle are theoretically flawed. Efficiency and equity cannot be so easily separated. Some consideration of equity, such as how much we are concerned with the utility of consumer versus producer, is essential for a rational discussion of policy.[3]

Before discussing applications, let us briefly review the logic behind the compensation principle. The compensation principle says that, if the winners can compensate the losers, then potential welfare has increased. To understand what is meant by potential welfare, look at Figure 6.2. There are two persons and two states of the world from which we can choose, and u_1 and u_2 represent the total utility of persons one and two, respectively. The diagram shows two utility possibilities curves $u(u_1, u_2)$ and $u'(u_1, u_2)$ corresponding to two different states. A utility possibilities curve shows the impact of lump sum transfers on the utility of each person. They are not meant to imply that making lump sum transfers is practical. Consider two points, point A on curve u and point B on curve u', which correspond to two states, call them *autarchy* and *trade*. Suppose the movement from au-

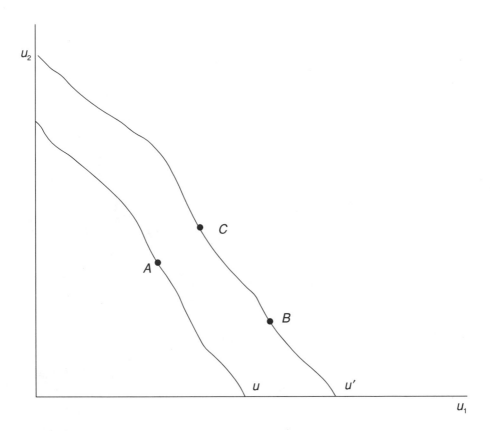

Figure 6.2 An illustration of the compensation principle.

tarchy to trade moves the economy from point A to B. Person one is made better off (u_1 is higher) and person two is made worse off (u_2 is lower) by moving from A to B. Looking at the diagram, it seems reasonable to say that potential welfare is higher at B than at A because B lies on a higher utility possibilities curve. We can always find a point like C where both persons are better off than at A. In other words, we can move from B to C if the winners compensate the losers. The actual payment of compensation would increase actual social welfare. In a situation like that illustrated in Figure 6.2, when one utility possibilities curve lies outside the other, the compensation principle does tell us when potential welfare has risen.

Now consider a case where the compensation principle does not appear to work. In Figure 6.3 the utility possibilities curves cross. Hence, we cannot say that one curve is potentially better than the other. Suppose a change will move the economy from point A to point B. Person one is better off but person two is worse off. It is possible for person one to compensate two by moving to point C. Hence, the compensation principle incorrectly identifies

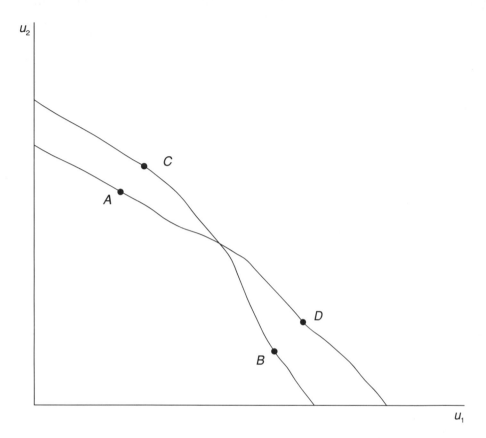

Figure 6.3 A problem with the compensation principle.

an increase in potential welfare where none has occurred. Alternatively, suppose a change will move the economy from point B to point A. In this situation, person two could compensate one by moving to point D. Hence, the compensation principle implies that welfare has increased if we move from B to A. Thus, the compensation principle provides contradictory answers depending upon which state we start with.

The discussion of Figure 6.3 suggests that a slightly more complicated compensation principle might alleviate our difficulties. We could, while at point A, apply the compensation principle to B to see if B has higher potential welfare. If B passes this test, a second test is applied. We could, while at point B, apply the test to see if A has higher potential welfare. If A by this test does not have higher potential welfare, we might conclude that B has higher potential welfare because a movement to B passes a double test implying that potential welfare is higher at B than A.

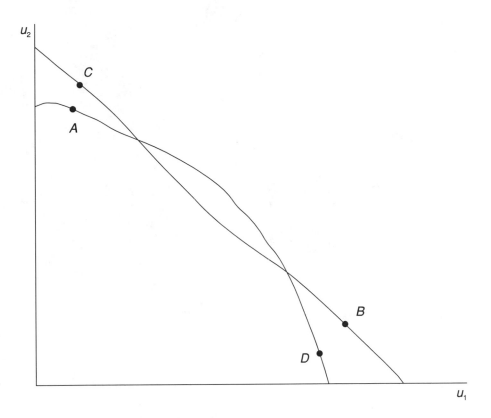

Figure 6.4 An ambiguous situation.

To illustrate this double test, consider Figure 6.2. A move from point A to B passes the first test because compensation to C would make everyone better off. A move from point A to B passes the second test because there exists no point along the utility possibilities curve u where both persons are better off than they would be at B. A case where the double test results in the conclusion that no statement can be made about potential welfare is illustrated in Figure 6.3 because as stated previously the double sided tests yields contradictory results.

Unfortunately, the double test does not always identify an increase in potential welfare. This can easily be seen by looking at Figure 6.4. By comparing points A and B, it can be seen that B passes both tests. C and B are on the same utility possibilities curve, so the losers in a move from A to B could be compensated by the winners because every one is better off at C than at A. Reverse compensation could not take place in a move from B to A. However, because the curves cross, we cannot conclude that potential welfare has increased.

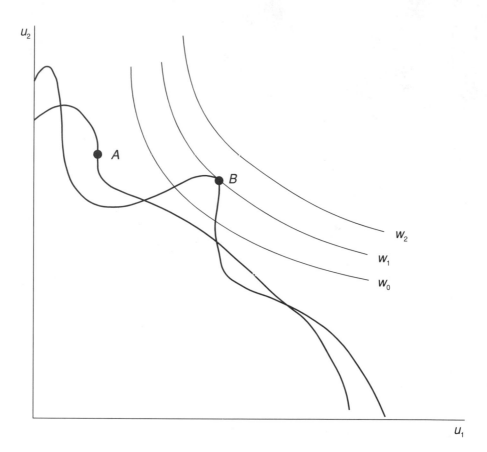

Figure 6.5 Value judgments.

It may not be possible to claim that potential welfare has risen, but we can identify situations where actual welfare has increased if we are willing to incorporate value judgments into the analysis. To illustrate the role of value judgments, consider Figure 6.5. The value judgment takes the form of specifying a social welfare function. Combinations of utility that yield the same social welfare are shown for $w(u_1, u_2) = w_0$, w_1, and w_2. The darker lines are utility possibilities curve. The social welfare functions do not cross and higher levels of social welfare are to the northeast; that is, $w_0 < w_1 < w_2$. Because $w(u_1, u_2)$ is less at A than B, actual welfare is improved by a movement from A to B. Therefore, we have a reason to choose B regardless of the ambiguity of the compensation principle.

We are now ready to return to more practical concerns. When should state B be chosen over state A? Several answers are commonly given. First, and least satisfactory, we might simply choose states according to the compensation principle. Second, we might choose states according to the compensation principle with the qualification that there should be no substantial worsening of the income distribution.[4] Third, explicit consideration of the distribution of income should be introduced into the analysis. In what follows, we will proceed with an analysis of social efficiency, always keeping in mind that the improvements in welfare just discussed are only potential, in the sense of the compensation principle, unless value judgments are made about income distribution.

SHADOW PRICES: VALUING OUTPUTS AND INPUTS

In the last section, the theoretical basis was discussed for analyzing economic policy in terms of its impact on social welfare. We will now see how we might approach a number of problems that are of interest in development economics. In evaluating the net change in consumer and producer surplus, we must know the value of the various inputs and outputs involved. Value and price are the same if the economy is at a competitive, general equilibrium. All factors are paid their marginal product and the ratio of all goods prices equal the marginal rate of substitution between those goods. Otherwise, value and price will differ. Because in development economics market imperfections of various kinds are emphasized, some attempt to measure the value of inputs and outputs in this circumstance seems appropriate. These values are called *shadow prices*, and we will now turn to various discussions of shadow prices and how they deviate from actual prices.[5]

A question central to dualistic and Keynesian views of development concerns the shadow price of labor. In deciding the true costs of a government project in the industrial sector, what wage rate should be used? The actual wage rate may be higher than the shadow wage rate because of distortions in the labor market. One extreme but simple answer is that wage costs should be ignored because the marginal product of labor is zero in the rural sector. Consequently, the opportunity cost, in terms of lost output, of shifting a rural, underemployed worker to the urban sector is zero.

Another extreme view is suggested by the Harris–Todaro migration model. An implication of this model is that the shadow price of urban labor is the urban wage rate even if that wage rate is set artificially high. To see why this conclusion flows from the Harris–Todaro model, recall that rural workers are assumed to be fully employed at a constant wage rate. Suppose that this constant wage rate equals the marginal product of labor that is constant but above zero. Although there is no rural unemployment, urban unemployment exists due to an artificially high urban wage rate. Workers will move from rural to urban regions until $\delta w = s$, where δ is the urban employment rate, w the urban wage rate and s the rural wage rate. The employment rate is the equalizing factor in the model. For example, if $w = 100$ and $s = 60$, the urban employment rate will be 0.6. If $\delta = 0.8$, then

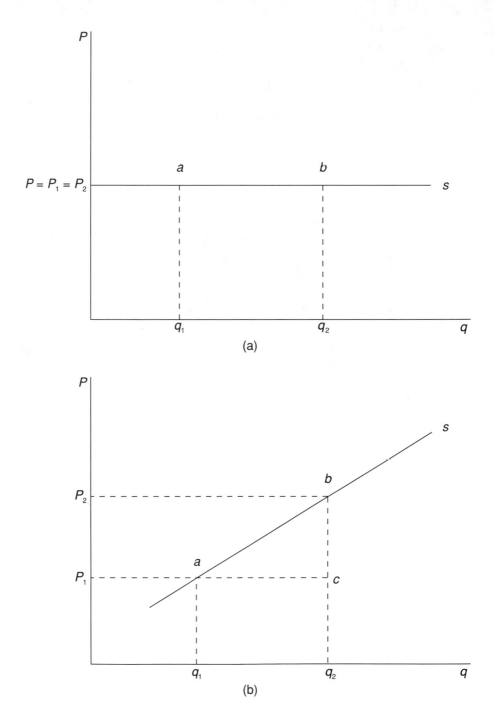

Figure 6.6   Effects of government purchases.

migration will occur because $\delta w = 80 > 60$. Thus migration will reduce δ until it falls to 0.6. For δ to equal 0.6, each urban job must result in $(1/\delta)$ = 1.67 rural workers moving to the urban area. Recall that each rural worker produced $s = 60$ units of output. Hence, $(1/\delta)s = s/\delta$ is the cost in terms of lost rural output of employing an urban worker. However, because $\delta w = s$, $s/\delta = w$. Thus the urban wage rate w is the correct shadow price of labor in this simple version of the Harris–Todaro model even if it is set artificially high.

A more complicated view of the shadow price of labor is that rural workers are paid above their marginal product but that their marginal product is positive. In this case, the shadow price of labor would be between zero and the urban wage rate. In considering whether to move to the urban sector, rural workers may be concerned with comparing the average product of labor in the rural sector, and not the marginal product of labor, to the urban wage rate. As we learned in Chapter 5, this can occur with family enterprises where family workers share in the rent. When the worker takes a job in the modern sector, output does not fall by the average product of labor, which appears to be the wage rate, but by the marginal product of labor. Consequently, even if the Harris–Todaro model is correct, the shadow price of labor may be below the high urban wage rate. Furthermore, this conclusion in no way depends upon the existence of disguised rural unemployment. Instead, it depends upon the sharing of rent by persons working in family enterprises.

The shadow price of labor has been treated as though the supply of labor is perfectly elastic. Shadow prices are easier to evaluate when they can reasonably be assumed to be fixed. For many problems, it may be reasonable to assume fixed shadow prices. Imports or exports might be bought and sold in world markets that are large with respect to the decision in question, which consequently will have little or no impact on world prices. In domestic markets, however, there is a greater likelihood that a decision will affect prices in the smaller domestic market. For many decisions, world demand and supply may, for practical purposes, be assumed to be horizontal while domestic demand will be downward sloping and domestic supply upward sloping. We will now see how such decisions can be treated.

Consider a government project that involves the purchase of certain inputs. The activities of the government may or may not influence the input price, and these two possibilities are illustrated in Figures 6.6(a) and 6.6(b). In both figures the government increases its purchases from q_1 to q_2. Because supply gives marginal costs, the change in total costs, ΔTC, is area q_1abq_2 in both diagrams. The quantity $q_2 - q_1$ is the increase in purchases and ΔTC is the total value of this increase. Hence the value per unit, or the shadow price of these purchases, is

$$\pi = \Delta TC/(q_2 - q_1). \tag{6.1}$$

For Figure 6.6(a) ΔTC, however, is simply

$$\Delta TC = P(q_2 - q_1). \tag{6.2}$$

By substituting equation (6.2) into equation (6.1), we find

$$\pi = P. \tag{6.3}$$

In this case, if private marginal costs reflect marginal social costs, then prices equal the shadow price. For Figure 6.6(b),

$$\begin{aligned}\Delta TC &= P_1(q_2 - q_1) + 0.5(P_2 - P_1)(q_2 - q_1) \\ &= 0.5(P_2 + P_1)(q_2 - q_1) \\ &= \overline{P}(q_2 - q_1),\end{aligned} \tag{6.4}$$

where $\overline{P} = 0.5(P_2 + P_1)$ is the average price. Equation (6.4) is found by adding the area of rectangle q_1abq_2, $P_1(q_2 - q_1)$, to the area of triangle abc, $.5(P_2 - P_1)(q_2 - q_1)$. The formula holds for a linear supply curve. The shadow price is then

$$\begin{aligned}\pi &= \Delta TC/(q_2 - q_1) \\ &= \overline{P}(q_2 - q_1)/(q_2 - q_1) \\ &= \overline{P}.\end{aligned} \tag{6.5}$$

In this case, even if prices reflect social cost, the price does not equal the shadow price because government purchases influence the price. Therefore, an average price must be calculated and, because this is simple to do for a linear supply curve, linearity will be assumed in our examples.

Governments also produce output as the result of some of their activities. If the demand for the output is horizontal and represents marginal social value, the shadow price, π, of the good in question is simply its price, P. When demand is downward sloping its shadow price is simply the average of the market price with and without the government action. In Figure 6.7, the government action increases the output of good q from q_1 to q_2. Market price falls from P_1 to P_2. The total value of purchases of this increased output is area q_1abq_2. The value per unit of extra output is

$$\pi = \overline{P}, \text{ where}$$
$$\overline{P} = (P_1 + P_2)/2. \tag{6.6}$$

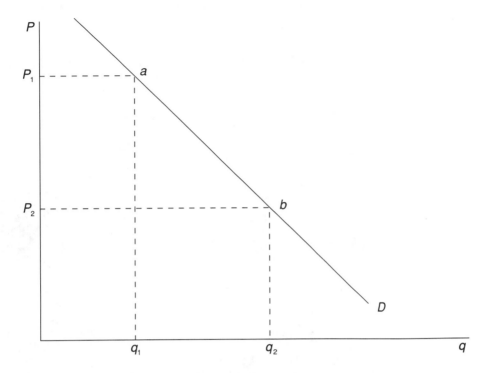

Figure 6.7 Government output.

Price and marginal social value or cost may, of course, differ because of numerous public and private distortions such as taxes or externalities. An important example of public distortions are tariffs. Tariffs affect the exchange rate and hence prices. To see how tariffs affect the analysis of the shadow price of foreign exchange, we will consider a government purchase when there are no tariffs and then introduce tariffs into the analysis. The demand for foreign exchange is determined by the demand for purchases of foreign assets or goods.

Demand would rise if the government decided to import more foreign capital goods. To purchase these goods, the government would need to obtain the necessary foreign exchange. Hence, the demand for foreign exchange would rise. The supply of foreign exchange is determined by the supply of exports and by foreign demand for the exports and assets of the economy.

The price of foreign exchange is called the *exchange rate, e*. For example, if the domestic country is Mexico, *e* gives the pesos necessary to purchase a given quantity of foreign exchange. The units might be thought of as pesos per dollar. If the peso price of dollars (foreign exchange) rises, Mexican exports will rise ceteris paribus. To see this, suppose a Mexican produced

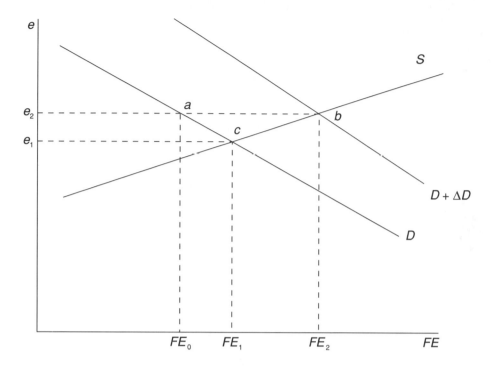

Figure 6.8   Effect of importing capital on foreign exchange.

gadget sells for $1.00 in New York. If $e = 3.00$ pesos per dollar, then the Mexican exporter earns $3.00 ($ denotes pesos) for each gadget sold in New York. If the exchange rate rises to $e = 5.00$ the Mexican exporter now receives $5.00 for each gadget sold.

This increase in the peso price that the Mexican gadget producer can earn by selling gadgets in New York will provide an incentive for the Mexican producer to export more gadgets to New York. The quantity of dollars (i.e., of foreign exchange) supplied to Mexico will thereby rise. Similarly, U.S. producers will find that their incentive to export to Mexico has been diminished. Consequently, the quantity of foreign exchange demanded by Mexican buyers to import U.S. goods will fall. Consequently, the demand for foreign exchange is a downward sloping function of e and the supply is upward sloping.

We are now ready to consider the shadow price of foreign exchange.[6] Suppose that the government makes a decision that increases the demand for foreign exchange. An example of such a decision might be the decision to purchase imported capital. The impact of this purchase on foreign exchange is illustrated in Figure 6.8. Before the action, the exchange rate is e_1 and the quantity of foreign exchange demanded and supplied is FE_1. Demand is shifted to the right by ΔD with the purchase. The exchange rate rises to e_2 and FE rises to FE_2. In the diagram

$$\Delta D = FE_2 - FE_0, \tag{6.7}$$

where FE_0 is foreign exchange used for purposes other than the purchase in question.

Note that this increase in foreign exchange comes from two sources. The quantity demanded for other uses has fallen from FE_1 to FE_0 and the quantity supplied has risen from FE_1 to FE_2. We can then write

$$\Delta D = \Delta M + \Delta X, \tag{6.8}$$

where $\Delta M = FE_1 - FE_0$ and $\Delta X = FE_2 - FE_1$.

In evaluating the foreign exchange costs of the action note that the value of ΔM is area $FE_0 acFE_1$ and the value of ΔX is area $FE_1 cbFE_2$. With a linear demand curve, the value of ΔX is $\bar{e}(\Delta X) = 0.5(e_1 + e_2)\Delta X$. Consequently, the shadow price of ΔX is $\pi = \bar{e}$. Similarly, with a linear supply curve the value of ΔM is $\bar{e}(\Delta M)$ and its shadow price is also $\bar{e}$. Consequently, the shadow price of foreign exchange is $\bar{e}$ as we would expect given our assumption that there are no distortions affecting the foreign exchange market.

Of course, most economies, both DCs and LDCs, distort the foreign exchange market by tariffs or other barriers to trade. It is easy to augment the discussion of the shadow price of foreign exchange to include tariffs. Consider Figure 6.9, where $e(1 + \tau)$ is the total price of a unit of foreign exchange and τ is an ad valorum tariff rate paid on all imports. For example, if a widget can be purchased for $1.50 in New York, $e = 5.0$, and $\tau = 0.1$, then the same widget (excluding transportation costs) will cost $1.50(5.0)(1 + 0.1) = \$8.25$ in Mexico. The demand for foreign exchange gives the quantity of foreign exchange demanded as a function of its total price $e(1 + \tau)$.

The level of exports and hence the supply of foreign exchange, S, is a function of the exchange rate and unaffected by a tariff because a tariff is a tax on imports. S gives the quantity of foreign exchange supplied at each exchange rate. $S(1 + \tau)$ gives the total costs of foreign exchange at each quantity supplied. For example, at exchange rate e_1, FE_1 units of foreign exchange would be supplied and $e_1(1 + \tau)$ is the total costs of foreign exchange for FE_1. For $e_1(1 + \tau)$ the quantity of foreign exchange demanded is FE_3. Consequently, there is an excess demand of $FE_3 - FE_1$ for foreign exchange. The exchange rate will rise until it reaches e_2 with a total cost of foreign exchange of $e_2(1 + \tau)$. At $e_2(1 + \tau)$ the quantity supplied and

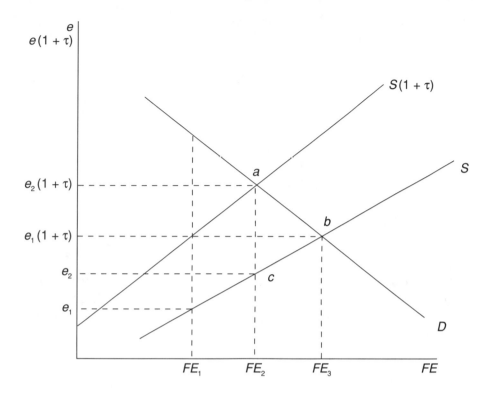

Figure 6.9 Shadow price of foreign exchange with tariffs.

demanded of foreign exchange is FE_2. As with any tax other than a lump sum tax, there is a loss of both consumer and producer surplus. Here this loss is the area of triangle *abc*.

We are now ready to consider the impact on the foreign exchange costs to Mexico of the purchase of capital in the case of a tariff. The impact of the purchase is shown in Figure 6.10. The exchange rate before the purchase was e_1 and after the purchase it rose to e_2. The foreign exchange required for the purchase was $\Delta D = FE_2 - FE_0$. Again there are two sources for ΔD. They are the decrease in the quantity demanded for other purposes, $\Delta M = FE_1 - FE_0$, and the increase in the quantity supplied, $\Delta X = FE_2 - FE_1$. Now, however, ΔM and ΔX have different shadow prices due to the tariff.

The shadow prices can be found by considering the total costs of the ΔM and ΔX. The value of ΔM is as before area FE_0acFE_1. The value of ΔX is FE_1ghFE_2. The area *gcbh* represents an internal transfer to the government and, hence, is not a net social cost. The value of ΔM is

$$0.5(e_1 + e_2)(1 + \tau)\Delta M = \bar{e}(1 + \tau)\Delta M. \tag{6.9}$$

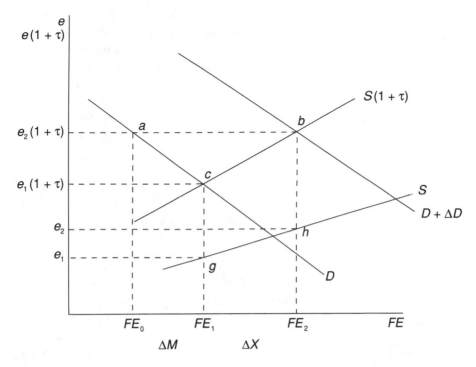

Fgure 6.10 The case of a tariff.

The value of ΔX is

$$0.5(e_1 + e_2)\Delta X = \bar{e}\Delta X. \qquad (6.10)$$

The total value or cost of the foreign exchange required for the purchase is the combined expressions (6.9) and (6.10),

$$\bar{e}(1 + \tau)\Delta M + \bar{e}\Delta X. \qquad (6.11)$$

The real cost per unit of foreign exchange (its shadow price) is found by dividing (6.11) by ΔD. This yields

$$\pi = \bar{e}(1 + \tau)\Delta M/\Delta D + \bar{e}\Delta X/\Delta D. \qquad (6.12)$$

For $\tau = 0$, equation (6.12) becomes

$$\pi = \bar{e}(\Delta M + \Delta X)/\Delta D. \qquad (6.13)$$

Because $\Delta D = \Delta M + \Delta X$, equation (6.13) simply states $\pi = \bar{e}$, which we found earlier when there was no tariff.

A nice feature of this analysis is that it is easily extended to the more realistic case where there are multiple tariffs. In equation (6.12) the last term, $\bar{e}\Delta X/\Delta D$, does not depend upon the tariff rate so we need to be concerned with only the first term. First, for each good imported we need to find ΔM with $\Delta M_i = P_i\Delta(q_{Di} - q_{Si})$, where P_i is the foreign price of good i and q_{Di} and q_{Si} are the domestic quantity demanded and supplied of good i at price P_i. Then, $q_{Di} - q_{Si}$ is the quantity imported. Next, we need to find the tariff rate τ_i for each imported good. Then we need to replace $\Delta M(1 + \tau)$ with $\sum_{i=1}^{n} P_i(1 + \tau)\Delta M_i$ yielding

$$\pi = \bar{e}\left(\sum_{i=1}^{n} P_i(1 + \tau)\Delta M_i\right)/\Delta D + \bar{e}\Delta X/\Delta D. \qquad (6.14)$$

This analysis of the shadow price of foreign exchange is relatively straightforward, but many additional complications must be considered in any application. An important practical consideration is the assumption that the exchange rate clears the market. This assumption may not be realistic, and chronic disequilibrium may exist. Furthermore, it was assumed that there are no nontariff barriers to trade. When nontariff barriers to trade exist, an implicit rate of protection for each good are needed to replace τ_i. If exchange rates are controlled, an implicit exchange rate needs to be found. Multiple exchange rates further complicate the analysis.

In conclusion, despite both conceptual and practical difficulties, the calculation and analysis of shadow prices provides a systematic foundation for calculating the costs and benefits of government action. Numerous other shadow prices are thought to be important for the evaluation of proposed actions by the government. They include the implicit value of risk, waiting, and intangibles like health, a clean environment, and indeed life itself. Numerous distortions influence the relationship between prices and shadow prices, including other taxes, monopoly power, price controls, and incomplete markets. We will not carry the analysis of shadow prices further to consider each possibility and shadow price. Instead, we will move on to more dynamic considerations, beginning with the analysis of investment decisions where the costs and returns take place over a number of years.

COST–BENEFIT ANALYSIS

Once shadow prices are determined, they can be used to evaluate whether a proposed action is worthwhile. The method for evaluating a proposed action in terms of the shadow prices of the action's likely consequences is called a *cost–benefit analysis*. Although the validity of conclusions reached using cost–benefit analysis depends upon the correct specification of shadow prices, the analysis itself can utilize any prices. We will briefly explain cost–benefit analysis and then see how it can be used for evaluating potential actions.

Cost–benefit analysis views any decision as an investment. Consider the decision of an individual investor when there is no risk. If funds are available at interest rate r, then an investment would be made by a rational investor if the net present value of the investment is positive. Net present value, denoted as NPV, is given by

$$\text{NPV} = -I_0 + \sum_{t=1}^{N} \frac{(B_t - C_t)}{(1 + r)^t} + \frac{S_N}{(1 + r)^N} \tag{6.15}$$

where I_0 is the initial investment cost, t is time, N is the total time the investment yields costs or returns, S_N is the salvage value, and r the cost of funds. For these assumptions, the investment would be made by a rational investor if NPV > 0.

A key relationship for equation (6.15) is between NPV and r. Because r appears in the denominator, it seems natural to suppose that there is an inverse relationship between NPV and r as illustrated in Figure 6.11(a). In Figure 6.11(a), NPV > 0 for $r < r_1$. Otherwise, the investment should not be made. An example that yields an (NPV, r) relationships like Figure 6.11(a) is an investment in fixed income securities. Here, $B_t - C_t = Y$, where Y is the fixed annual income generated by the investment. The only term in equation (6.15) that would be negative is the first term, $-I_0$, because the security would have a nonnegative salvage value, S_N. S_N is the redemption value of the security at time N. I_0 is also the only term not divided by a power of $(1 + r)$. Consequently, as r rises the positive terms, $Y/(1 + r)$, $Y/(1 + r)^2, \ldots, Y/(1 + r)^N$, and $S_N/(1 + r)^N$, will decline in value while the negative term, $-I_0$, remains constant. Hence, for a high enough interest rate, NPV becomes negative. The same result holds if all the negative terms are for early years. That is, if $(B_t - C_t) < 0$ for $t < \tau$ and $(B_t - C_t) > 0$ for $t \geq \tau$. Again, the positive terms are more sensitive to interest rates because they are discounted by $(1 + r)^t$ and the derivative of $(1 + r)^t$ with respect to r obviously rises with t.

The shape in Figure 6.11(a) comes from the assumption that the sign of the terms are initially all negative and then become all positive. If there is a subsequent sign reversal, where the terms are negative, then positive, and finally become negative, the shape of NPV seen in Figure 6.11(b) can occur. An example might be when there is a negative salvage value S_N. S_N is then the net cost of closing down the enterprise when it has outlived its usefulness. For a low r the present value of this cost $S_N/(1 + r)^N$ could be

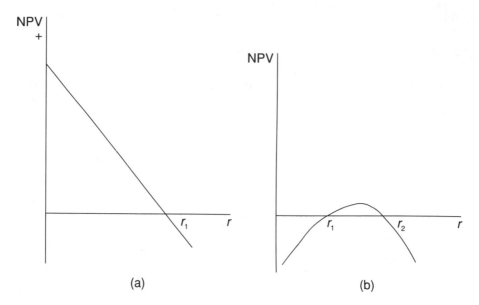

Figure 6.11 Relationships between the net present value and the cost of funds.

considerable. As r rises S_N is discounted by more than the intermediate positive returns so NPV increases and becomes positive. Finally, as r rises further, $-I_0$ begins to dominate the discounted terms and NPV becomes negative again. In this situation, evaluating a project at an arbitrarily low or high interest rate might provide a misleading picture of the intrinsic value of the project.

The discussion of cost–benefit analysis has thus far been for individual investors who can borrow all they want at a given interest rate. In applying the analysis to government projects, two questions come immediately to mind. First, is the private interest rate socially optimal? There are many reasons why the private interest rate might not represent the true social costs of funds. Taxes, imperfect capital markets, and imperfect product markets are just three sources of this divergence. Second, how should a suboptimality of the private interest rate be incorporated into cost–benefit analysis?

Let r be the private interest rate and δ, called the *social discount rate*, be the social opportunity cost of investment funds. It is usually assumed that $r > \delta$. This is certainly the assumption for public finance as applied to developed economies. In less developed economies, there may be several interest rates in a fragmented credit market. One of these interest rates, in the informal sector, might be well above the discount rate, while others might be below the discount rate. Indeed, it is not unusual in favored sectors to find negative real interest rates.

The divergence of r from δ matters if part of the funds needed for an investment project come from private savings and part of these funds come from consumption. Let λ be the fraction of funds that comes at the expense of private investment from the available savings. That is, λI_0 would have been invested earning $r\lambda I_0$ per year. And $(1 - \lambda)I_0$ comes from consumption, which, at the social discount rate δ, is valued at $\delta(1 - \lambda)I_0$ per year. The present value of the foregone consumption, $(1 - \lambda)I_0$, is simply

$$\sum_{t=1}^{\infty} \frac{\delta(1 - \lambda)I_0}{(1 + \delta)^t} = (\delta/\delta)(1 - \lambda)I_0 = (1 - \lambda)I_0, \qquad (6.16)$$

because $\displaystyle\sum_{t=1}^{\infty} \frac{1}{(1 + \delta)^t} = \frac{1}{\delta}$. The present value of the foregone investment, however, is

$$\sum_{t=1}^{\infty} \frac{r\lambda I_0}{(1 + \delta)^t} = (r/\delta)\lambda I_0. \qquad (6.17)$$

Hence, with the divergence of private interest rates and the social discount rate, NPV becomes

$$\text{NPV} = -\{(1 - \lambda) + \lambda r/\delta\}I_0 + \sum_{t=1}^{N} \frac{(B_t - C_t)}{(1 + \delta)^t} + \frac{S_N}{(1 + \delta)^N}. \qquad (6.18)$$

Note that equations (6.15) and (6.18) are the same only if $\lambda = 0$ or if $r = \delta$.

The divergence of r from δ introduces another complication when a project is not self-financing. For public projects, often many of the benefits are intangible or priced below their shadow price. Such projects may require annual financing from public funds. Let F_t be the required funds. These funds will again come partly from consumption and partly from savings. The present value, in year t, of F_t for funds coming from consumption is $(1 - \lambda)F_t$ and for funds coming from private investment is $\lambda(r/\delta)F_t$. Consequently, the present value of these funds in year t is then

$$PV_t = \{(1 - \lambda) + \lambda r/\delta\}F_t. \qquad (6.19)$$

PV_t will in general differ from F_t. $F_t - PV_t$ should be included in the calculation of NPV because of the divergence between the (present) value of current money and the present value of money raised by public financing. Hence, equation (6.18) becomes

$$\text{NPV} = -\{(1 - \lambda) + \lambda r/\delta\}I_0 +$$

$$\sum_{t=1}^{N} \frac{B_t - C_t + \lambda F_t(1 - r/\delta)}{(1 + \delta)^t} + \frac{S_N}{(1 + \delta)^N}. \qquad (6.20)$$

In interpreting equation (6.20), note that the shadow price of publicly raised investment funds is

$$\pi = (1 - \lambda) + \lambda r/\delta. \qquad (6.21)$$

If $\lambda > 0$, then these funds come partly from investment, and their opportunity cost is (r/δ). If $r/\delta > 1$, there is underinvestment in the private sector because the cost of private investment, r, is too high. The shadow price of these funds is r/δ. Hence, the shadow price of public investment exceeds unity, $\pi > 1$. Note that π is a weighted average of the shadow price of private consumption and investment. Substituting (6.21) into (6.20) yields

$$\text{NPV} = -\pi I_0 + \sum_{t=1}^{N} \frac{B_t - C_t + (1 - \pi)F_t}{(1 + \delta)^t} + \frac{S_N}{(1 + \delta)^N}. \qquad (6.22)$$

Equation (6.22) gives NPV in terms of the shadow price of public funds.

The situation is more complex in a less developed, fragmented economy. Let q be a low interest rate in a favored sector of the economy and r be the interest rate for the rest of the economy. For lack of better terms call these sectors the *formal* and *informal sectors*. Suppose q is set arbitrarily low and r is determined by the supply and demand for credit in the rest of the economy. This divergence might exist for many reasons, including government ownership or control of the financial system coupled with a desire to channel investment into favored areas. The shadow price of public funds will then depend upon whether they come from consumption, favored sector private investment, or private investment in the rest of the economy. The shadow price is then

$$\pi = (1 - \lambda) + \lambda\theta r/\delta + \lambda(1 - \theta)q/\delta, \qquad (6.23)$$

where $0 \leq \theta \leq 1$ and $\theta\lambda$ is the proportion of the investment coming from funds that would otherwise result in informal sector investment, and $(1 - \theta)\lambda$ is the proportion coming at the expense of formal sector investment.

To interpret equation (6.22), suppose that $q < \delta$. In other words, the costs of capital in the formal sector are below their social opportunity costs in terms of consumption. This distortion would, of course, result in an inappropriate technique of production, as was discussed in Chapter 5, to be adopted in the formal sector. The production technique would be too capital intensive. The production technique in the informal sector would, however, rely on too little capital because $r > \delta$. The shadow price of public funds now depends not only on the proportion of funds coming from private investment, λ, or consumption, $1 - \lambda$, but also upon, θ, the source of investment funds.

When only one interest rate exists and $\lambda > 0$ in equation (6.21), $\pi > 1$ if $r > \delta$. When two interest rates exist, one of which is below the social discount rate, and $\lambda > 0$, equation (6.23), there is the possibility that π will be less than unity: π will be less than unity if $q + \theta(r - q) < \delta$. Because, by assumption, $r > \delta > q$, then $\pi < 1$ if $\theta < (\delta - q)/(r - q)$. Therefore, if these funds come largely from the formal sector, the shadow price of public products will be below the nominal price.

Another complication concerning the shadow price of public funds occurs if the funds come from unproductive investment. Recall from Chapter 1 that in Keynesian models planned investment is below savings. These excess savings went into unproductive use. One reason given for this low investment was low entrepreneurship. Higher growth in Keynesian models could be achieved by increasing the marginal propensity to invest. No increase in the propensity to save is necessary. In a sense, this growth is free. Savings that would have gone into unproductive investment go into productive investment. In terms of the shadow price of public funds, the opportunity costs of these funds is zero. Suppose α is the proportion of public investment coming from funds that would otherwise be unproductive investment. The shadow price of these funds, modifying equation (6.23), is then

$$\pi = (1 - \lambda) + (1 - \alpha)\{\lambda\theta r/\delta + \lambda(1 - \theta)q/\delta\}. \qquad (6.24)$$

As an economy moves toward the full utilization of its resources, α falls and the shadow price of public funds rises.

The appropriate shadow price of public investment will depend upon the entire structure of the economy coupled with the way in which this investment is financed. If there is unproductive investment in the economy, there may be an opportunity to finance public expenditures partly at the expense of this unproductive investment. If this is the case, public investment will yield large social dividends. If, however, public funds come largely at the expense of informal sector investment and if returns to investment in this sector are high, public investment will be much less desirable. Keynesian models suggest the possibility of a low cost of public investment as do some dualistic models because in these models public financing can come largely from unproductive savings.

PUBLIC REVENUES

Having discussed the expenditure side of public economics, it is time to turn to revenues. The major source of government revenues is taxation. For some countries such as Saudi Arabia, returns from government owned enterprises are a major source of funds, but the major source of government revenues is taxation. The patterns of taxation, difficulties in obtaining sufficient tax revenue, and tax reform have received considerable attention and will be discussed in this section.

Patterns of Taxation

There are several differences in the way tax revenues are raised between industrial and less developed countries. About two thirds of tax revenues in developed countries come from direct taxes on firms and individuals and one third from indirect taxes. The opposite is true for developing countries.[7] Perhaps the most striking difference is in the individual income tax, which raises a very low percentage of tax revenues in developing countries. This small role for individual income taxes is the result of the dominant role of the traditional sector. Much of the output in the traditional sector is either consumed by the family that produces the output or traded for goods produced by other traditional sector families. Consequently, income is hard to measure and is therefore difficult to tax.

Traditional sector income is also difficult to tax, partly because a large part of traditional sector income is nonmonetary income. Suppose total real income is

$$Y = F + M \tag{6.25}$$

where F represents goods produced and used directly by the family, in consumption or investment, and M represents goods sold on the market. If a tax rate of α is placed on all income, then total taxes would be

$$T = \alpha(F + M). \tag{6.26}$$

However, taxes need to be paid in money. The proportion of market earnings paid in taxes, β, are given by dividing equation (6.26) by M, yielding

$$\beta = \alpha(F/M) + \alpha, \tag{6.27}$$

where β might need to be very large to collect a small α because the preponderance of income may come in the form of nonmarket family production. For example, if 80 percent of income is from nonmarket production, $F/M = 4$. A tax rate, α, of 10 percent on all income would require a tax rate of 50 percent on market earnings. If this revenue were raised by directly taxing visible market earnings at a rate of β, the high tax rate would surely discourage market activity.

To tax the traditional sector, some method of taxing F, nonmarket production, must be found. Otherwise, the high tax rate, β, on market earnings would drive production back into nonmarket household production and thwart the transformation of the traditional sector. Taxes on land are one way of taxing nonmarket production. Land taxes can encourage market production because they hit the nonmonetized sector but must be paid in money. Farmers, who need more cash to pay the tax, will shift their efforts to the market sector in order to raise more cash.[8] Taxing land has the further advantage of being administratively easy to implement. However, political resistance to land taxes has been high and for the most part they have been an unimportant source of revenue.[9]

The major role played by indirect taxes, largely import duties, excise taxes, a value added tax, a general sales tax, and turnover taxes is partly due to sales being harder to hide than income. However, the major reason for the heavy reliance on indirect taxes is because of the political popularity of import duties. Although only 2.7 percent of tax revenues come from import duties in industrial countries, 24.3 percent of tax revenues comes from import duties in developing countries.[10] Foreign producers will be easier to tax than domestic producers if protectionist sentiments run high.

Another source of revenue that is easier to tap in developing countries is seignorage. Consider a government budget constraint of the form

$$E = T + rD + \Delta D + \Delta M + R, \tag{6.28}$$

where E is government outlays, rD is the interest payments on government debt, ΔD is the government deficit (or surplus), ΔM is the growth (or decline) of the monetary base, and R is revenues from government enterprises. For a constant velocity of money, the seignorage, ΔM, will not be inflationary unless ΔM grows at a faster rate than real output. This result comes directly from differentiating the log of the equation of exchange,

$$MV = PQ \qquad (6.29)$$

which yields

$$\hat{M} + \hat{V} = \hat{P} + \hat{Q}. \qquad (6.30)$$

$\hat{P}$, the inflation rate, is zero if $\hat{M} = \hat{Q} - \hat{V}$. If V, the velocity of the monetary base, is constant, $\hat{V} = 0$ and $\hat{M} = \hat{Q}$. $\hat{M}$ is the rate of seignorage. Total seignorage is

$$\hat{M}M = \hat{Q}M. \qquad (6.31)$$

For an economy experiencing inflation but with $\hat{V} = 0$, total seignorage is

$$\hat{M}M = (\hat{Q} + \hat{P})M. \qquad (6.32)$$

$\hat{P}$, in equation (6.32) is an inflation tax on holding money.

In some cases, there might be heavy reliance on seignorage. This could occur particularly when there is some unanticipated shortfall in revenues or expansion in spending. Borrowing may be difficult and the ability to levy new taxes may be limited. Indeed, if, for structural reasons, tax revenues rise less rapidly than government spending as the economy grows, then the result might be an increase in the money supply and inflation. However, reliance on an inflation tax is possible. If the inflation tax is excessive, it will disrupt monetary exchange in the economy, retarding the development of traditional and modern sectors alike.

Tax Reform

Three types of tax reform will be mentioned in discussing developing countries. The first type of reform involves raising more taxes. As a portion of GDP, taxes are 31.2 percent in industrial countries and only 18.1 percent in developing countries.[11] A second type of reform involves changing the type of taxes to improve allocative efficiency in the economy and to encourage economic growth. The third type of reform involves making the burden of taxes more equitable.[12]

Any tax reform measure must cope with entrenched political interests. For example, it has long been argued that more reliance on land taxes would improve allocative efficiency in the economy and could make the tax system fairer. A pure land tax, based on the fertility of agricultural land, would not affect allocative decisions and would, hence, not distort economic activities. In addition, land taxes are relatively easy to administer and implement. Furthermore, land taxes may be much more progressive than the tax system

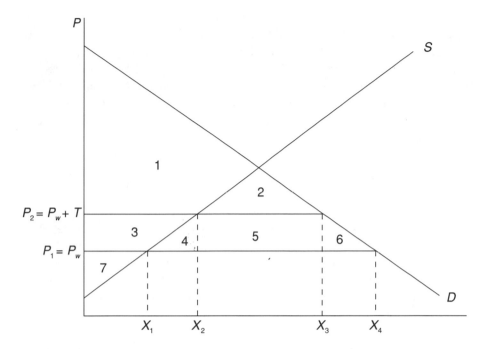

Figure 6.12 Protectionism: quotas versus tariffs.

as a whole. The incidence of land taxes falls on the landlord and cannot be shifted forward onto the tenants. As the economy becomes more monetized and more open to imports, landlords may be able to change the tax system in a way that shifts the tax burden from themselves to the general population. The monetization of the economy and the expansion of imports, increases the ability of policy makers to substitute indirect taxes such as sales taxes, excise taxes, and tariffs for land taxes. These indirect taxes shift the burden from landlords to the general population and are highly favored by landlords. Indeed, this tax shifting has occurred in a sometimes dramatic fashion.[13] Tax reform may prove impossible if it deals with equity in a dramatic way.[14]

One type of tax reform that may be fairly easy to enact is to replace import licenses and quotas with tariffs. Quotas are inferior to tariffs as a means of protectionism because they raise little revenue. To see this difficulty with quotas, consider Figure 6.12. D is domestic demand for a good and S is domestic supply. P_w is the world price, which is unaffected by the quantity of imports. At $P_1 = P_w$, X_1 is produced domestically, X_4 is demanded, and $X_4 - X_1$ is imports. A tariff will increase the price by the amount of the tariff, to $P_2 = P_w + T$. Domestic production will rise to X_2, consumption will fall to X_3 and imports will fall to $X_3 - X_2$.

The costs of the tariff can be seen by looking at consumer and producer surplus. With no tariff, producer surplus is area (7) and consumer surplus is area $(1 + 2 + 3 + 4 + 5 + 6)$. With the tariff, producer surplus rises to $(3 + 7)$, consumer surplus falls to $(1 + 2)$ and the government receives (5) in revenues. The area $(4 + 6)$ represents the loss in total surplus from imposing a tariff. The costs of an import quota, which restricts imports to $(X_3 - X_2)$ exceed the costs of the tariff. Price still rise to P_2. Consumer and producer surplus are the same as with the tariff. Area (5), however, may largely go to foreign producers. Replacing a quota with an equivalent tariff acts as a type of tax reform in that the tariff revenues can be used to replace a domestic tax with no cost to the domestic economy.

Another type of possible tax reform is to replace indirect taxes with direct taxes on income and profits. The direct taxes have two disadvantages in implementation. First, inadequate records, for both cultural and economic reasons, may make it difficult to ascertain income or profits. The lack of a sophisticated financial system may mean that most transactions are in cash. Cash transactions are particularly easy to underreport, especially when receipts are not routinely kept, as they are not in many sectors. Second, widespread noncompliance undermines voluntary compliance, making tax payment a penalty for a lack of cleverness rather than a civic responsibility. Direct taxes fall unfairly on those sources of income and profits that are the most difficult to underreport.

The last type of tax reform, which will be discussed, is the replacement of excise and sales taxes with a value added tax (VAT). A VAT has two advantages over sales and excise taxes. First, it is more neutral in the sense that it has a broader tax base. Second, a VAT reduces the incentive to evade the tax. To see this point, note that value added is the value of sales minus the value of purchases of intermediate inputs. The seller of intermediate inputs has to remember that the purchaser may be claiming these purchases as reducing value added. Consequently, evasion might be detected. Perhaps for this second reason, value added taxes have become more widely used in recent years.

CONCLUSION

Public economics deals with the role of government in allocative and distributive decisions in developing countries. Its scope is narrow in that it normally concerns these decisions given the current structure of the economy. Nonetheless, public economics is rich in that it incorporates aspects considered to be important for developing countries into a formal analysis of what that country's government should or could do to improve social welfare. In Chapter 8, the impact of policy in changing the structure of the economy will be considered.

NOTES

1. Abram Bergon, "A Reformulation of Certain Aspects of Welfare Economics," *Quarterly Journal of Economics* (February 1938): 310–334, formally introduced the concept of a welfare function. For a textbook on welfare economics, see Robin W. Boadway and Neil Bruce, *Welfare Economics* (London: Basil Blackwell, 1984).
2. This compensation principle was proposed by Nicholas Kaldor, "Welfare Propositions in Economics," *Economic Journal* 49 (December 1939): 549–552; and Sir John R. Hicks, "The Foundation of Welfare Economics," *Economic Journal* 49 (December 1939): 696–712.
3. The compensation principle identifies actual increases in economic welfare, for small changes, if the income distribution is already optimal. See Hal R. Varian, *Microeconomic Analysis*, 3rd ed. (New York: Norton, 1992), pp. 409–410.
4. See I. M. D. Little, *A Critique of Welfare Economics* (Oxford: Oxford University Press, 1949), pp. 198–205.
5. For an introduction to shadow prices, see Robin W. Boadway and David E. Wildasin, *Public Sector Economics*, 2nd ed. (Boston: Little Brown and Company, 1984).
6. See Partha Dasgupta, Stephen Marglin, and Amartya Sen, *Guidelines for Project Evaluation* (New York: United Nations, UNIDO, 1972) and, for an alternative approach, see I. M. D. Little and J. A. Mirrlees, *Manual of Industrial Project Analysis in Developing Countries*, vol. 2, *Social Cost–Benefit Analysis* (Paris: Development Center of OECD, 1968).
7. See Robin Burgess and Nicholas Stern, "Taxation and Development," *Journal of Economic Literature* 31 (June 1993): 762–830, for a detailed discussion of taxation in developing countries. This section draws much from Burgess and Stern and from Stern, "Walras-Pareto Lecture, 1–3 May 1991, University of Lausanne Public Policy and Economic Development" (unpublished manuscript, London School of Economics).
8. See Stephen R. Lewis, Jr., "Agricultural Taxation in a Developing Economy," in Agricultural Development and Economic Growth, ed. H. M. Southworth and Bruce F. Johnston (Ithaca, N.Y.: Cornell University Press, 1967), pp. 453–492.
9. See Jonathon Skinner, "Prospects for Agricultural Land Taxation in Developing Countries," in *Tax Policy in Developing Countries*, ed. J. Khalizadeh-Shiazi and A. Shaw (Washington, D.C.: World Bank, 1991).
10. Burgess and Stern, "Taxation aqnd Development," p. 773.
11. Ibid., p. 772.
12. See Nicholas Kaldor, *Essays on Policy I* (New York: Holmes and Meier, 1984), Chapters 10, 11, and 12, for early views on tax reform.
13. See Ehtisham S. Ahmad and Nicholas H. Stern, *The Theory and Practice of Tax Reform in Developing Countries* (Cambridge: Cambridge University Press, 1991).
14. For example, see Michael H. Best, "Political Power and Tax Revenues in Central America," *Journal of Development Economics* 3 (March 1976): 49–82.

7

International Trade

The role that international trade has played and should play in the process of economic development has divided development economists. Some economists have argued that trade is a mechanism by which the wealthy nations of the world exploit the poor by extracting economic surplus. Some of these theories were touched upon in Chapter 1. Others argue that, although trade may not necessarily harm a nation, its impact is too diluted to provide the necessary stimulus to generate development. Therefore, a nation should turn inward and search for its own solution to the develop‐ment problem independent of the flows of international trade. Finally, there are those who argue that outward oriented growth is the only feasible long‐term strategy for development.

Theories of the role of international trade in economic development have been heavily influenced by perceptions of the underlying causes of historical development successes. The success of England in exporting to new markets, created in part by the discovery of the new world, influenced classical and traditional Marxist views of trade and development. The recent successful performances of the Japanese, Taiwanese, and South Korean economies have also lent support to the view that export expansion is a key to development. The recent success of these economies might serve to indicate that rapid development can be achieved by following an outward oriented, export promotion strategy of development. The controversy has centered on three questions. First, because these Asian countries also protect many activities, did they really follow an outward oriented growth strategy? Second, early in their growth processes, all these nations engaged in practices that sharply restricted and regulated international trade, so does their example suggest that countries might best follow import substitution policies followed later by export promotion? Finally, do the experiences of these countries represent very special cases from which there are few lessons to be learned by today's developing countries?

233

To shed light on these and other issues, trade theory as it relates to development will be explored in this chapter. In the first section of the chapter the comparative static analysis of the impact of trade in the small and large country cases will be discussed. Classical and neoclassical trade theory will be introduced in terms of the support these theories provide for the existence of positive allocative gains from trade, in a static framework.

The second section of the chapter will explore various critiques of the conventional view of the role of trade. Since Marxian and Keynsian critiques were discussed in Chapter 1, little more will be said concerning these views. Instead, various forms of the infant industry argument will be analyzed. Specifically, the existence of distortions and externalities, within a dual economy setting, will be discussed within the context of an import substitution strategy as being a second best policy solution.

The third section of the chapter will discuss in some detail the import substitution or inward oriented strategy of economic development. The results of such strategies in terms of economic performance will then be explored. The overall conclusion is that for some countries the strategy has been successfully applied, but for the bulk of today's developing nations this approach has been a failure.

The reasons for the failure of the import substitution strategy will also be analyzed. Of course, there are the efficiency, mainly allocative, losses stemming from inward oriented strategies of development. However, it will be argued that the main reasons for the failure of the import substitution strategy are to be found elsewhere. Specifically, most less developed nations initially pursued a first stage import substitution strategy geared toward the domestic production of consumer goods. In the vast majority of cases the industries established were not internationally competitive and thus continued industrialization depended upon second stage import substitution in which intermediate input industries were promoted. These industries also failed to become internationally competitive. Alternatively, East Asia turned outward after its first stage of import substitution. That is, the industries created in this first stage were forced to become internationally competitive. The difference in experiences is linked to government policy making.

TRADITIONAL PERSPECTIVE

Gains from Trade

It has long been argued that as long as opportunity costs differ among nations, all countries will benefit (at least potentially) from specializing in the production and export of that commodity in which it has a relative or comparative advantage. The reasons for these differences in opportunity

Table 7.1   Classical example.

	Food	Manufacturing
Home	5	15
Rest of world	10	10

costs include differences in technology, in the proportion of potentially mobile factors (between sectors) such as capital and labor, or in the availability of specific, nonmobile factors (between sectors) such as land or natural resources. The two dominant theoretical models explaining comparative advantage and trade are the classical model and the neoclassical model. The classical model stresses differences in natural resources or in technology,[1] whereas the neoclassical model stresses differences in the proportion of capital to labor. In the next few pages, both classical and neoclassical views will be analyzed.

In the classical view of production and trade, labor is the only factor of production, and there are constant returns to labor. To illustrate the classical theory, assume that there are only two countries producing two goods, food and manufactured goods. One of these countries is a small country, called the *home country,* and the other country is the rest of the world. The home country is small in the sense that it may buy or sell all it wants at world prices. The production functions for the home country and the rest of the world are illustrated in Table 7.1, which gives the hours of labor required to produce food and manufactures. In the home country, 5 hours of labor are needed to produce a unit of food and 15 hours are needed to produce a unit of the manufactured good. Consequently, the real cost of manufactures in terms of food in the home country is $15/5 = 3$ and will be denoted as P_M/P_F. For the rest of the world $P_M/P_F = 10/10 = 1$, which, because the home country is small, is the real price for which manufactured goods can be obtained in the world market.

The home country's choices are illustrated in Figure 7.1. HH' is the production possibilities curve for the home country. Because constant returns to labor is assumed, HH' is linear. Its slope is $-P_M/P_F = -3$. Its location is determined by the size of the labor force, which is fixed in the short run. The curves TT, $T'T'$, and $T''T''$ all have the slope $-P_M/P_F = -1$ and represent isoincome curves giving combinations of food and manufactures that can be purchased for the same income, at world prices. For example, the home country could produce at A and trade to any point along TT. The highest obtainable national income (isoincome line) can be reached by producing at H and trading along $T'T'$. Points along $T''T''$ are not obtainable.

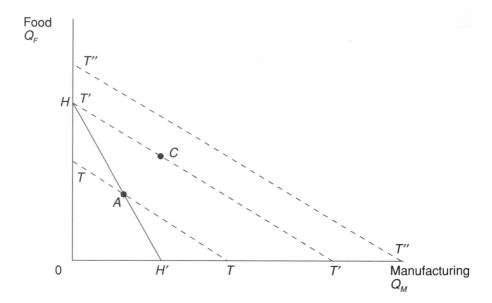

Figure 7.1 The home country's choices.

The classical theory provides a powerful argument for free trade. For any point on *HH'* (other than *H*) such as *A*, we can always find a point on *T'T'* where the home country could consume more of both commodities. It does not even matter what determines the slope of the isoincome line. The small home country is better off producing at *H* and trading along *T'T'*.

One difficulty with the classical theory, at least for the two goods model, is that it implies complete specialization. However, complete specialization is seldom observed. Consequently, the two goods classical model is not consistent with the empirical evidence. This complete specialization comes from the linearity of *HH'*. If *HH'* were strictly convex, as is the case in Figure 7.2, complete specialization would seldom occur. National income would be maximized if the country produced at the point on *HH'* with a slope equal to the real world price. This occurs in Figure 7.2, at point *B*. The country should produce at *B* and trade, at world prices, along *TT*. For any other point on *HH'*, such as *A*, we can always find a point on *TT* where more of both commodities could be consumed.

In the neoclassical view[2] of production and trade, both labor and capital are factors of production. Differences in relative costs of producing commodities are determined by differences in factor proportions. The production functions are linearly homogeneous but there are diminishing marginal returns to capital and labor. The production possibilities curve for each country is strictly convex, as was the case in Figure 7.2. Consequently, complete specialization is not expected. The reason for focusing on the proportion of

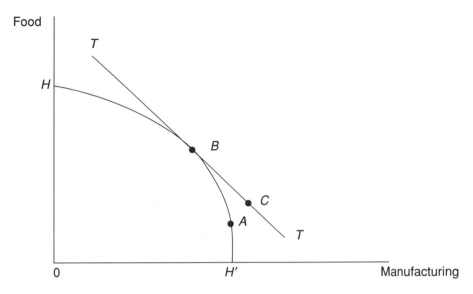

Figure 7.2 The home country's choice without complete specialization.

capital to labor is because the neoclassical theory is designed to explain real wage and profit rates. To do so, production and consumption of each good needs to be determined both with and without trade. The demand for goods is described by introducing community indifference curves. The role of community indifference curves will be seen in discussing Figure 7.3.

As with the classical model, assume that the home country is small. It produces on a production possibilities curve *HH*. The goods produced are simply designated as Y_1 and Y_2. Its community indifference curves are denoted as C_0, C_1, and C_2. Under conditions of autarchy the highest production and consumption point that can be attained is represented by point *A*. At this point the domestic marginal rate of transformation (the slope of the production possibilities curve) equals the domestic price ratio (the slope of line *PP*), which is equal to the marginal rate of substitution in consumption (represented by the slope of C_0).

Now assume that the home nation is opened to trade. The slope of the isoincome lines *TT* and *T'T'* is determined by the international terms of trade. If the slopes of *PP* and *TT* differ, trade will be beneficial. For example, in Figure 7.3, the home country would maximize utility by producing at *D* and trading along *T'T'* to *C*. Hence, compared with autarchy (no trade) where *A* is produced and consumed, the home country will shift domestic resources from producing Y_1 toward producing Y_2. The costs of producing Y_2 will rise and the costs of producing Y_1 will fall until the domestic price

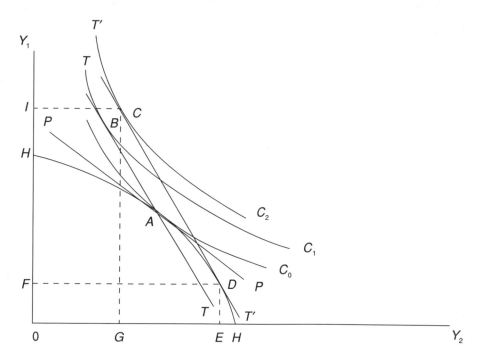

Figure 7.3 Neoclassical model of trade.

ratio equals the terms of trade. Further specialization in the production of Y_2 is not profitable. In addition, the home nation can trade Y_2 for Y_1 by moving along the international terms of trade line given by $T'T'$, until the highest possible indifference curve is attained, given by C_2 at point C.

After trade occurs, $0E$ of Y_2 will be produced, but only $0G$ is consumed. Thus, the home nation exports GE trading along $T'T'$. Hence, $0I$ of Y_1 is consumed but only $0F$ is produced. FI represents the amount of Y_1 which is imported by the home country.

The home nation certainly benefits from trade because trade allows the country to go from indifference curve C_0 to C_2. These gains from trade can be divided into two parts: production gains and consumption gains. Beginning at A, the autarchy point, assume that the home country is opened to international trade but that no change in production is allowed to occur. The international terms of trade are given by the slope of line TT, and the home nation is allowed to trade along this line as long as the production point remains at A. The highest indifference curve that can be achieved in this situation is C_1 at B. Thus the movement from A to B represents the consumption gains from trade that follow from allowing consumers in the home nation to buy Y_1 at the cheaper international prices. The movement from B to C represents gains that accrue as the result of the home country specializing in the production of the good in which it has a comparative advantage in Y_2.

In summary, utility maximization is achieved via trade when

$$DRT = FRT = DRS. \tag{7.1}$$

In this expression DRT is the domestic rate of transformation and is given by the slope of the production possibilities curve. FRT is the foreign rate of transformation and is represented by the slope of the terms of trade line. Finally, DRS is the domestic rate of substitution and is represented by the slope of the community indifferences curve.

It is obvious from examining Figure 7.3 that any restriction of trade, under the given circumstances, would reduce the nation's level of welfare. Thus, the conclusion follows that free trade represents the best of all possible worlds. However, both neoclassical and classical theories recognize one exception to the free trade argument. In a large country, where the home country's decisions affect the terms of trade, the home country possesses some monopoly power over the international terms of trade and can take advantage of this power in its trading decisions. This possibility underlies the case for an optimum tariff.

The ability to alter the terms of trade will influence a country's desired exports and imports. For example, in Figure 7.4, two different terms of trade, for T_1T_1 and T_2T_2 are considered, where T_2T_2 represents a higher relative price for Y_1, the export good. Note that as the terms of trade rise, desired imports rise from $(D_2 - S_2)$ to $(D_2' - S_2')$, and desired exports rise from $(S_1 - D_1)$ to $(S_1' - D_1')$. Thus if a nation can raise the terms of trade ratio, it can increase both desired exports and imports. There will be a gain to the home country because it can now sell its exports at a higher relative price. The terms of trade could be changed by the imposition of a tariff. There would, however, be an efficiency loss due to the distortion caused by the tariff.[3] However, initially the terms of trade gains will outweigh the misallocation losses if the tariff is small. For high tariffs, the misallocation losses will be larger than the terms of trade gains. At some intermediate level, an optimal tariff will be found.

The optimum tariff can be illustrated by utilizing offer curves as in Figure 7.5. The slope of straight lines out of the origin represent relative price ratios. Thus the steeper the curve, the higher is the price of good one (the export good of the home country and the import good of the foreign country) relative to good two (the export good of the foreign country and the import good of the home country). Curve $0H$ shows how much of Y_1 the home country is willing to give for imports of Y_2. Note that as the relative price of Y_1 rises, the home country is willing to offer or sell more of Y_1 to

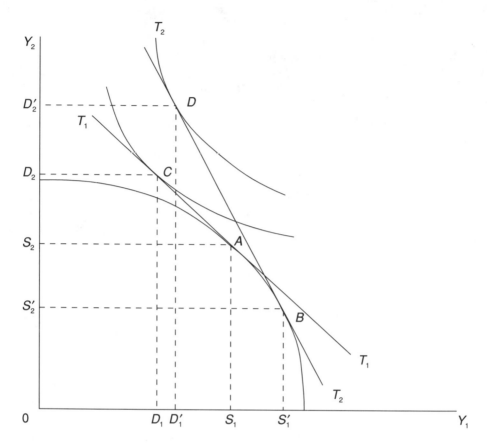

Figure 7.4   The terms of trade.

obtain additional Y_2. Alternatively, $0F$ represents the foreign country's offer curve. The two offer curves intersect at the equilibrium terms of trade (relative price ratio).[4]

Note that C_0 and C_1, represent community indifference curves for the home country. They are positively sloped because as more Y_1 is given up (exported) additional quantities of Y_2 must be received in return to attain the same level of welfare. Improvements in utility occur as one moves from C_0 to C_1 (obtaining more of Y_2 for the same amount of Y_1). The important point to see is that a higher level of utility can be attained if the home country can shift its offer curve up and to the left. This can be achieved by the home country imposing a tariff on Y_2. For example, if the tariff is levied in terms of Y_1, then for each amount of Y_2 the foreign country will receive less Y_1 (the tariff can also be levied in terms of Y_2). As can be seen, it would be possible to achieve a higher level of utility (C_1) through the use of a tariff.

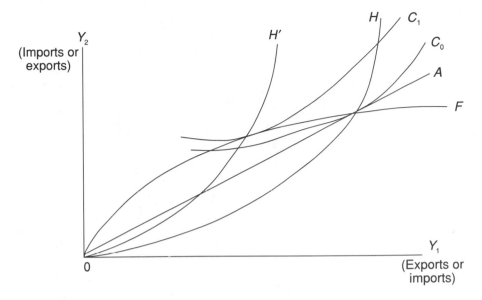

Figure 7.5 The optimum tariff.

The main criticism of the optimum tariff notion is that such a protection-ist policy is basically a zero sum game situation. That is, the benefits to the home country of such a policy come at the expense of one's trading part-ners. As a result, this sort of policy invites retaliation. As retaliation occurs, all of the terms of trade gains are negated and the amount of trade is reduced, resulting in a loss of welfare (operating on a lower level indiffer-ence curve) for both the home country and its trading partners. Thus the neoclassical argument, despite admitting the theoretical possibility of an ex-ception to the optimality of free trade, generally implies that a free trade policy is overall the best. Hence, the neoclassical theory, like the classical theory provides a powerful argument for free trade.

Factor Payments and Trade

Factor payments are changed by trade. A primary advantage of neoclassical theory is its emphasis on the market determination of prices including factor prices. One of the most interesting and simultaneously one of the most troubling implications of neoclassical trade theory is the factor–price equali-zation theorem. For the model developed thus far, free trade will result in each factor earning the same rate of return in both countries. This theorem is troubling because it does not appear to be consistent with observation. Wage rates, for the same skill level, are not the same in developed versus less developed countries. These differences might be explained by trade

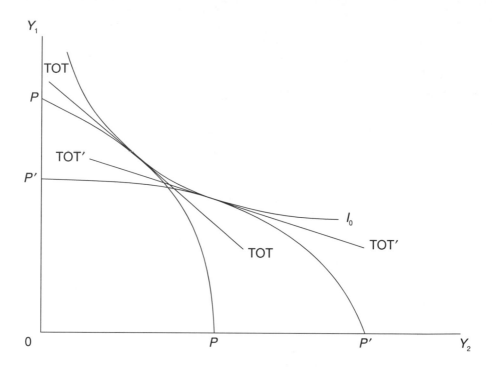

Figure 7.6 The Hecksher–Ohlin theory of trade.

restrictions, transportation costs, economies to scale, nontradeable goods, differences in technology, complete specialization, or production externalities. Another explanation draws from the new growth theory discussed in Chapter 1. Before discussing these possible explanations, let us briefly consider how factor price equalization works. The theory we will discuss is referred to as the Hecksher–Ohlin[5] theory of trade.

To simplify the Hecksher–Ohlin theory, assume that there are two countries each producing two different goods (Y_1 and Y_2) that require two inputs, capital (K) and labor (N), in the production process. Furthermore, assume, for all possible factor price combinations, that the production of Y_1 always requires a higher capital to labor ratio than Y_2 (the production of Y_1 is capital intensive relative to Y_2). The production functions for the two goods in country one are assumed to be identical to those in country two and preference patterns are also assumed to be identical. Finally, let country one be relatively capital abundant while country two is labor abundant ($K_1/L_1 >$ K_2/L_2).

Given these assumptions, Figure 7.6 can be used to illustrate the Hecksher–Ohlin theory of trade. Production possibilities curve PP represents country one, the capital abundant nation, and $P'P'$ represents the production possibilities curve for country two, the labor abundant nation. It simplifies the presentation to assume that these countries are near enough in size so that *PP* and *P'P'* intersect. Notice that it is assumed, for any given ratio of goods, that the slope of country one's production possibilities curve is greater than that for country two. This implies, for the same capital–labor ratio, that the opportunity cost of producing Y_2, the labor intensive good, is higher in country one and the opportunity cost of producing the capital intensive good is higher in country two. The indifference curves are identical in the two countries and the slopes of the points of tangency with the two production possibilities curves gives the relative prices of Y_1 and Y_2 in the two countries (TOT and TOT'). For illustration, the points of tangency are drawn to lie on the same indifference curve.

In the situation depicted in Figure 7.6 country one possesses a comparative advantage in the production of Y_1 and country two in Y_2. Thus one of the main conclusions of the Hecksher–Ohlin theory is that countries tend to have a comparative advantage in goods whose production is intensive in factors with which they are abundantly endowed and export goods in which they have a comparative advantage. Therefore, in our example the capital abundant nation (one) has a comparative advantage in the capital intensive good and the labor abundant nation (two) has a comparative advantage in the labor intensive good (Y_2).

As trade occurs between these two countries, there will be a tendency for output prices to converge. Under standard assumptions, complete convergence will occur with relative output prices becoming identical in the two countries. This is illustrated in Figure 7.7.

The convergence of output prices also has an influence on relative factor prices as well. Before trade, the ratio of the price of capital to labor was lower in country one relative to country two, because country one was relatively capital abundant, country two was relatively labor abundant, relative factor prices were identical to relative factor marginal productivities, and the technologies for production were identical between the two countries. As trade occurred, the production of the capital intensive good expanded in country one, causing the relative price of capital to rise. Alternatively, as the production of the labor intensive good rose in country two, the relative price of labor rose. Eventually, factor price equalization occurred.[6]

Thus two important conclusions follow from the Hecksher–Ohlin theory of trade. First, a nation has a comparative advantage in the good that is intensive in the use of the factor of production that is most abundant in the nation. Second, factor prices (e.g., wage rates and profit rates) are equalized. Hence, not all groups within a country benefit from trade. For example, in the preceding discussion, the wage rate of labor in the capital abundant nation declined, which implies that labor was made worse off as a result of

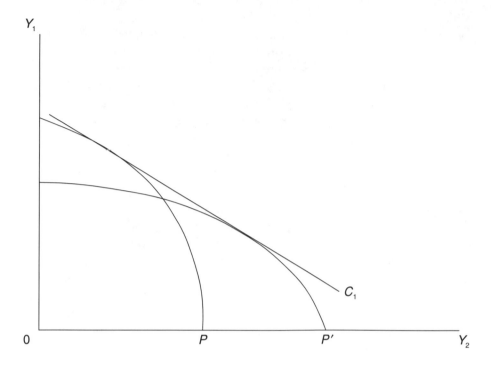

Figure 7.7   The convergence of output prices.

trade. Alternatively, in the labor abundant nation, the return to capital declined, implying that the owners of capital were harmed as the result of trade. These two conclusions of the Hecksher–Ohlin trade theory suggest two empirical tests to see if these implications hold.

One test of the Hecksher–Ohlin theory of trade concerns whether the theory predicts which goods a country exports. For example, in the immediate postwar period the U.S. economy was by far the world's wealthiest nation. In addition, it was the world's most capital intensive nation as well. Therefore the Hecksher–Ohlin theory would seem to predict that U.S. exports would be capital intensive whereas U.S. imports would be labor intensive. However, in a study carried out in the late 1950s, Leontief[7] found that U.S. exports were less capital intensive than U.S. imports. This result has come to be known as the *Leontief paradox*. Further tests[8] using data for a large number of countries confirm the Leontief paradox. It would seem that trade does not follow the pattern predicted by Hecksher–Ohlin theory.

The Leontief paradox is not easily resolved, and without a resolution the Hecksher–Ohlin theory is of little use. One possible resolution is to introduce another factor of production, like human capital. In terms of the two factor model, capital can be thought of as existing both in physical and human forms. A country's exports can then be capital intensive, both physical and human, without being physical capital intensive. Another possible explanation is that comparative advantage is determined by differences in technology between countries, similar to the classical theory of trade analysis earlier. However, the neoclassical theory of factor proportions would still determine comparative advantage if the technologies are the same, and in neoclassical theory factor payments would still be affected by trade.

The other prediction of Hecksher–Ohlin is that factor prices should be equalized. This prediction is called the *factor price equalization theorem*. This prediction obviously contradicts reality. As discussed in the labor chapter, Chapter 5, wage rates for the same type of labor are not equalized. This divergence may result from differences in technology or because there are external returns to education. Also production externalities may affect relative factor payments. The role of externalities was discussed in Chapter 1.

One implication of the factor price equalization theorem is that some will gain from trade while others lose. How is this conclusion to be reconciled with those derived from Figure 7.3? Specifically, the discussion of Figure 7.3 indicated that nations are made better off as a result of trade. One can make these ideas compatible by going back to the nature of community indifference curves. To draw such indifference curves one could assume that all individuals have the same tastes and the same share of all resources. Thus as the return to the one factor of production rises and the return to the second falls, all individuals will still be better off, because the rise in returns to one factor of production outweighs the reduction in returns to the other factor (since trade improves overall allocative efficiency in the economy). Alternatively, one can assume that after trade takes place the government will pay off the losers (laborers in the capital intensive nation and the owners of capital in the labor intensive nation), still leaving the winners with more than they had before trade. Lacking this, the most that can be concluded is that trade results in an increase in potential welfare. After trade it would be possible for the winners to compensate the losers and for the former to still be better off after trade.

Factor Price Equalization, Factor Mobility, and the New Trade Theory

In discussing the implications of Hecksher–Ohlin, we mentioned that, although much attention has been paid to the Leontief paradox, little attention has been paid to failures of factor price equalization because it is obvious that factor prices are not the same in every country. Wage rates, for labor of any skill level, are clearly higher in developed than in less developed countries. There are numerous reasons why factor price equalization might

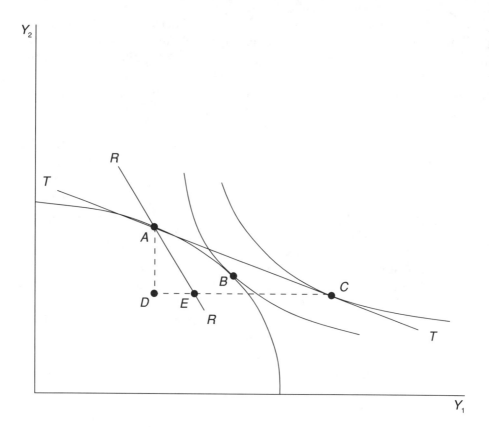

Figure 7.8   Nontraded goods example.

fail, including protectionist trade policies, complete specialization due to large
differences in relative factor endowments, the existence of nontraded goods
or services, the existence of returns to scale or positive production externalities, positive externalities to education, and differences in technology. Three
reasons for factor prices to fail to equalize that will be discussed here are the
existence of nontraded goods, externalities, and differences in infrastructure.

Nontraded Goods and Factor Mobility

The existence of nontraded goods means that the prices of these goods will
not be equalized between countries. Many services are by their nature not
traded at all. Unless factors of production are mobile, factor price equalization will not occur if there are nontraded goods. Consider a two goods
model, illustrated in Figure 7.8. Y_1 is a tradeable good and Y_2 is a nontradeable
service. The country in question is assumed to have a small, less developed
economy with labor as its most abundant factor of production. The good is

assumed to be capital intensive, and the service is assumed to be labor intensive. Suppose that *TT* represents the international terms of trade, but that the transactions costs of exporting services are prohibitively high. If there were no transactions costs, the country would produce at *A* and trade to *C*, where *TT* is tangent to a community indifference curve. The country would trade *AD* services for *DC* goods. Instead the country produces and consumes at *B* with the relative price of labor in the less developed country remaining below that of the rest of the world and the return to capital being relatively higher.

When trade cannot occur, factor mobility can lead to the achievement of the free trade result (point *C*).⁹ The Rybczynski theorem is useful in demonstrating this point. According to this theorem, increasing the endowment of any factor of production while leaving the other factor fixed will increase the output of the good that uses the increased input intensively while decreasing the output of the other good. The reverse holds for a decrease in a factor of production; in this case, labor. This is represented in the diagram by the Rybczynski line (*RR*), which shows the locus of outputs when the endowment of labor declines (or increases), ceteris paribus. This line is drawn through *DC* at *E*. *E* represents a possible production equilibrium as labor services are exported. This is a possible equilibrium because at *E* labor remittances, in payments of *EC*, when added to the outputs at *E* permit consumption at point *C*. If all of labor's income earned abroad is sent home this result must follow. This follows because *EC* equals the decrease in national income due to the export of labor services, the decrease in labor multiplied by the marginal product of labor in the home country. The decrease in home country labor must be equal to the increase in foreign country labor. In addition, the marginal productivity of labor will be identical in the two countries (as a result of factor mobility). Therefore, the decrease in domestic income due to the export of labor services must be equal to labor's income earned abroad.¹⁰

There are, of course, numerous barriers to migration between countries even though migration, like trade, is potentially beneficial to the residents of these countries. Workers in capital abundant countries are likely to oppose immigration because it would reduce wage rates. Capital may move more freely and thus could flow from capital abundant countries to labor abundant countries. The results would be symmetrical to those with labor migration in that profit rates would fall in the labor abundant country and rise in the capital abundant country until factor prices are equalized. Again, there are barriers to capital mobility just as there are barriers to migration. Capital owners in labor abundant countries are likely to oppose foreign investment because it would reduce profit rates. Consequently, factor price differences could persist because factors of production are not very mobile.

In discussing the impact of nontradeables on factor prices, it is important to note that the existence of nontradeables causes wages to be lower and profit rates to be higher in the labor abundant country when factors are immobile. As we saw from the discussion of education and productivity in Chapter 5, these profit rates would have to be enormous if factor proportions alone were to explain income differences between countries. Specifically, even though wages are lower in poor countries than in rich ones, there is no indication that profit rates are higher in the former relative to the latter. In fact, both profit rates and wage rates, adjusted for risk, may be higher in rich relative to poor nations. Consequently, even though nontraded goods and factor immobility undoubtedly have something to do with wage rate differentials, they do not provide a complete answer as to why factor prices fail to equalize.

Specialization, Economies of Scale, and the New Trade Theory

Some theorists have sought to utilize models with economies of scale to analyze the effects of trade.[11] There are two variants of this approach: the first based on external economies in competitive markets and the second based on monopolistic competition. With the first, the economies of scale are external to each firm but internal to the industry. This type of externality is generally associated with information or knowledge. The externality occurs as knowledge spills over to other firms in two forms. First, direct information may flow from firm to firm through day to day contact. Second, as workers move from firm to firm they carry the skills and knowledge that they have learned.

As the reader will remember, these economies are external to the firm but internal to the industry. Thus, as the industry expands in scale, costs to each individual firm will fall as external economies are generated. This implies that comparative advantage may often be the result of historical accident in the sense that a particular country that happens to begin producing a particular product, subject to these external economies, before anyone else will find its productivity growing and its per unit cost falling. This will allow the country to gain a long-run advantage in the production of the good. Alternatively, a farsighted government's policy aimed at promoting a particular industry would result in it becoming a major exporter.

Externalities also provide an explanation as to why factor price equalization may not occur. Such externalities are likely to increase the productivity of both capital and labor. Hence countries experiencing such externalities are likely to experience high returns for both labor and capital.

Economies of scale can also be internal to a firm. A simple way of introducing the discussion of such economies is to consider a simple model

hegelan
e Drive
ginia 22101
A

hor/Artist	Format	List Price	Our Price	Total
hard Grabowski, :hael P. Shields	Hardcover	41.95	41.95	41.95
:ald M. Meier itor)	Paperback	41.95	41.95	0.00
ert L. Koegel itor), Lynn Kern egel (Editor)	Paperback	32.95	26.36	0.00
Frith (Editor)	Paperback	22.95	22.95	0.00

Subtotal	41.95
Shipping & Handling	10.95
Order Total	52.90
Paid via Amex	52.90
Balance Due	0.00

.com, and please come again!

3 million titles, everyday savings of up to 40%

amazon.com

Books, Music & More

Our Return Policy

Our return policy is simple. Within 30 days of receipt of your order, you may return:

- any book in its original condition
- any unopened CD

We will issue a full refund for the price of any item you return that meets these conditions. We can only refund shipping costs if the return is a result of our error.

Please fill out the return information and include this packing slip with your return. Please wrap the package securely.

Send it to:

Amazon.com
Returns Department
One Centerpoint Boulevard
New Castle, DE 19720-4172
USA

For your protection, please use UPS or Insured

Problems, Questions, Suggestions?

If you have any questions regarding this order, please contact us via telephone (1-800-201-7575 or 1-206-346-2992), e-mail (orders@amazon.com), or FAX (1-206-346-2950).

Reasons for return:

_____

_____

_____

_____

Thank You!

http://www.amazon.com

Thanks for shopping at Amazon.com!

BOOKS, MUSIC & MORE
amazon.com

http://www.amazon.com
orders@amazon.com

Rand
1716 !
Mclean,

Amazon.com   Toll–Free: (800) 201–7575
1 Centerpoint Blvd   Voice: +1 (206) 694–2992
New Castle, DE 19720   FAX: +1 (206) 694–2950
USA

Your order of September 02, 1998 (Order ID 002–9683636–1700465)

Quantity	Title

In This Shipment

| 1 | Development Economics *(47–4–655)* |

Already Shipped

1   Leading Issues in Economic Development

1   Teaching Children With Autism : Strategies for Initiating Positive
Interactions and Improving Learning Opportunities

1   Autism and Asperger Syndrome

Thanks for shopping at Am

129/19115638/1b/1pn/4195/next/226515

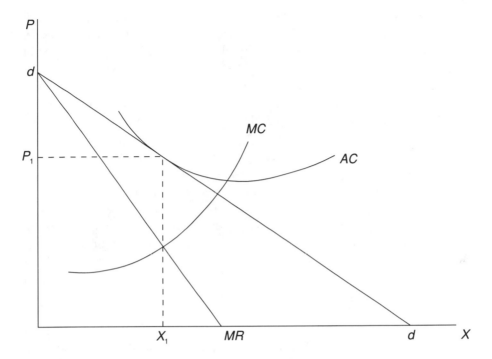

Figure 7.9 Long-run equilibrium.

of monopolistic competition. Remember, in this kind of market each firm has a monopoly in the product that it produces, but there are many close substitutes. Thus in long–run equilibrium all economic profit is squeezed out. This long-run equilibrium is illustrated in Figure 7.9, where *dd* represents the demand curve, *AC* average cost, and *MC* marginal cost for a particular firm. The firm will produce at X_1, where $MR = MC$ and charge price P_1. As the country engages in trade and market size increases, still more firms will enter the market producing close substitutes for the goods of existing firms. The uniqueness of each firm's product will be eroded, making *dd* flatten. This will make the tangency of *dd* with *AC* move to a lower level on the average cost curve. Thus firms in such an industry will find productivity improved and costs lowered as market size increases.

The new trade theory stresses that any trade liberalization will make the market larger and, hence, reduce costs. These externalities will be general gains and do not in themselves explain divergences from factor price equalization. They do offer an additional source of gains from trade, however, in that trade will enlarge the market and make it more competitive; that is, more allocatively efficient. To the extent that larger national markets are more allocatively efficient, however, the new trade theory suggests that both labor and capital will be more productive. Thus, countries with large and growing markets are likely to find, ceteris paribus, the returns to capital and labor being higher relative to those countries with small and stagnant markets. Factor price equilibrium does not occur because of these higher returns in large and growing economies.

A recognition of these externalities is important in trade debates. For example, in the United States there was considerable discussion about possible distributive effects of NAFTA (The North American Free Trade Agreement). Opponents of NAFTA argued that NAFTA would increase the profits of U.S. multinationals and wage rates in Mexico but reduce wage rates in the United States until U.S. and Mexican wage rates converged. This convergence is precisely the factor price equalization theorem. They also argued that this process would be accelerated by capital flowing from the United States to Mexico to seek lower production costs, due to the lower Mexican wage rates. Proponents of the agreement contended that better infrastructure and education made U.S. costs lower and U.S. labor more productive. U.S. wage and profit rates would rise because freer trade would shift production along lines of comparative advantage.

The new trade theory suggests two effects of freer trade. First, there would be a Hecksher–Ohlin effect. Wage rates would fall and profit rates rise in the United States. The opposite would occur in Mexico. Second, there would be an increase in allocative efficiency within each country. Wage rates and profit rates would rise in each country. Hence, these two effects would both have a positive impact on Mexican wages and U.S. profits. Their impact on U.S. wages and Mexican profits would be offsetting. Hence, the question of whether NAFTA would increase or reduce U.S. wages is empirical. The answer depends upon the relative strength of these two effects.

Considerable empirical work had been done on NAFTA spurred by speculation and a previous U.S.–Canada free trade agreement. For example, Robert Stern, Alan Deardorff, and Drusilla Brown used a computable general equilibrium (CGE) model, which assumed monopolistic competition and, hence, increasing returns, to estimate the impact NAFTA would have on the U.S. economy.[12] They found that NAFTA would increase both U.S. and Mexican wage rates but that Mexican wage rates would rise by much more than wage rates in the United States, if the agreement were implemented.

Some Additional Benefits to Trade

Trade also works as a restraining influence in situations of monopoly and oligopoly. If domestic markets are so small that only one or at most a few firms can take advantage of the existing economies of scale, then allocative inefficiency may arise as these firms exert monopoly power. By opening the country up to trade, domestic firms will be subject to competition from foreign firms and thus the extent of inefficiency would be reduced.[13]

Classical economic theory argued that trade might very well lead to improvements in technical efficiency. That is, less developed countries, which are closed off, for the most part, from international trade, may have surplus land and labor that are not currently being utilized in the production process. In other words, an economy may be operating inside of its production possibilities curve as the result of a lack of demand for those products the surplus labor and land could produce. However, once the country is opened up to trade, external demand for these products would now make it profitable to utilize the surplus land and labor in the production process. Thus the economy moves from a point inside the production possibilities curve to a point on the curve. It follows then that the economy is benefiting from "free" growth, an expansion in production for which the opportunity cost is zero. This has often been labeled the *vent for surplus* theory of trade and has played an important role in the work of Hla Myint.[14]

In summary, through a variety of mechanisms, trade promotes a more efficient economy in that it promotes improvements in allocative and technical efficiency. These are the comparative static effects of trade. They will increase income, but once the improvements in efficiency are exhausted, the rate of growth will return to the previous trend.

These ideas can be illustrated, in a simple way, by extending the discussion into the realm of neoclassical growth theory. Suppose that an economy can produce a number of goods, utilizing capital and labor, and that the production process is characterized by constant returns to scale. In addition, assume that the economy under consideration represents the small country case (prices are given exogenously). Under these conditions, it is possible to define a composite or surrogate production function by taking the inner envelope of a set of isoquants for the goods that have the same value at international prices. Findlay[15] has called this the *foreign exchange production function*. This is illustrated in Figure 7.10 where I_o, J_o, and K_o represent different production functions for different goods that represent the same value of international prices.

As a result, a composite production function can be constructed that represents a foreign exchange production function, and this is illustrated by $F(k)$ in Figure 7.11. This is, of course, identical to the apparatus that is usually used to present the neoclassical theory of growth. Now, however, the composite production function replaces the single good production function. Thus, given the marginal propensity to save (s) and the rate of growth of the effective labor force (n), the equilibrium capital to labor ratio $k*$ is easily derived.

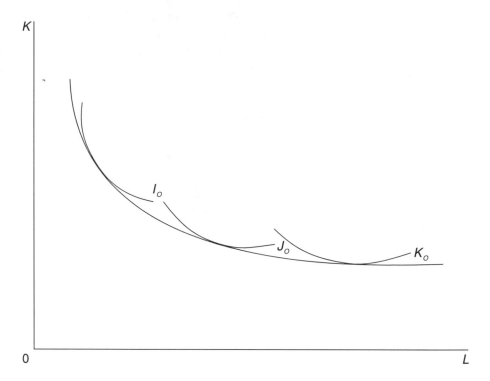

Figure 7.10   Composite production function.

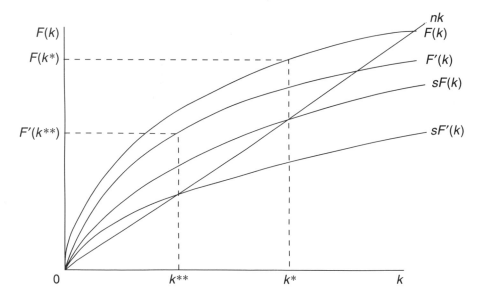

Figure 7.11   Neoclassical growth.

To compare this trade situation with autarchy, presume that a composite production function is now constructed using domestic rather than international prices. Thus the isoquants will represent the inner envelope of isoquants for various goods that represent the same value. In Figure 7.11 this is represented by $F'(k)$, and as can be seen, the equilibrium capital to labor ratio and the per capita income level will be lower for the same s and n, but the growth rate will still be equal to n. Thus trade allows a country to achieve a higher level of income per capita, but not a higher long-run growth rate.

Initial empirical estimates of the comparative static gains from trade, that is, the size of the shift from $F'(k)$ to $F(k)$, have proven to be rather small. However, estimates such as these have been subjected to a significant amount of criticism at both the technical and theoretical levels. At the theoretical level, it is argued that no account has been taken of the waste of resources that occurs as the result of rent seeking activities generated by protectionist policies. Quotas are particularly harmful in generating rent seeking behavior.

Quotas reduce the quantity available of a particular imported good below the domestic demand for this good. So some mechanism must be used to allocate scarce foreign exchange to determine who will be allowed to import the good. Import licenses, which are allocated to individuals, permit them to import limited quantities of the good. In effect, recipients of such import licenses receive a valuable property right, allowing them to sell a product that is in short supply domestically. This property right is valuable and leads to the allocation of resources, by various individuals and groups, with the sole purpose of gaining access to these licenses. A frequently encountered example of this resource expenditure is that individual firms requiring an imported raw material or intermediate good are often allocated licenses for the imports in proportion to their share of the industry's capacity (the industry to which they belong). It follows then that firms may be expected to add to capacity, even when they are not operating at full capacity, to gain access to additional import licenses.[16] Other examples of rent seeking activity include the expenditure of time and resources by business owners and their representatives in an attempt to obtain licenses. Other theorists have extended the rent seeking notion to tariffs as well. They have argued that the imposition of tariffs creates the opportunity for firms to earn excess revenues and that this will also lead to rent seeking behavior.[17]

All of these rent seeking activities add to the costs of protection. As a result, comparative static losses to an economy that follows protectionist trade policy are likely to be higher than originally thought. In addition, these losses are no longer merely one time, comparative static losses. However, the main determining factor of a country's rate of growth would still be those factors within a country that influence the rate of growth of productivity. In terms of Figure 7.11, the autarchy production function may actually be below $F'(k)$ because of rent seeking activities that use resources. Steady state income would then be below $F'(k^{**})$. However, n and s would still be the major factors influencing the growth rate.

It follows then that development is not so much the result of exports or that trade is an engine of development (export led).[18] Alternatively, as Kravis[19] has stated, trade is more of a handmaiden to economic growth and development. That is, trade does not lead the development process, but only enhances the gain achieved through growth. For him the main sources of growth are on the supply side. If appropriate conditions are created within the developing country, then the rate of growth of supply will rise. If the country also pursues an outward oriented strategy, the gain, in terms of per capita income, will be even higher.

Before closing this section reference should be made to one additional argument concerning the gains from trade. Deepak Lal and Sarath Rajapatirana[20] have argued that Kravis and others have downplayed the extent to which a liberal trade regime can help to create a domestic economic situation that is conducive to higher growth rates. For them, the entrepreneur is the key to rapid economic growth.

Economic decisions almost always involve some consideration of future events. Conventional economics views such decision making as being risky. That is, one cannot be certain what will happen to the future returns to an investment. However, one can attribute probabilities to all of the potential possibilities. One can then continue to apply conventional maximizing methodologies with the entity to be maximized changed from profit to expected profit. In this context there is no role for the entrepreneur to play because all calculations are relatively easy to make, once the probabilities of various alternatives are known.

Lal and Rajapatirana argue that decisions which involve possible future events are subject to ignorance, not risk. Probabilities cannot be accurately attributed to various alternative future possibilities. In fact, the future possibilities are not even well known. In this situation, the entrepreneur takes on a key role. He or she must search out investment opportunities and gamble on a future that is to a large extent unknown and unknowable. Entrepreneurial activities cannot, for reasons of incentives as well as information, be centralized.

This uncertainty adds a new dimension to the role of free trade. Governments often undertake programs that interfere with market operations based on the justification that significant externalities exist. However, often such government activity only makes the distortions worse, leading to large losses for the economy at large. For example, tariffs and quotas are used to assure domestic producers that they will have domestic markets for their goods. However, in a free trade environment, the options that the government has at its disposal are much reduced. That is, the government is not capable of assuring domestic producers access to export markets. In other words, Lal and Rajapatirana see free trade as a mechanism for confining government action to its proper place. This would help create an environment that encourages entrepreneurship and productivity.

In summary, mainstream economists have for a long time argued the superiority of a free trade policy. The gains from trade include improvements in allocative efficiency, monopoly prevention, the achievement of economies of scale, and so forth. In addition, trade may provide an environment that restrains government activities. However, for the most part it seems that trade is a handmaiden to growth. Also there are reasons to think that managed or controlled trade via protective policy may be necessary for rapid growth. It is to these ideas that we turn next.

PROTECTIONIST ARGUMENTS

Classical Theory

Two of the strongest arguments for protectionism have their foundation in the growth models considered in Chapter 1. Recall that the Keynesian growth model could be used to explain and justify import substitution. Protectionist policies might stimulate productive investment. The savings for this investment are already there, they are simply not being put to productive use. This argument is similar to the argument made in Keynesian stabilization policy. Trade restrictions by reducing imports increase aggregate demand and, hence, move the economy toward full employment. At the same time, investment in import substitution industries is stimulated, leading to growth in potential output (thus productively utilizing savings). Of course, this generates resource misallocation in the short run because the country is not taking advantage of comparative advantage. However, in the long run the growth rate is higher.

Ironically, we will see that the classical model, discussed earlier, which provides a powerful static argument for free trade, also provides a long-run argument for protectionism. The classical trade model, if the reader will remember, assumes that comparative advantage is driven by differences in technology. Classical trade models typically imply complete specialization in producing one commodity for a small country and incomplete specialization for a large country.

The model presented in the previous section of this chapter is, however, not fully developed in that agriculture, and diminishing returns are ignored. A classical model incorporating these factors was developed in Chapter 1 and can be easily extended to consider international trade. The model is

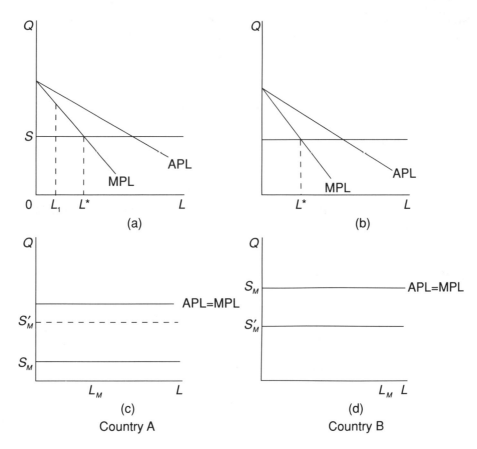

Figure 7.12   A classical model of specialization.

illustrated in Figure 7.12. Consider two countries, where Country B is already at a stationary state, where there are no profits in agriculture or manufacturing, and Country A is just beginning the development process. L_1 is the agricultural labor force in Country A, and there are positive profits where the agricultural labor force in Country B is already at L^*. The subsistence wage rate in agriculture, S, is the same in both countries. In terms of the simple Malthusian model discussed in Chapter 4, this assumes that the habits and customs underlying the subsistence level are the same in both countries.

Initially, there is no trade. This means that relative prices between manufacturing and agriculture are different in the two countries. Because manufacturing is expensive in Country A, its relative price is high and consequently the real wage rate, S_M is lower. Recall that this real wage rate is in terms of the agricultural good, which is relatively cheap in A. Let q be the price of subsistence, S, in the manufacturing sector so that $S_M = qS$. When trade is introduced, competition will lead to these relative prices being equalized between the two countries. The price of agricultural output, q, will rise in Country A and fall in Country B. Consequently, $S_M = qS$ will then rise in Country A and fall in Country B to the point where S_M is the same in both countries at a level like S_M'.

This opening of trade will initially benefit both countries. In Country A, agricultural employment and output will initially expand and manufacturing employment and output will contract to take advantages of the higher profits in agriculture. In Country B, the opposite will occur. Profits again will become positive in manufacturing causing labor to be shifted from agriculture to manufacturing and output in agriculture to fall. Note that, although in each country profit rates between agriculture and manufacturing are equalized, profit rates between the two countries are not the same. Profits will differ between countries because the technologies are assumed to be different. Factors of production, in this case labor, are assumed to be immobile in the classical model, but this immobility of resources does not play a crucial role in the long-run implications of the model.

The introduction of trade implies that q in both countries will be equal, and this will cause S_M in both countries to be equal. Once S_M is equalized in the two countries (at S_M'), both begin again to move toward a stationary state, with agricultural and manufacturing output growing in both A and B. As agricultural output expands in A, S_M will rise until $S_M = APL = MPL$ in Country A. At this point there will still be profits in Country B but Country A will be in a stationary state. This stationary state is not unique, however. As manufacturing output in Country B continues to rise it would cause the relative price of agricultural goods in both B and A to rise causing S_M to rise above $APL = MPL$ in Country A. This would make profits in manufacturing negative in A, which will cause manufacturing output to fall, driving q and hence S_M down to the zero profit level.

Thus, manufacturing output in A will decline along $S_M = APL = MPL$ as output in B expands along S_M. This process means that much of the labor force in A will become redundant. Eventually all of A's manufacturing labor force will become redundant as A becomes completely specialized in agriculture. After this time, B will again move toward a stationary state as the economy expands, S_M rises, and profits fall.

Note that, in the example, the introduction of trade caused A's manufacturing output to initially decline. It then rose as both economies grew until A reached the stationary state. At this point, A's labor force and manufacturing output began a long decline to oblivion. Such a decline is hardly beneficial to A and would almost certainly be resisted by implementing protectionist policies. Hence, classical growth theory provides a powerful argument against free trade. This argument is not dependent upon the particular story that we tell. For example, we could have started with both countries at a stationary state with A specialized in agriculture. The introduction of a prohibitive tariff by A would cause A's manufacturing to grow until it reached a high employment steady state. B would suffer a loss in employment and manufacturing output.

In summary, the classical view presented in the first section of this chapter has been found to be incomplete. Once a two sector model is developed, with one sector subject to diminishing returns (agriculture), then a more complex story emerges. Initially, both countries would seem to benefit from trade. Country A expands its production of food and B its production of manufactured goods. However, the operation of the law of diminishing returns causes subsistence costs to rise in A such that eventually all industrial production there ceases and surplus labor exists. In the long run, trade certainly does not benefit Country A.

Infant Industry Protectionist Arguments

One of the oldest arguments used to justify protectionist policies has come to be known as the *infant industry argument*. It is often based upon the existence of significant economies of scale for particular manufacturing firms. In this situation, firms in developed nations that have been operating a long period of time have been able to move down their long–run average cost curves to take advantage of these economies. New firms in developing nations producing relatively small amounts will be unable to reap such economies and thus will not be able to compete. It is argued that these new industries must be protected until they can achieve economies of large scale production and thus become internationally competitive. Once this occurs, the protection would be removed and the infant firms would compete internationally.

There is an immediate problem with this argument. If such infant industries can, in the long run, become profitable, then private investors ought to be able to see this and provide the funds necessary to cover the short–run losses until the firm can become internationally competitive. Of course, a capital market capable of providing such funds rarely exists in such an economy. Therefore, market failures occur, which slow the growth of manufacturing.

The establishment of such a capital market is likely to be beyond the current abilities of most less developed nations, so some sort of government action is necessary. One could choose to protect the industry using tariffs or quotas to promote the expansion of domestic production at the expense of imports. This protection will allocate resources toward the infant industry and away from other activities. However, this does not occur without cost. The reader will remember, the gains from trade can be divided into production and consumption gains. By using tariffs or quotas to reallocate resources toward infant industries a cost is imposed upon consumers because they must now pay a higher relative price for the imported good or its substitute. Thus, protection, although achieving a more appropriate allocation of resources for production, comes at a cost to consumers. A better policy would be to address the market failure problem directly. That is, the first best policy[21] would be to promote a better development of capital markets. This would result in a better allocation of resources (by providing resources to the infant industry) without any attendant costs to the consumer. However, it has often been argued that less developed countries lack the administrative expertise to carry out the first best policy and, therefore, their only choice is the second best protectionist policy. From this point on, we will ignore the question involving the best policy to use in dealing with market failure and other distortions. Instead, it is recognized that first best policies are usually not available to developing countries and that tariffs, quotas, and other trade barriers are a second or even third best alternative.

Another basis for the infant industry argument, in addition to the economies of scale argument, assumes that technology is costly to transfer. Neoclassical theory often assumes that technology is known to all and costless to assimilate. However, as Pack and Westphal[22] point out, neither is completely true. They emphasize the tacitness of technology, the fact that one cannot really master a new technology without actually applying it and utilizing it in production. In the process of doing so, new adaptations of the technique are likely to generate additional cost savings with experience. Also, one can tailor the technology to the particular local circumstances, which may generate further benefits. In summary, it is being assumed here that new technology is not perfectly tradeable, and thus, experience in actual production is necessary to successfully assimilate new technology.[23]

The preceding situation is related to the fundamental development problem facing poor nations today. The technological frontier is constantly shifting outward as a result of the efforts of developed nations aimed at innovation. To successfully industrialize, a nation must set in motion a process by which it can catch up to this technological frontier. As Alice Amsden[24] has pointed out, this may even be the situation of labor intensive goods such as textiles. The experience of Taiwan and South Korea would seem to indicate difficulty for labor abundant nations in claiming a comparative advantage in labor intensive goods. Even here, catching up to the technological frontier is essential to international competitiveness.

The implication of the above would seem to be that, in order to promote the rapid assimilation of technology, domestic producers in particular industries are going to have to be protected from foreign competition. As a result, they can expand domestic production utilizing new technologies and, using

the experience gained, close the technological gap for that particular commodity. Import substitution would thus seem to be the first step in becoming internationally competitive. After the technology has been assimilated,
then the firms indeed can turn outward.

The emphasis on differences in technology between developed and less
developed countries and the role of technological learning in development
imply a very close link between the classical model of trade and infant
industry arguments. The reader will remember, in the classical model, trade
between nations is not based upon differences in relative factor supplies, but
instead on differences in technology. The implication of the classical model
was that free trade would destroy the manufacturing sector in the nation
in which manufacturing utilizes a less productive technology. In this case,
infant industry protection is necessary to allow the assimilation of new technology, so that when trade does occur, the manufacturing sector in the developing country can survive.

RESULTS OF IMPORT SUBSTITUTION

Analysis

The evidence concerning infant industry protection and development can
be characterized as mixed. Historically, most of today's developed European
nations followed a process of industrialization involving periods during which
they selectively withdrew from international trade. During these periods the
domestic market was protected and domestic producers were able to catch
up to the technological frontier. Thus Dieter Senghaas[25] characterizes most
of the European experience as one in which trade was selectively controlled
and periods of free trade were exceptions. He argues that such a process was
essential to European industrialization.

More recently, evidence concerning Taiwan and South Korea has come
to light that seems to be consistent with this European experience. In particular, Jaime de Melo[26] has analyzed the sources of structural change in these
two countries. He finds that a similar pattern emerges at both the aggregate
and subsector levels. Import substitution production precedes export expansion
in both countries. This lends support to the notion that a nation must catch
up technologically by production for the domestic market before successful
exportation can occur.

This view is further supported by the work of Robert Wade.[27] He divides
views on East Asian economic success into three categories: free market,
simulated free market, and governed market. The first view attributes the economic success of this region to the fact that the state did not actively interfere
with economic activity. Instead, the state merely provided an environment

suitable for such economic activity. However, most analysts have come to the conclusion that this view is incorrect. The state has actively interfered with economic activity in Taiwan and South Korea as well as in Japan. Thus the economic success there is not due to laissez-faire economic policies.

The second view accepts the fact that the state has played an important role. It argues that the economies of most less developed countries are riddled with distortions in relative prices, both those stemming from government policy (protection) and "those remaining from government failure to change distortion-inducing institutions directly (e.g., segmented financial markets)."[28] The state in Taiwan, South Korea, and perhaps Japan undertook policies to correct such distortions. So, for example, if the production of a particular intermediate good was protected, then firms utilizing this good in the process of production would receive rebates or subsidies to offset the protection costs. Thus the relative prices that would result are similar to those that would have arisen in a free market. As a result, a free market is simulated in which prices (relative) are right.

Wade proposes an alternative view, which he labels the *governed market theory*. This theory argues that East Asian success is the result of a number of factors. First, extremely high levels of investment have resulted in the rapid accumulation and transfer of new technology. Second, more investment has occurred in certain key industries than would have occurred without government intervention. Finally, many industries were eventually exposed to international competition. Thus the state is perceived to be leading rather than following the market. By *leading* Wade means that government incentives or initiatives are large enough to lead firms to do things that they would not have done in the absence of such incentives.[29]

By examining evidence both at the macroeconomic and microeconomic levels, Wade is able to show that import substitution generally preceded exports, that state policies were important in providing resources to selected industries, and that much of the catching up occurred with respect to technology. Whether or not this was the critical factor in East Asian development is still a subject for much debate. However, there is a growing literature supporting this view.

The historical evidence concerning import substitution strategies in Europe and East Asia thus points to the probable success of such a strategy in promoting rapid industrialization. However, one must proceed with caution. Against this picture of success, one must pose an alternative picture of the failure of this strategy for most developing nations in the post-World War II period. Such policies certainly promoted an expansion of manufacturing in the Third World, but they have for the most part failed to stimulate rapid development. Instead, inefficient industrial structures have evolved that operate at below capacity and rarely have they become internationally competitive.

How is one to understand this failure? Some of the explanation can certainly be found in the particular steps that were followed. Specifically, most developing nations began with first stage import substitution for imports of nondurable consumer goods (clothing, shoes, household goods) and their inputs (textile fabrics, leather, and wood). These commodities utilize technologies that are more labor intensive, smaller in scale, and less complex. In this first stage, domestic production rises more rapidly than domestic consumption, because it replaces imports as well as supplying increases in demand. However, eventually the rate of growth of production declines to the rate of growth of consumption as stage one import substitution is completed.

To maintain a high industrial growth rate, the less developed nation must either begin exporting these manufactured goods or move to second stage import substitution. Many of today's developing nations chose the latter approach, which involved the replacement of the imports of intermediate goods and producer and consumer durables by domestic production. This type of production involved the utilization of complex, capital intensive technologies. Alternatively, much of East Asia chose to begin exporting those products, which had initially been protected during the first stage of import substitution. Simultaneously, protection was shifted toward secondary, intermediate industries.

What made the difference was that East Asia, through primary import substitution, was able to create a set of industries that were internationally competitive and at the next stage protect more complex industries, which themselves eventually became dynamically efficient. For most of the rest of the developing world, primary import substitution created industries that were not competitive internationally. Thus the only mechanism to maintain industrial growth was to turn to secondary import substitution, which created intermediate goods that were not internationally competitive.

Explanation

The preceding analysis indicates that most developing nations failed, through a primary import substitution strategy, to establish dynamically competitive industries. Part of the explanation for this failure can be found in the behavior of the state. Here, this idea will only be introduced, with a detailed analysis to come in the next chapter, on the role of the state.

The initial difference, for Amsden, between successful and unsuccessful application of import substitution relates to the principles governing subsidy allocation. "In all late-industrializing countries, states have intervened to get prices 'wrong' because initially firms could not compete even in labor-intensive industries on the basis of low wages. Subsidies have been a condition for industrial development in the absence of pioneering technology."[30]

However, in the slow growing countries governments have imposed no performance standards on the industries receiving subsidies. In the fast growing economies "subsidies have been allocated according to the principle of reciprocity, in exchange for concrete performance standards (with respect to output, exports, product quality, investments in training, and, more recently, research and development)."[31]

The role of the state just discussed has often been characterized by contrasting hard and soft states.[32] Hard states are able to set economic priorities that are independent of interest groups within the nation. More important, they are able to effectively carry out policies to achieve these priorities. Alternatively, a soft state has been captured by special interest groups. It is unable to independently establish priorities, and its policies serve as tools to be utilized by special interests to enhance their well-being. East Asian states have been seen to be hard whereas government in much of the rest of the developing world is characterized as being soft. Of course, the interesting issue concerns the factors that give rise to hard and soft states. These issues are addressed in the next chapter.

CONCLUSION

In this chapter an attempt has been made to analyze the relationship between trade and development. Initially a simple classical model was used to illustrate the principle of comparative advantage. Then a neoclassical model was used to illustrate the benefits from trade as well as the Hecksher–Ohlin explanation of comparative advantage, which emphasizes differences in factor proportions as explaining trade flows.

That free trade is more efficient than protection is undisputed. Thus a nation involved in the former will have a higher level of income than if it engages in the latter (assuming a small country case). However, the neoclassical theory sheds little light on trade and growth in the level of income. Reference is often made to economies of scale and other sorts of dynamic benefits, but little theoretical development has occurred.

The classical model was then extended to the two sector, agriculture and manufacturing, case. The former was assumed to be subject to diminishing returns and the latter constant returns. It was further assumed that trade between two nations was based on differences in technology. It was found that in this situation, trade between a developed nation and less developed nation was likely to eliminate the manufacturing sector in the latter.

This theoretical perspective was then linked to the notion that economic development is a process of catching up technologically and that the mastery of new technology is dependent upon actually utilizing it in the production process. Thus infant industry protection was seen as necessary to allow backward nations to catch up with the technological frontier. Once this is accomplished, these manufactured goods would be exported and the expansion of their exports would dominate growth.

The results of utilizing protective policies to promote infant industries has, however, been mixed. Much of the early European experience involved such protection and the eventual success of industrialization was attributed to this strategy. The same can be said for much of East Asia. However, the vast majority of todays developing countries have had a different experience. Import substitution resulted in the creation of a set of infant industries that never became internationally competitive.

The explanation of these results concentrated on the state. In those countries that succeeded using an import substitution strategy of development the state was able to require performance standards upon the part of firms receiving subsidies. Thus firms either became competitive or they no longer received support. Alternatively, the failure of import substitution in many less developed nations stemmed from the lack of such standards. In effect, subsidies were received without corresponding productive investment. The subsidies became, for all intents and purposes, giveaways.

Therefore, the key to successful development would seem to be related to the state and its effectiveness. This issue is dealt with in the chapter on the state.

NOTES

1. See H. D. Evans, *Comparative Advantage and Growth: Trade and Development in Theory and Practice* (New York: Harvester Wheatsheaf, 1989).
2. Much of this discussion is based on Paul R. Krugman and Maurice Obstfeld, *International Economics: Theory and Policy* (Glenview, Ill.: Scott, Foresman, and Co., 1988).
3. See James E. Meade, *A Geometry of International Trade* (London: Allen and Unwin, 1952).
4. The discussion of optimal tariffs is taken from Charles P. Kindleberger and Peter Lindert, *International Economic* (Homewood, Ill.: Richard D. Irwin, 1978), pp. 511–517.
5. See Bertil Ohlin, *Interregional and International Trade* (Cambridge, Mass.: Harvard University Press, 1933).
6. See Wolfgang Stolper and Paul Samuelson, "Protection and Real Wages," *Review of Economic Studies* 9 (1941): 58–73.
7. W. Leontief, "Domestic Production and Foreign Trade: The American Capital Position Re-examined," *Proceedings of the American Philosophical Society* 97 (September 1953): 331–349.

8. Harry P. Bowen, Edward E. Leamer, and Leo Sveikauskas, "Multicountry, Multifactor Tests of the Factor Endowment Theory," *American Economic Review* 77 (December 1987): 791–809.

9. See Robert Mundell, "International Trade and Factor Mobility," *American Economic Review* 47 (1957): 321–335.

10. See M. B. Krauss, "The Economics of the 'Guest Worker' Problem: A neo-Hecksher–Ohlin Approach," *Scandinavian Journal of Economics* 78 (1976): 470–476; and M. G. Quibria, "A Note on International Migration, Non-Traded Goods and Economic Welfare in the Source Country," *Journal of Development Economics* 31 (1989): 117–183.

11. See F. Helpman and P. Krugman, *Market Structure and Foreign Trade: Increasing Returns, Imperfect Competition and the International Economy* (Cambridge, Mass.: MIT Press, 1985) and Peter H. Lindert, *International Economics* (Homewood, Ill.: Irwin, 1991), pp. 98–106.

12. Robert M. Stern, Alan V. Deardorff, and Drusilla K. Brown, "A U.S.–Mexico–Canada Free Trade Agreement: Sectoral Employment Effects and Regional/Occupational Employment Realignments in the United States," Report to the National Commission for Employment Policy. University of Michigan Working Paper, October 1992. For a survey on CGE models emphasizing LDC and trade issues for LDCs, see Jayatilleke S. Bandara, "Computable General Equilibrium Models for Development Policy Analysis in LDCs," *Journal of Economic Surveys* 5 (1991): 3–69.

13. Bela Balassa, *Trade Liberalization among Industrial Countries* (New York: McGraw-Hill, 1967).

14. Hla Myint, "The Classical Theory of International Trade and the Underdeveloped Countries," *Economic Journal* 68 (1958): 317–331.

15. Ronald Findlay, "Growth and Development in Trade Models," in *Handbook of Internal\tional Economics*, vol. 1, ed. R. W. Jones and P. B. Kennan (New York: Elsevier Science Publishers, B.V., 1984), pp. 534–535.

16. Anne Krueger, "Trade Policies in Developing Countries," in *Handbook of International Economics,* vol. 1, ed. Jones and Kennan, pp. 534–535.

17. J. N. Bhagwati and T. N. Srinivasan, "Revenue Seeking: A Generalization of the Theory of Tariffs," *Journal of Political Economy* 88 (1980): 1069–1987.

18. R. Nurkse, *Equilibrium and Growth in the World Economy* (Cambridge, Mass.: Harvard University Press, 1961).

19. Irving Kravis, "Trade as a Handmaiden of Growth: Similarities between the 19th and 20th Centuries," *Economic Journal* 80 (1970): 850–872.

20. Deepak Lal and Sarath Rajapatirana, "Foreign Trade Regimes and Economic Growth in Developing Countries," *Research Observer* 2 (July 1987): 208–211.

21. See H. G. Johnson, "Optimal Trade Intervention in the Presence of Distortions," In R. E. Baldwin et al., *Trade, Growth and the Balance of Payments* (Chicago: Rand McNally, 1965), pp. 3–34.

22. Howard Pack and Larry E. Westphal, "Industrial Strategy and Technological Change," *Journal of Development Economics* 22 (1986): 108.

23. Ibid.

24. Alice H. Amsden, *Asia's Next Giant: South Korea and Late Industrialization* (New York: Oxford University Press, 1989).

25. Dieter Senghaas, *The European Experience: A Historical Critique of Development Theory* (Dover, N.H.: Berg Publishers, 1985).

26. Jaime de Melo, "Sources of Growth and Structural Change in Korea and Taiwan," World Bank Discussion Paper (October 1983).

27. Robert Wade, *Governing the Market: Economic Theory and the Role of Government in East Asian Industrialization* (Princeton, N.J.: Princeton University Press, 1990).

28. Ibid., p. 23.

29. Ibid., pp. 24–29.

30. Alice H. Amsden, "A Theory of Government Intervention in Late Industrialization," in *State and Market in Development: Synergy or Rivalry*, ed. Louis Putterman and Dietrich Rueschemeyer (Boulder, Colo.: Lynne Rienner Publishers, 1992), p. 61.

31. Ibid.

32. Gunnar Myrdal, *Asian Drama: An Inquiry into the Poverty of Nations* (New York: Partheon, 1968).

8

The State

Appropriate government policy was both explicitly and implicitly considered in previous chapters. For the most part, the state was considered only in terms of the potential role, positive or negative, various government policies would play in the development process. The state itself and the role it plays in development will now be considered. Different theories of the state will be reviewed and their implications for the success or failure of various development policies will be analyzed.

The role of the state in the process of economic development has become a topic of much debate. Theoretical work after World War II indicated a major role for the state in the promotion of industrialization through planning and direct involvement in the production process. The justification for this approach was that market failures in developing countries were pervasive and the state would have to substitute for the market in numerous ways. Examples include the Keynesian and the dualistic growth models discussed in Chapter 1. In Keynesian growth models, entrepreneurial failures provide a rationale for import substitution industrialization. In dualistic growth models, the irrationality of the traditional sector provides the rationale for urban bias. In these models, market failures are pervasive and cannot be corrected at the source. In this way development economics was viewed to be different from standard economics, where less pervasive market failures can be corrected much more directly.

Eventually, this activist role of the state came under close scrutiny. Concern shifted to government failure and why the state may fail to solve problems stemming from inadequate markets. In fact, government attempts to deal with inadequate markets may make matters worse because of government mismanagement of the economy. The latter may be the result of a government that maintains its power and position at the expense of long-term growth.

The purpose of this chapter is to analyze the role of the state in the development process, so a number of competing theories of the state will be reviewed. In the first section the enlightened state theory will be examined, and the second section will review theories that view the state as an obstacle to development. The third section will analyze the developmental state perspective. In this analysis the key factors in the industrialization process will be reviewed. In addition, various theories as to how an effective developmental state can arise will be discussed. The final section will summarize the chapter.

CONCERNING MARKET IMPERFECTIONS

In much of the early thinking on development and in much of neoclassical theory the state is viewed as benign in terms of its goals and objectives. Specifically, the state's objective is to maximize social welfare. Individuals as consumers and producers were assumed to maximize their individual welfare, but the state's job is to consider the welfare of the group. It is recognized that the state often does not act with social welfare in mind. The welfare of powerful special interests may take precedence over social welfare. However, the state is viewed as being basically concerned with society's welfare.

In this setting the case for government intervention in an economy was based upon the existence of certain market inadequacies.[1] These inadequacies include externalities, public goods, incomplete or missing markets, and imperfectly competitive markets. These imperfections were seen as requiring government intervention so as to improve social welfare.

One can think of externalities as being those costs or benefits created by a particular individual or firm but borne by or accrued to other individuals or firms. There are two broad types of externalities: technological and pecuniary. The former diffuse to others in the absence of market transactions whereas the latter flow through market transactions.[2] Because these spillover benefits or costs do not enter into the calculations of the individual or firm engaged in the activity, either too much will occur, in the case of negative externalities, or too little, in the case of positive externalities. In the former the government is supposed to tax and in the latter subsidize the particular activity to achieve a socially optimal level of production.

Expenditures aimed at training and educating the workers of a particular firm provide an example of an activity characterized by positive technological externalities. Firms that spend significant sums on such employee training are hoping to raise their productivity. Once the training is completed, the worker may decide to leave the firm, with the result that the benefits of the expenditures accrue to other firms rather than the firm undergoing the expense of training. Thus firms in general will have a tendency to spend too little on employee training and education.

Expenditures on technological research are also thought to be characterized by significant spillover benefits. New ideas and devices are often easily copied, and therefore the firm that expends the money to finance the research sees most of the benefit accruing to others. Obviously, this can be overcome if property rights in new ideas exist and can be enforced. However, institutional mechanisms for this are often missing in less developed countries.

So far all of the examples of externalities have been technological in nature. However, a number of development economists have argued for the importance of pecuniary externalities. The best known example of this is provided in the original work of Rosenstein-Rodan[3] and recently formalized by Murphy, Shliefer, and Vishny.[4] Firms contemplating investment in a modern technology may often be deterred by the smallness of the market for the product being produced. However, if investments by other firms occur simultaneously, a large enough market for all the goods might be generated. Thus where a single investment proves unprofitable, simultaneous investment by a number of firms in different industries proves to be profitable for all. Because, in the new growth theory discussed in Chapter 1, investment might result in technical progress external to the firm, pecuniary externalities to investment could lead to additional technical externalities.

Rosenstein-Rodan illustrated his idea with an example of a shoe factory. A single shoe factory established in a less developed region will likely fail for lack of a market. However, if a number of factories were established in a variety of industries, each would provide a market for the other's product. Thus, as a group the firms would succeed. In this case the role of the state is to coordinate the simultaneous investment in a big push sort of industrialization process.

One might argue that the big push argument is valid only in the case of a closed economy. In that case the smallness of the domestic market might inhibit profitable investment. Alternatively, in an open economy setting, market size could not act as a constraint because the domestic firm could also produce for export. However, the argument may still be valid in the case of an open economy because the ability to export is often linked to previous production for the domestic market. The reader will remember from Chapter 7, that the learning and adaption of new technology by less developed nations often requires previous experience gained by production for the domestic market. More simply, import substitution generally precedes exportation, and in this case, the big push analysis discussed previously is applicable.

In addition to externalities, the existence of public goods also provides a justification for government interference. These goods possess the characteristics of nonexcludability and jointness in consumption. A good is excludable if it can be made available to some individuals but withheld from others. A good is characterized by jointness in consumption if the good can be consumed by increasing numbers of individuals without reducing the amount available to any single individual (marginal cost of provision is zero). In this case, market production of the commodity will not occur because no private firm will have an incentive to do so. Hence, production by the state must serve as a substitute.

There are a number of such public goods. National defense is probably the best example, but internal order and peace are perhaps equally good examples. With respect to the latter, a market exchange economy cannot operate efficiently if a secure system of property rights and a legal system to enforce these rights does not exist. Thus the state has an important role in providing these public goods.

Because markets for public goods may not arise, there is a role for the state in providing these goods. This statement assumes that there are certain goods that, because of their very nature, have characteristics that inhibit private production. However, it must also be pointed out that markets for goods that are by nature private (excludable and nonjointness in consumption) may also fail to develop. This possibility emerges when one allows for the transactions costs involved in carrying out market exchange.

Simple neoclassical theory tends to examine markets in terms of supply and demand. Figure 8.1 shows the intersection of demand and supply that determines equilibrium price. However, this ignores the costs of transacting that drive a wedge between the demand and supply price. As the wedge gets bigger (A–B, C–D, E–F), the amount of exchange goes down. Obviously, if transaction costs are high enough, exchange will cease altogether.

According to North[5], the costliness of information is the most important element of transaction costs. Specifically, there are search costs in finding partners to a potential exchange, costs of measuring the attributes of products, costs of coming to agreement over the terms of exchange, costs of protecting rights, and costs of policing and enforcing the terms of exchange. Institutions, defined as rules both formal and informal, are often created in an attempt to reduce such transaction costs. In fact, according to North, institutions make sense only in an environment characterized by such costs.

With this perspective in mind, one can then construct two types of societal settings. In the first type of society most exchange takes place between individuals who know each other and in settings in which future transactions among the same set of people are likely to occur over and over again. In this situation, the transaction costs involved in exchange are likely to be very low. However, the personalized nature of such exchange implies that it occurs on a very small scale, and therefore, specialization in production is not likely to be extensive. Although transaction costs are low, production costs are high and market size is small.[6]

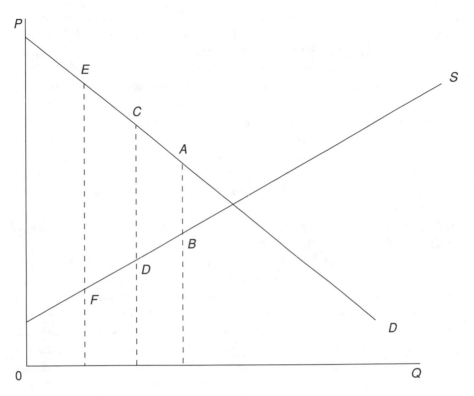

Figure 8.1 Market supply, demand, and transaction costs.

Alternatively, one can envision a society in which exchange is impersonal and on a large scale. Therefore, specialization in production will be extensive, but the costs of transacting are likely to be quite high. However, institutions have been established that dramatically reduce the transaction cost per unit of product exchanged. The result is a modern market economy that reaps the productivity gains stemming from specialization.[7]

The key to this process of transformation would seem to be the establishment of the institutional structure necessary to reduce per unit transaction costs. Without such an institutional structure, markets for many private goods are unlikely to develop. Thus the state serves an important role in constructing this institutional infrastructure.

A final market inadequacy has to do with the distribution of income. Specifically, even if a system of well-functioning markets exists, the resulting distribution of income may be unacceptable to the society. Usually when market inadequacies are discussed, the term is restricted to apply only to departures from Pareto efficient outcomes and therefore excludes the equity problem. However, Charles Wolf argues that the concept of a public good can be applied to considering income distribution. "An equitable redistribution does not result from freely functioning markets because philanthropy and charity yield benefits that are not appropriable by donors."[8] Thus if redistribution is left to the activities of private individuals, the result will be too little redistribution. Thus a role for government would be to generate a more socially acceptable distribution of income and wealth.

Implicit in the preceding analysis is a particular perspective concerning the state. This view regards "governments as agencies whose task is to secure the best interests of their societies."[9] Thus when market inadequacies are found, the government's role is to design the appropriate policy to deal with the inadequacy. Much of this research involving these inadequacies has concentrated on the manufacturing or modern sector to the neglect of the traditional or agricultural sector. This bias is probably related to the theoretical dominance of dualistic models of development.

Recall that the models of Lewis[10] and Ranis and Fei[11] are actually built around the notion of market inadequacy. It is assumed that the wage rate in the traditional sector is above the marginal product of labor and thus does not reflect the true social opportunity cost of labor. Labor is paid its average product either because family workers share in the firm's rent or because some nonmarket traditional mechanism for setting the wage rate serves as a substitute for an inadequate labor market. Thus not enough labor is being employed in the modern sector and a transfer of labor from the traditional to modern sector will expand output. It is further assumed that this market imperfection in the traditional sector cannot be corrected at the source. Hence, the implication of this view is that the government should foster the expansion of the modern relative to the traditional sector.

Although this tendency of correcting for market inadequacies by investing in manufacturing has been dominant, Myint[12] has argued that market inadequacies are more characteristic of the traditional sector than the manufacturing sector. For example, markets are more likely to be missing in the rural traditional sector. The capital market is likely to be much more developed in the urban, industrial setting whereas such markets are not likely to exist or exist only to a limited extent in rural areas. High transactions costs in the latter hinder market development.

The market inadequacies concerning public goods and externalities are also likely to be much more applicable to the rural areas. Agricultural technology possesses many of the characteristics of a public good, and it is very difficult to design a property rights system to protect the development of this kind of technology (see Chapter 3 on the traditional sector). Externalities connected with education and training are also likely to be more important for agriculture. This is because educational levels are so much lower in this sector, relative to the modern sector, that investment in the former is likely to lead to higher social returns than such investment in the latter sector.[13] Thus this perspective on the state would seem to point to the importance of the government's role in the development of the traditional sector.

PROTECTING RULING COALITIONS

In the previous section the state was seen as playing a positive role in the development process. The theories reviewed in this section view the state as an obstacle, either passive or active, to economic development.

The first view argues that the policy choices made by the state are determined by the interplay, competition, and struggle between interest groups within society. From this perspective, the state has no real independence in decision making. The resulting combination of policies is thought to be growth inhibiting rather than promoting.

The latter conclusion is based on Olson's theory of group behavior.[14] He argues that the goals of a group can best be perceived as a collective good. If successfully achieved, the benefits will be available to all members of the group whether or not they contributed resources toward the achievement of the goals. In this situation, individuals maximizing their own utility are not likely to contribute such resources. If the success of the group is dependent on the extent to which it can mobilize resources, then the free rider problem is likely to spell doom for the organization of groups.

However, Olson[15] argues that one must make a distinction between large groups and small groups. Large groups are highly unlikely to be organized because free riders are not likely to be easily detected and punished. Alternatively, small groups are more likely to organize because strategic interaction often occurs in such groups. That is, the group is small enough that each member knows that his or her action will affect the choices made by other members of the group. Thus if one chooses to free ride, other members may respond by punishing one's free riding behavior. This possibility increases the likelihood of a cooperative result in which all members contribute to the achievement of the group's goal.

This importance of cooperative results was illustrated in Chapter 2, where a prisoners' dilemma was used to illustrate limits to rationality in household tasks. We return to the prisoners' dilemma game as presented in Figure 8.2. There are two players, I and II, and each has the choice of two strategies, A and B. Strategy A represents a cooperative choice with the individual contributing resources to the achievement of the group's goal and strategy B represents a noncooperative choice in which an individual refuses to contribute. The numbers in each cell represent the payoffs to individuals I and II respectively.

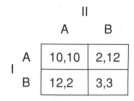

Figure 8.2   The prisoners' dilemma.

If this game is played one time it is obvious that neither player has an incentive to cooperate and both will choose strategy B. As a result, a socially inferior outcome results. However, the situation changes somewhat when the game is played an infinite number of times or if the number of plays is indefinite. With the extended play situation, the possibility of retaliation emerges. For example, if individual I chooses strategy A (cooperates) and individual II strategy B (free rider), then II certainly benefits at the expense of I. However, individual I may choose to punish individual II for the rest of the game by choosing strategy B. Now individual II must weight the short-run gains from free riding (12 instead of 10) against the long-run losses (3 instead of 10) resulting from retaliation. If the long-run losses are sufficiently important (the discount rate is low enough), then individual II is likely to choose strategy A as well.[16] Thus both will choose to contribute and the group will form.

With large groups, however, the situation is very different. Specifically, with larger groups the possibility for strategic interaction is less because the actions of any single individual have little impact on other members of the group. In this case free riding is more likely because the group is less likely to respond to the cooperative or uncooperative behavior of an individual. The implication, then, is that small groups will likely organize whereas large groups will not. If political power is dependent upon such organization, then the smaller groups are likely to have greater influence over policy making.

What sort of economic goals will these small groups pursue? Olson argues that because of their small size they are highly unlikely to be interested in policies that benefit society at large. The main reason for this is that in a small group situation the group bears all of the cost of bringing about a wealth enhancing policy, but the benefits accrue mainly to individuals outside of the group. As a result, small groups are likely to be interested in policies that benefit the few at the expense of the many. These would be policies that redistribute wealth or income or the possibilities of earning wealth or income. Policies that harm the rest of society are of little or no concern to the group because these costs would be borne by members outside of the group.[17]

The result of Olson's scenario is that as time passes interest groups will likely gain control of the policy making process and, as a result, their policies are likely to be inimical to long-term economic growth. What shape are these policies likely to take? It seems probable that they would favor the urban, industrial sector at the expense of the rural, agricultural sector. This would result in what Michael Lipton has called the *urban bias* in policy making.[18] The reasons for this urban bias will be briefly explored in the next few paragraphs.

The most obvious reason for expecting urban, industrial groups to be very powerful relative to rural, farming groups is, of course, size. Due to economies to scale each industry in a less developed country is often made up of a few firms, making organization easy. Alternatively, peasant farmers generally make up a large group in the countryside. Thus they are less likely to be able to successfully organize to achieve their goals.

A second view is related to the formation of ruling coalitions. In most developing nations, policy is not made by a single interest group but instead by a coalition of such groups. Bates and Rogerson[19] argue that agrarian interest groups are unlikely to ever be members of such ruling coalitions. They explains this by assuming that people specialize in production but generalize in consumption. "That is, they earn their incomes from the production of a particular good and they spend their incomes broadly, allocating only a portion to the consumption of the good which they themselves produce and the remainder to the purchase of a wide variety of other goods."[20] Thus their real income depends on the price of what they produce relative to the prices of the things they consume. Hence, the aim of any governing coalition will be to raise the price of the products produced by its members.

Given this analysis, we can see why farming interest groups make unattractive coalition partners. In most less developed countries individuals devote a large share of their budgets to the purchase of food. If farming interests became a member of a ruling coalition and the relative price of farm products increased, other members of the coalition would likely suffer greatly. Alternatively, for coalitions made up of urban, manufacturing interests this is less likely to be a problem. No group belonging to such a coalition is likely to spend a large share of its budget on a product produced by another coalition member.

In summary, the special interest theory of the state argues that policies are likely to be aimed at redistribution rather than productivity enhancement. In addition, such policies are likely to be biased in favor of urban, industrial interests and against rural, agricultural interests. The implication is that there is likely to be an underallocation of resources to agriculture. This is very similar to the conclusion, although the reasons are different, drawn in the previous section's discussion of the benign state perspective.

The interest group theory has been further extended by modifying the perspective to consider the state as having its own interests. In the interest group theory, the state is seen as being passive in nature. Bates[21] has argued that a more active view of the state should be taken. That is, the state should also be viewed as a group or coalition of groups with its own interests that may be separate from the interests of the rest of society. In addition, Bates assumes that the state seeks to pursue these interests, chief of which is to maintain itself in power.

The state's reluctance to utilize markets can now be better explained. Any interference with a market that moves the existing price away from equilibrium creates either a surplus or shortage of the product or service in question. With a shortage, a mechanism for allocating the product among competing demands must be developed to substitute for the market. The state generally institutes a scheme for allocating a scarce product, service, or input. The advantage to the state of instituting such a scheme is that it can now use this allocation process to reward its supporters and punish its foes. For example, when a country's currency is overvalued as the result of government policy, a shortage of foreign exchange results. The allocation of such exchange can now be used by the state as a tool to promote its own power.

Of course, the state, to remain in power, must be able to establish a ruling coalition. Those groups likely to be most powerful, according to the interest group theory presented earlier, are likely to be urban, manufacturing groups. Alternatively, agricultural groups are not likely to be organized. In this case, the state is likely to be actively involved in lowering the price of agricultural goods relative to manufacturing goods. Of course, scarce food would then have to be allocated by the state, which would certainly use this opportunity to reward the urban, manufacturing interests.

In this section the state has been viewed as either a passive or active obstacle to economic development. It tends to pursue policies that suppress markets, discriminate against agriculture, and generally favor redistribution rather than productivity enhancement. The implication would then seem to be that a key to development would be to minimize the state and thus remove this obstacle to development.

FOSTERING DEVELOPMENT AND INSTITUTIONAL CHANGE

In this section a very different view of the state will be taken. It will be argued that under certain circumstances the state can play a very positive role in the process of economic development. More strongly, without active state involvement economic development is unlikely to succeed. This will be called the *developmental state perspective.*

In this perspective the extreme version of the utility maximizing individual is modified. In much of the discussion in this chapter and book, it has been assumed that individual choice is dominated by individual interests, even if such interests conflict with those of the group, as illustrated in the prisoners' dilemma game. However, North provides an alternative perspective. He sees individual behavior as being constrained by a number of factors other than the individual's budget. Specifically, there are formal and informal constraints that can be thought of as the institutional infrastructure of a society. However, he also emphasizes that self-imposed codes of behavior constrain maximizing behavior.

These self-imposed codes are extremely difficult to explain. North[22] however contends that some progress can be made by viewing the problem as involving marginal tradeoffs. That is, individuals are likely to have a greater willingness to express these self-imposed codes through their choices, if the cost of doing so is relatively low. More simply, he sees a negatively sloped demand curve in which "the lower the cost of expressing one's convictions the more important will the convictions be as a determinant of choice."[23] He believes that it is impossible to "make sense out of history (or contemporary economies) without recognizing the central role that subjective preferences play in the context of formal institutional constraints that enable us to express our convictions at zero or very little cost."[24]

Governments made up of such individuals may indeed be willing to pursue policies aimed at general wealth enhancement. They may, in other words, be willing to replace their individualistic internal code of behavior with a code that sets the good of the group above that of particular individuals. However, the willingness of the governing elite to do this would be a direct function of its costliness to the individuals making up the elite. This costliness would certainly depend upon the probability of success that a productivity enhancement strategy would have, as well as the timing of the benefits stemming from such a policy. The more quickly the benefits of such a policy become available, the lower are the costs to the governing elite of pursuing such a strategy. However, if exogenous factors reduce the probability of success or there is a long delay before benefits occur, the cost of such a policy to the ruling elite rises dramatically. These higher costs increase the likelihood that the state will choose to become an obstacle to development.

Successful industrialization is dependent upon the ability of the society to rapidly adapt new technologies. A successful developmental state is one that is capable of fostering a rapid learning process. This must involve the actual production of goods and services utilizing new technologies. The process of production allows firms to absorb and adapt new knowledge, thus reaping economies of learning. It was argued in the chapter on international trade that such learning generally requires an initial period of import substitution followed by export of the product to foreign markets.

Most newly independent nations after World War II were governed by elites who did indeed seek to pursue policies aimed at productivity enhancement. For the most part, they embarked on policies aimed at protecting domestic producers. However, for most of these nations this strategy failed. As the cost of pursuing policies aimed at enhancing the welfare of the society increased, governing elites increasingly turned to policies aimed at redistribution and the concentration of power. Thus import substitution became a mechanism for allocating subsidies to political supporters rather than a means to promote the establishment of internationally competitive industry. The state increasingly became an obstacle to development as outlined in the previous section.

However, there were a number of countries, mostly in East Asia, for which import substitution served as a mechanism for creating internationally competitive industry. The success of these countries has been attributed to the development of an autonomous or hard state. Rodrik[25] has given some analytical content to this concept by viewing the interaction between the state and the private sector as a game. "The natural way to think about the autonomy of the state in this context is by considering the question of which group acts as the Stackelberg leader."[26] The latter refers to a game sometimes used to analyze the behavior of duopolists in microeconomic theory. In applying this game to this setting it is assumed that both the government and the private sector have control over some particular action. This action influences the utility of each individual player. Thus, the two players are interdependent. In this context Rodrik defines an autonomous state as a Stackelberg leader. By this he means that the state when choosing its policy takes into account the private sectors reaction to this policy. The private sector merely reacts to the policy.

The alternative is, of course, that the state could behave as a follower or, in other words, behave in a subordinate fashion. In this situation the private sector chooses its policy by taking into account the best reaction of the state. The state merely reacts to the policies set by the private sector. "Put differently, the subordinate state lacks a mechanism that would commit it to reward or punish the private sector according to whether the desired behavior is carried out or not."[27] Of course, the strong state does have the ability to commit itself to such rewards and punishments.

This fits in nicely with Amsden's[28] explanation as to why East Asian nations have been much more successful than the bulk of the developing world in promoting industrialization. The critical difference between these two groups of countries is not in terms of the types of policy instruments utilized. They have all had extensive government intervention utilizing similar policies. All of these interventions have involved subsidizing, in one way or another, some industries at the expense of others. In late industrializing nations, subsidies may be necessary for industrial development to encourage the learning and adaptation of new technologies.

The critical difference seems to be the principles used to govern the allocation of subsidies. Amsden argues that in countries which have failed to industrialize no performance requirements were imposed upon the industries receiving subsidies. Instead, these subsidies were often provided as give-aways. "In the case of financial incentives, for instance, subsidized loans often have not been repaid altogether, or they have been used for purposes for which they were not intended, or they have been bottled up in investments that never approach international standards of productivity or quality."[29] In those countries (East Asia) where successful industrialization has occurred, subsidies have been allocated on the basis of performance. Performance itself was judged on the basis of standards involving the level of output, exports, product quality, investment in training, and expenditures on research and development.

Sometimes the performance of East Asia has been attributed to low wage rates and the activities of the state aimed at keeping wage rates low. However, wage rates are very low in much of the developing world, and governments in many of these countries have also sought to repress wages. "What accounts for differences in rates of growth of industrial output and productivity among late-industrializing countries is not the degree to which the state has disciplined labor but the degree to which it has been willing and able to discipline capital."[30]

If an autonomous or hard state is the key to successful industrialization, then how do they evolve? What main factors account for such states? Is it possible for a weak, subordinate state to become autonomous? Of course, these are extremely difficult questions, and only some tentative answers will be presented in the following few paragraphs.

It is believed by some scholars that one of the reasons hard states came about in East Asia was connected to the massive social dislocations these nations endured.[31] Both Korea and Taiwan were parts of the Japanese Empire and both suffered, along with Japan, from the destruction of World War II. The occupation of Japan by the United States also resulted in a number of major social reforms. South Korea was further disrupted by the outbreak of the Korean War and Taiwan had to adapt to the influx of about 2 million mainland people between 1945 and 1949.

Olson's[32] theory of groups provides some support for the importance of these social disruptions in the development of strong states. The reader will remember, Olson argued that over time small interest groups will come to dominate decision making by the state. These groups are generally interested in redistribution rather than productivity enhancement. To reorient government policy, the influence of small interest groups must be dramatically reduced. This can occur as the result of massive social dislocation caused by war. In effect, World War II and, in particular, its aftermath swept away most of these small groups. The state was then left free to formulate and implement policies aimed at promoting overall growth.

A second factor, often suggested as an explanation of the evolution of a hard state, is related to the existence of serious external military threats. Both South Korea and Taiwan faced serious military threats in the form of North Korea and the People's Republic of China. During the 19th century Japan was also threatened with the possibility of colonization by Western powers. Thus governments in these three countries faced some very stark choices. The costs of state failure were indeed very high.

Evans[33] has pointed out a third important factor. Economic exchange has sometimes been thought of as occurring quite naturally. However, as pointed out previously in this book, the successful establishment of markets requires the establishment of an institutional infrastructure. The state must play an important role in the creation of such a structure. Specifically, an established market society requires the structure and order provided by a modern bureaucratic state.[34] The success of the bureaucracy depends "on the bureaucracy being a corporately coherent entity in which individuals see furtherance of corporate goals as the best means of maximizing their individual self-interest."[35] This corporate coherence requires that members of the bureaucracy be somewhat insulated from the demands of society. This insulation is promoted by conferring status and rewards to such bureaucrats in a meritocratic fashion.[36] Indeed, all three East Asian nations developed skilled and independent bureaucracies. Entrance into and promotion within was, to a great extent, based on merit, and these organizations were, to a great extent, independent of the influence of societal interest groups.

A final factor of importance in explaining the evolution of a strong state may involve the influence of external powers. In all three cases the United States government played important roles in determining the direction of policy. Foreign aid was often made contingent upon the receiving government following the economic, as well as political, policies laid out by the United States.

A good example of this is provided by land reform. In many developing nations the ownership of land is highly concentrated. Because land is the main factor of production, this concentrates economic, social, and political power in the hands of a few. This landowning elite has often manipulated government policies to protect its position. The result has been a set of policies that has made overall economic development difficult to achieve. Land reform may provide a mechanism by which such a growth retarding group can be eliminated. However, because of the political strength of this group, land reform is often impossible to implement. Therefore, the United

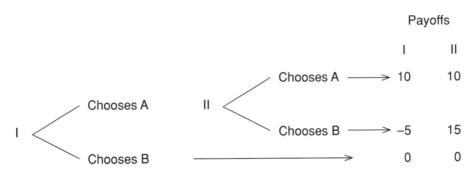

Payoffs

	I	II
Chooses A	10	10
Chooses B	-5	15
Chooses B	0	0

Figure 8.3 The prisoners' dilemma game between the government and an industry.

States used its influence and resources to promote land reforms in all three East Asian countries. The removal of this group gave the government of each country a great deal more latitude in designing and carrying out government policy.

The discussion of forces leading to strong states is not very encouraging about the prospects of creating strong states. Much of this discussion suggests that external, exogenous forces, which for the most part are out of the control of any particular government, are responsible for the evolution of hard, autonomous states. In what follows, the discussion will center on some factors that might be under the control of the government in most developing nations and that could be manipulated by relatively weak states with the ultimate objective of becoming more autonomous and, thus, more effective at carrying out economic policy.

The reader will remember, it is being assumed that individuals will choose to sacrifice their individual interests to those of the group as long as the cost is not too great. As the cost rises, individual interests come to replace those of the group. One can illustrate this through the use of a one-sided prisoners' dilemma game as represented by Figure 8.3.[37] The two players are the government (I) and an industry or group of firms (II). Each has the choice of two strategies, A and B. The government can choose to subsidize an industry (A) or not subsidize an industry (B). Alternatively, the industry can choose to use the subsidy in a productive manner (A), investment in new technology, or an unproductive manner (B), higher salaries or expenditures aimed at convincing the government to continue the subsidy. The payoffs can be thought of in terms of utility. For the firms, that utility is directly linked to the money it earns. For the government it is assumed that the utility is linked to the degree of expansion in manufacturing that occurs. It is thus presumed that the government's goal is to foster the expansion of manufacturing.

If the state chooses not to grant the subsidy, then there are no payoffs to either party. If the government chooses to subsidize this industry (A) and the industry responds productively (A), then both parties gain because the government gets an expansion of industry and the industry gets profits. However, if the industry chooses to waste the subsidy its winnings are even greater, because no expenditures on costly technologies must be made and the state loses the subsidy.

If this game is played only once, conventional theory tells us the leaders of industry would rationally choose B and the result will be suboptimal from the group's perspective. Of course, this is too simple of a game. If it is assumed that the game is played an infinite amount of times or an indefinite number of plays, the results may very well be different. If the government chooses to subsidize the industry (A) and the industry chooses the unproductive response (B), it is indeed true that the industry will reap abnormally high returns (15 relative to 10) on the first play of the game. However, the state may choose to punish the industry by withdrawing the subsidy. In this case, in all future plays of the game the industry will find that its relative returns are reduced (from 10 to 0). Thus the industry must weight the short-run gains against the long-run losses that result from choosing strategy B. If the long run is sufficiently important or if the discount rate is low enough, then the industry will decide to choose A and the Pareto optimal solution results.

In this analysis the discount rate is very important. However, some additional insights can be gained. If the payoffs to government and industry from choosing strategy A are raised dramatically (10 to 14), this increases the likelihood that the industry will choose to sacrifice its short-run interest in B for its long-run interest in A. What has happened here is that the cost of choosing strategy A has been reduced or the cost of choosing B has been increased.

The intuition behind the analysis can be made a little cleaner. The tenor of the problem was altered by increasing the returns to both players from the productive use of the subsidy. One can think of a government granting tariff protection to the firms in a particular industry. What will determine how the firms utilize this subsidy? Obviously, this game will be replayed an indefinite number of times and, thus, one of the important factors will be the discount rate applied by the firms. In other words, how important will those future losses, stemming from the states withdrawal of protection, be to the firm. However, of equal importance is what the firms can expect to earn if they invest the subsidy in the development of productive technology.

If the domestic market for this particular product is very small, the returns to productive investment of the subsidy are likely to be very small (lower the returns for both I and II of choosing A from 10 to 5). In this situation the cost to the firms of choosing A has increased or, in other words, the relative return to choosing B has increased. The reader will remember, the key to successful industrialization is the mastery of new technology, and such mastery generally is the result of experience gained from actual production. If the domestic market is very small, the learning economies that will be reaped are likely to be small in size. The firms will likely never become internationally competitive, and thus the returns to productively using the subsidy are very low.

Contrast the preceding with a situation in which the domestic market is large and growing. In this case, the returns to productive utilization of the subsidy by the firms will rise (10 to 14). As argued in the new growth theory, large and growing markets mean that the economies of learning that can be reaped will be large. The likelihood that the firms will successfully master the new technology and become internationally competitive is much greater. This implies that firms are more likely to productively use the subsidy.

These notions are reinforced if one keeps in mind that less developed nations not only operate inside the production possibilities curve, but that the curve itself is rapidly shifting outward. Therefore, to develop means to catch up with the technological frontier via the learning process. Thus the faster the domestic market grows, the faster the nation can learn and so close the gap.

One of the most important determinants of market size for less developed countries is the productivity of the agricultural sector. Because the bulk of the population earns its living in agriculture, productivity here determines per capita income levels. The more productive agriculture is the more income farm families have to spend on nonagricultural goods.

Indirectly, the productivity of agriculture also has an effect on the size of the market for manufactured goods. Specifically, where agricultural productivity is growing rapidly, the relative price of food will tend to fall. Hence, families in urban and rural areas will not have to devote as large a share of their income to the purchase of food and other related agricultural goods. In other words, the demand for food is inelastic. This means that a larger share of income can be devoted to the purchase of manufactured goods, thus expanding the domestic market for such goods.

Given the preceding, it is not surprising to learn that the East Asian nations all experienced rapid productivity growth in their agricultural sectors. The Japanese experience has already been discussed in Chapter 3. Taiwan and Korea were both colonies of Japan prior to World War II. Japan's objective was to use its colonies as a source of rice and other agricultural products. Because both colonies were rice based economies similar in many ways to Japan, Japan attempted to transfer much of its own agricultural technologies to its colonies in order to raise productivity there.

Japan formally acquired Taiwan in 1895 and initially changed little in Taiwan's economy. However, in 1897, the Japanese began an extensive land survey to determine land values for tax purposes as well as to secure property rights in the land.[38] In addition, a system of research and experiment stations was established with the aim of adapting seed varieties that had been successfully utilized in Japan to Taiwanese circumstances. To diffuse this technology, the Japanese created farmer's associations and agricultural cooperatives. The cooperatives worked to supply credit to farmers, and the associations served as coordinators and suppliers of information and inputs.

The results were that throughout the entire prewar period total agricultural output in Taiwan grew at an average annual rate of 3.6 percent.[39] Although much of the benefits arising from this productivity growth accrued to the Japanese in the form of relatively cheap rice for its people, it seems that standards of living among the Taiwanese also rose through time. This was reflected in rising food availability as well as rising agricultural wages.[40]

A similar story can be told for Korea. Compared to Taiwan, Korea's economy was much less commercialized and lacked much of the necessary infrastructure. Just as in Taiwan, the development program began with a land survey that was completed by 1918. This identified unused land and clarified property rights to the land. The land tax was converted to require cash payments, forcing farmers to market a greater proportion of their crop.[41] In addition, significant investments were made in roads, railroads, and harbor facilities. Finally, significant investments were also made into agricultural research and extension systems.[42]

The efforts aimed at raising productivity in Korea were much less successful than those in Taiwan. For the period 1912–1937 agricultural growth was a little over 2 percent per year compared with the prewar 3.6 percent growth rate in Taiwan. The difference in performance has been attributed to the slower diffusion of new fertilizer responsive seed varieties and a less intensive use of commercial fertilizers. Those differences have in turn been linked to the lack of development of irrigation facilities at the time of colonization.[43] Furthermore, the Japanese government in Korea invested far less in agriculture than it did in Taiwan.[44]

Although living standards in Taiwan seemed to rise with agricultural improvements brought about by the Japanese, the same cannot be said for Korea. The slower growth there combined with large exports of rice to Japan meant that household consumption of rice must have declined. Kuznets in fact uses the term *starvation exports*[45] to describe Korean sales of rice to Japan. However, it must be remembered that in both Korea and Taiwan a foundation for future growth in agricultural productivity was provided.

The creation of a large domestic market, based upon expenditures from agriculture, in Korea and Taiwan awaited the land reforms that occurred after World War II in Japan, Korea, and Taiwan. In Japan the landlord class had been so weakened prior to World War II that the postwar land reform was merely a continuation of this process. In Korea and Taiwan the end of World War II meant the elimination of Japan as a colonial taskmaster and the rice, which the latter had extracted, could now be captured by domestic producers. The land reforms implied that incomes in the countryside would be relatively equally distributed and that future increases in productivity would also be so distributed. Thus the foundation for a large domestic market had been realized as governments in all three nations continued to invest in their agricultural sectors resulting in continued rapid productivity growth.[46]

Such large domestic markets increased the likelihood that high priority industries in the private sector in East Asia would respond in a productive way to the provision of subsidies by the state, and indeed the private sector did respond productively. However, large markets influenced the effectiveness of government policy in another way. As was pointed out previously, the success of government policy in East Asia has depended on the state's ability to discipline the firms to which subsidies and protection are granted. This was illustrated in the discussion of Figure 8.3. In that figure it was seen that, if the firms protected by the state (II) choose to utilize the subsidy unproductively (B), the state (I) could then punish the firms by withdrawing the subsidy (B). For this to occur the threat by the state to withdraw its subsidy must be credible. Indeed, in the situation outlined in Figure 8.3, the threat is credible because punishing the firms for unproductive use of the subsidy (B) will reduce the state's loss from −5 to 0. It is rational for the state to punish the firms.

However, if the situation is altered slightly to that represented in Figure 8.4, the results change dramatically. As can be seen, any attempt by the state to punish uncooperative firms in an industry will actually worsen the state's position. Thus the rationality of such retaliatory behavior is suspect or, in other words, the state's threat to impose punishment on unproductive firms lacks credibility.

What is the intuition behind the above discussion? Remember the state's goal is to promote manufacturing. Hence, the more successful it is at this, the larger its reward. When markets for all manufactured goods are relatively small, there may be no viable alternative for the state to pursue. Thus even if firms in a particular industry misuse the protection they receive, there may be no valid alternative to the state in promoting manufacturing because the markets for all other manufactured goods are also limited. Therefore, to withdraw protection will mean the sacrifice of all domestic production of that good whereas protection provides for at least some domestic manufacturing.

If the markets for a wide variety of manufactured goods are extensive, then alternatives are open to the state to promote other industries. Thus to

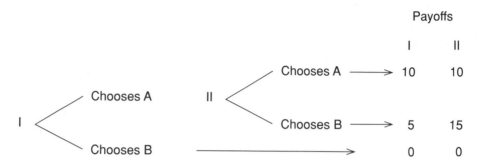

Figure 8.4 An alternative prisoners' dilemma game between the government and an industry.

continue to subsidize an unproductive industry would result in a net loss for the state (the game resembles Figure 8.3) because it has the alternative of promoting potentially successful manufacturing elsewhere.

From the perspective outlined here, the effectiveness or hardness of the state is no longer altogether externally determined, although these external factors are important. Instead, the effectiveness of state industrial policy is seen to be directly linked to the size of the domestic market for manufactured goods. The larger this market is and the faster it grows, the more effective the state will be in carrying out its policies to promote domestic industry. The importance of market size is because larger markets generally increase the likelihood that private firms will respond productively to government policy and larger markets increase the credibility attached to government threats to reallocate the distribution of subsidies. In turn it was also pointed out that the size of domestic markets is generally dependent on the productivity of the agricultural sector. The importance of agricultural productivity was illustrated with reference to East Asia.

CONCLUSION

In this chapter a number of different views of the state have been examined. First, the benign state view sees the state as making up for inadequacies of the market. The result of the state's actions will be an overall improvement in the efficiency with which resources are allocated. From this perspective the state is seen to be the custodian of the interests of society in general. Although this may be a naive view of the state, one important conclusion did emerge. Because the preponderance of such market inadequacies are likely to be found in rural, agricultural areas rather than in urban areas, much of the state's policies should be oriented to the former rather than the latter sector whenever possible.

A second view sees the state and its policies as an obstacle to overall development. State choice with respect to policy is greatly influenced by small special interest groups. These groups are generally urban, manufacturing interests. Thus government policy tends to be biased toward policies that redistribute resources from rural to urban areas. These policies often retard productivity growth rather than promote it. The interesting implication is that, similar to the benign state view, state policy needs to be reoriented toward rural areas and agriculture so as to eliminate urban bias.

A third view sees the state as being neither completely benign nor malevolent. Instead, states are seen to pursue the interests of society in productivity growth as long as the cost to the state, both political and economic, is not too great. As the cost of productivity enhancing policies rise, the state and its leaders will increasingly turn to the pursuit of their own selfish interests and their political survival. This implies a turn toward predatory policy making.

Productivity enhancing policies generally involve the short-run protection of selected industries to promote the learning of new technology, with the goal being to become internationally competitive. The latter will involve sales to foreign markets. Of course, the key to the success of this policy is just how responsive the private sector will be. Will it use the subsidies selectively granted to particular industries in a productive or unproductive manner? It was argued that the private sector is likely to be more responsive the greater is the size of the domestic market. This increases the profitability of expending resources to become dynamically efficient because the larger market increases the probability that the firms will be able to successfully master modern technologies. Very small markets imply that the likelihood of successfully mastering modern technologies is low and that consequently the incentive for domestic firms to attempt to become internationally competitive is reduced.

Large market size enhances the effectiveness of government policy in another way. In situations where markets are large and growing, the credibility of government threats to withdraw subsidies from poor performers is increased. With large markets, the state can withdraw support from one industry and allocate it to another with some hope of success. However, when markets are small it is unlikely that there are many or any industries that can become competitive internationally. Thus the threat to take away the subsidies for a particular industry loses some of its credibility, because the removal of subsidies will result in the loss of most or all domestic manufacturing.

The point is that governments are likely to be more effective in carrying out policy when domestic markets are large and growing rapidly, because the cost to the state of carrying out productivity enhancement is likely to be relatively low. Alternatively, where the domestic market is small, the cost of such policies is likely to be higher and governments are likely, therefore, to become more self-centered and predatory in nature.

Finally, this view, as do the previous two, emphasizes the importance of the agricultural sector. Long-run productivity growth here will provide for a large and rapidly growing domestic market for manufacturing. Therefore, whether one sees the state as benign, malignant, or otherwise, investment by the state in agriculture is pivotal to overall development.

NOTES

1. Much of this discussion is based on Charles Wolf, Jr., "A Theory of Non-Market Failure: Framework for Implementation," *Journal of Law and Economics* 22 (April 1982): 107–139.
2. Howard Pack and Larry E. Westphal, "Industrial Strategy and Technological Change: Theory Versus Reality," *Journal of Development Economics* 22 (1986): 87–128.
3. Paul N. Rosenstein-Rodan, "Problems of Industrialization of Eastern and Southeastern Europe," *Economic Journal* 53 (June–September 1943): 202–211.
4. Kevin W. Murphy, Andrei Shliefer, and Robert W. Vishny, "Industrialization and the Big Push," *Journal of Political Economy* 97 (October 1989): 1003–1026.
5. Douglass North, *Institutions, Institutional Change and Economic Performance* (Cambridge: Cambridge University Press, 1990), p. 27.
6. Ibid., p. 34.
7. Ibid., p. 35.
8. Charles Wolf, Jr., "A Theory of Non-Market Failure," p. 111.
9. Robert H. Bates, "Governments and Agricultural Markets in Africa," in *The Role of Markets in the World Food Economy*, ed. D. Gale Johnson and G. Edward Schuh (Boulder, Colo.: Westview Press, 1983), p. 162.
10. W. A. Lewis, "Economic Development with Unlimited Supplies of Labour," *The Manchester School* 28 (1954): 139–191.
11. G. Ranis and J. Fei, "A Theory of Economic Development," *American Economic Review* 51 (September 1961): 533–565.
12. Hla Myint, "Agriculture and Economic Development in the Open Economy," in *Agriculture in Development Theory*, ed. Lloyd G. Reynolds (New Haven, Conn.: Yale University Press, 1975), pp. 350–351.
13. Ibid.
14. See Mancur Olson, *The Logic of Collective Action: Public Goods and the Theory of Groups* (Cambridge, Mass.: Harvard University Press, 1971).
15. Ibid.
16. David M. Kreps, "Corporate Culture and Economic Theory," in *Perspectives on Positive Political Economy*, ed. James E. Alt and Kenneth A. Shepsle (Cambridge: Cambridge University Press, 1990), pp. 90–143.
17. Mancur Olson, *The Rise and Decline of Nations: Economic Growth, Stagflation, and Social Rigidities* (New Haven, Conn.: Yale University Press, 1982).

18. Michael Lipton, *Why Poor People Stay Poor* (Cambridge, Mass.: Harvard University Press, 1977).

19. Robert H. Bates and William P. Rogerson, "Agriculture in Development: A Coalitional Analysis," *Public Choice* 35 (1980): 513–527.

20. Ibid., p. 215.

21. Robert H. Bates, "Governments and Agricultural Markets in Africa," in *Toward a Political Economy of Development* (Berkeley: University of California Press, 1988), pp. 343–356.

22. North, *Institutions, Institutional Change and Economic Performance*, pp. 36–45.

23. Ibid., p. 43.

24. Ibid., pp. 43–44.

25. Dani Rodrik, "Political Economy and Development Policy," *European Economic Review* 36 (April 1992): 329–336.

26. Ibid., p. 331.

27. Ibid.

28. Alice Amsden, "A Theory of Government Intervention in Late Industrialization," in *State and Market in Development: Synergy or Rivalry?* ed. Louis Putterman and Dietrich Rueschemeyer (Boulder, Colo.: Lynne Rienner Publishers, 1992), pp. 53–84.

29. Ibid., p. 61.

30. Ibid.

31. These factors were originally discussed by Joel Migdal, *Strong Societies and Weak States: State-Society Relations and State Capabilities in the Third World* (Princeton, N.J.: Princeton University Press, 1986). References to his work were taken from Robert Wade, *Governing the Market: Economic Theory and the Role of the Government in East Asian Industrialization* (Princeton, N.J.: Princeton University Press, 1990), pp. 337–342.

32. Olson, *The Rise and Decline of Nations*.

33. Peter Evans, "The State as Problem and Solution: Predation, Embedded Autonomy, and Structural Change," in *The Politics of Adjustment: International Constraints Distributive Conflicts, and the State*, ed. Stephan Haggard and Robert R. Kaufman (Princeton, N.J.: Princeton University Press, 1992).

34. As Evans points out, this represents the work of Max Weber, *Economy and Society*, ed. Guenter Roth and Claus Wittich (New York: Bedminister Press, 1968).

35. Evans, "The State as Problem and Solution," p. 146.

36. Ibid.

37. This game is taken from David M. Kreps, "Corporate Culture and Economic Theory," in *Perspectives on Positive Political Economy* (Cambridge: Cambridge University Press, 1990), p. 100.

38. Ramon Myers and Adrenne Ching, "Agricultural Development in Taiwan under Japanese Colonial Rule," *Journal of Asian Studies* 23 (August 1964): 560–562.

39. Teng-hui Lee and Yuch-eh Chen, "Agricultural Growth in Taiwan," in *Agricultural Growth in Japan, Taiwan, Korea, and the Philippines*, ed. Yujiro Hayami, Vernon Ruttan, and Herman M. Southworth (Honolulu: University Press of Hawaii, 1979), p. 61.

40. Samuel P. S. Ho, *Economic Development of Taiwan, 1860–1970* (New Haven, Conn.: Yale University Press, 1978), pp. 91–102.
41. Ramon Myers and Yamada Saburo, "Agricultural Development in the Empire," in *The Japanese Colonial Empire, 1895–1945*, ed. Ramon H. Myers and Mark R. Peattie (Princeton, N.J.: Princeton University Press, 1984), pp. 429–430.
42. Ibid., pp. 433–434.
43. Samuel P. S. Ho, "Colonialism and Development: Korea, Taiwan and Kwantung," in *The Japanese Colonial Empire, 1895–1945*, ed. Ramon H. Myers and Mark R. Peattie (Princeton, N.J.: Princeton University Press, 1984), pp. 361–362.
44. Myers and Saburo, "Agricultural Development in the Empire," p. 439.
45. Paul W. Kuznets, *Economic Growth and Structure in the Republic of Korea* (New Haven, Conn.: Yale University Press, 1977), p. 17.
46. See Yujiro Hayami, Vernon Ruttan and Herman Southworth, eds., *Agricultural Growth in Japan, Taiwan, Korea, and the Philippines* (Honolulu: University Press of Hawaii, 1979).

Index

dynamics of, 73, 79–82
and manufacturing, 105–9
rates of return in, 89
taxation and, 226–7
wage rates in, 169, 184
traditional society economic stage, 16
transaction costs, 73, 74–6, *271*
transition theory, 122, 125–30
trap. *See* demographic trap models; low-
level trap

underdevelopment, 4–5, 7–8
unemployment, 170–5
and shadow prices, 211–13
See also disguised unemployment
urbanization, 169, 275
and labor migration, 172–3, 200
utility functions
and household choice, 57–9,
61, 68
and international trade, 239
and manufacturing, 281
and rationality, 51
Uzawa, Hirofumi, 40

Vishny, Robert W., 269
de Vries, Jan, 109

Wade, Robert, 260–1
wage rates, 122–3, 135–6, 142, 146,
173–4, 177, 237
and education, 194, 199
and free trade, 250
and industrialization, 279
and labor, 169
versus shadow prices, 211, 213
and technical change, 98
wages and labor, 18–20
wages fund constraint, 19
Warren, Bill, 8
wealth, 10, 233, 244, 277
Weber, Max, 10–12, 13, 50
Weber-Tawney hypothesis, 11, 12, 13
welfare economics, 65, 154, 204–10
Westphal, Larry E., 259
Wheeler, Mark, 130
Williamson, Jeffrey G., 131
Winegarden, C. R., 130
Wolf, Charles, 271